Hardin County, Kentucky Marriage Records

1813–1850

❦

Frances T. Ingmire

Heritage Books
2025

HERITAGE BOOKS
AN IMPRINT OF HERITAGE BOOKS, INC.

Books, CDs, and more—Worldwide

For our listing of thousands of titles see our website
at
www.HeritageBooks.com

Published 2025 by
HERITAGE BOOKS, INC.
Publishing Division
5810 Ruatan Street
Berwyn Heights, MD 20740

International Standard Book Number
Paperbound: 978-0-7884-7767-6

GROOM	BRIDE	DATE
ABELL, Edmund	SWAN, Elizabeth	8/14/1832
F: Samuel	F: Thomas	
ABELL, Samuel C.	RATCHFORD, Flora	9/25/1832
	F: Robert	
ABLE, Robert M.	FAIRLEIGH, Mary L.	10/27/1847
	F: Thos.	
ABNEY, Joshua	SANDERS, Ann	6/23/1845
		S: Colmore Lovelace
ACRES, John	AMENT, Elizabeth	4/ 3/1819
	Ament, John said	S: Henry Ament
	she was of age.	S: James Cunningham
	F: Anthony	
ACRES, Joseph	GARRET, Sally	12/22/1814
		S: Philip Bunger
ACRES, John	AMENT, Elizabeth	4/ 3/1819
	F: Anthony AMENT	S: Henry
ACRES, Joseph	GARRET, Sally	12/22/1814
ADAM, Isaac C.	STONE, Mrs. Milly	2/26/1824
		S: Hodges, John
ADAMS, John	EDLIN, Rose Ann	5/13/1846
	John Edlin swore	S: S. Williams
	girl 21.	
ADAMS, Thomas	MCMILLEN, Letitia	10/ 7/1840
	F: John MCMILLEN	
ADAMS, James H.	CULVER, Elizabeth	2/15/1836
	F: Daniel	
ADAMS, Green	ENLOW, Genota	2/26/1819
	F: Jacob ENLOW	
ADKINS, Patrick	YOUNG, Lavina	2/27/1826
	F: John	S: David Hoskinson
ALBERT, William	DEWITT, Polly	4/22/1821
		S: Price Dewitt
ALBERT, William	LOGAN, Margaret	11/23/1833
		S: Wright, David
ALBERT, Peter	HAWKINS, Ruth F.	5/14/1846
	Jas. M. Hawkins proved	
	cert. of Harden HAWKINS, F:	
ALEXANDER, Alfred	WHETSTONE, Catherine	6/26/1836
F: Andrew	F: Peter	
ALEXANDER, Robert H.	HOWARD, Jemima	7/11/1831
	F: Samuel	S: Thurman, David
ALEXANDER, Jesse	COOMBS, Pamela	2/15/1832
	F: Adin	
ALEXANDER, Robt. Veasy	CLOSE, Mrs. Elizabeth	10/ 2/1815
		S: Geo. Highbough
ALEXANDER, James	HENDERSON, Prudence	10/29/1826
		S: Hugh Cole
ALSE, William	WARD, Olive	7/ 2/1831
	F: John IRWIN	S: Lovelace, Colmore
ALVEY, James	BREWER, Elizabeth	9/ 6/1845
	Wm. Cole swore girl	S: C. J. Coomes
	21.	

GROOM	BRIDE	DATE
ALVEY, Benedict	COLE, Agatha	1/ 2/1847
M: Susan	F: William	
ALVEY, Henry	SUMMERS, Rachel	4/15/1816
		S: Thomas Summers
ALVIN, Edward H.	MOORE, Elizabeth	1/ 5/1846
		S: Jacob Rogers
ALLEN, Abijah	SMITH, Mathilda	12/20/1813
		S: James Smith
ALLEN, Wm.	GRAVEN, Anna	3/ 4/1815
		S: James Allen
ALLEN, David	HARLAN, Mrs. Elizabeth	9/19/1824
		S: Thos. Whitson
ALLEN, Joseph	HARRIS, Nancy	9/10/1824
	M: Mary Ann HARRIS	S: Mary A. Harris
ALLEN, William	DRAKE, Sally	7/27/1824
	F: William BUNNELL	S: John Stith
ALLEN, Wm.	CRAVEN, Anna	3/ 4/1815
		S: James Allen
ALLEN, David	EMHLEY, Ruthey	4/19/1824
		S: S. Martin
ALLEN, Elijah	PICKREL, Sarah	5/ 6/1826
	F: Samuel	S: Pickrel
ALLEN, John	LYON, Susannah	12/23/1822
	F: Joseph LYON	S: Wm. Purcell
ALLEN, Abijah	SMITH, Matilda	12/20/1813
		S: James Smith
ALLEN, Jeremiah	SMITH, Susan	6/ 7/1820
		S: Jacob Enlow
ALLEN, Ben	KOHO, Polly	4/13/1818
	F: John KOHO	S: John Stith Jr.
	Aged 27 years old.	S: Soloman Brandenburg
ALLEN, Horace	LAINE, Elizabeth Ann	7/21/1827
	F: Squire	S: Laine, S.
ALLEN, John B.	DILLARD, Jane	11/16/1829
	F: James	S: Dillard, J.
ALLEN, Samuel	LAINE, Elizabeth	3/29/1827
F: William		S: Allen, William
ALLEN, William	PICKERELL, Elizabeth	8/ 4/1832
	F: Samuel	
ALLEN, John	ALLEN, Sally Ann	10/23/1832
	F: William A.	
ALLEN, Jeptha	WADLEY, Mrs. Nancy	6/17/1834
		S: Daugherty, James
ALLEN, William	HALL, Martha	9/25/1834
	F: Philip	S: Hamilton, Alfred
ALLEN, Simeon L.	MELTON, Lydia	3/16/1846
	F: Adam STADER	S: Colmore Lovelace
ALLEN, Pleasant	THOMPSON, Delila	8/19/1844
		S: Colmore Lovelace
ALLISON, John	NEFF, Sally	12/29/1820
	F: Henry NEFF	S: G. L. Rogers
		S: Wm. Neff

HARDIN COUNTY, KENTUCKY MARRIAGE RECORDS

GROOM	BRIDE	DATE
ALLISON, William	NEFF, Sarah Jane M: Ruth	12/20/1847 S: Green B. Williams
ALLOWAY, Abram	SMITHER, Catherine F: John	8/10/1835
ALLSTON, John	BRUMFIELD, Lucretia F: William	2/10/1835
AMBROSE, Davis	MILLE, Laney also Sena F: Jonathan	3/18/1845
AMENT, John	MILLER, Lucetta Benj. Miller swore girl 21.	2/19/1849 S: Geo. H. Hicks
AMENT, Anthony	LAMPSON, Eliza Ann F: Benjamin	12/12/1830 S: David Thurman
AMES, Samuel	BRACHERR, Elizabeth	10/ 1/1844 S: Alex. Guston
AMES, Samuel	DODGE, Mrs. Nancy	10/21/1831 S: H. G. Wagginer
ANDERSON, Benedict	DAUGHERTY, Celia M: Martha DAUGHERTY	9/27/1825
ANDERSON, John F: John Sr.	OSTER, Rebecca	8/13/1824
ANDERSON, Josiah	VANDIGRIPH, Isabel F: Samuel VANDIGRIPH	7/19/1824
ANDERSON, John	GILLELAND, Sally M: Margaret MILLER SF: Wm. MILLER	2/28/1824
ANDERSON, Speair?	ANDERSON, Nancy F: John B. ANDERSON	7/12/1821 S: James Haycraft
ANDERSON, Seth	SULCER, Polly	3/24/1821 S: James Haycraft S: Wm. Sulcer
ANDERSON, John A.	BURCHAM, Rebecca	10/10/1818 S: Jacob Enlow S: David Burcham
ANDERSON, Robert	LAINE, Lucinda F: Jonathan	8/24/1826
ANDERSON, John	MORGAN, Sarah Jane F: James	11/14/1828 S: J. Morgan
ANDERSON, John F.	HANNA, Louisa Ann F: John	6/20/1844
ANDERSON, Henry S.	SAMUELS, Mary F: James	5/23/1850
APPLEGATE, William H.	TRIPLETT, Eliza	6/25/1846 S: Colmore Lovelace
ARMOUR, David	MCCLELAND, Treasy	4/10/1817 S: Reddy Parcel
ARMOUR, Dempsey	GOFORTH, Ruth	7/23/1825 S: Hugh Cole
ARMS, James	HOLDREN, Harmony F: Jacob	10/18/1830 S: J. Holdren
ARNEL, Henry	ROUT, Prudence F: Richard ROUT	10/ 8/1825

HARDIN COUNTY, KENTUCKY MARRIAGE RECORDS

GROOM	BRIDE	DATE
ARNOLD, Georgw	CARLISLE, Mrs. Penelope	7/30/1820
	S: John Jackson	
	S: Wm. Slack	
ARNOLD, Jacob	LONG, Sarah	1/19/1820
	S: John Jacokson	
	S: John Madley	
ARNOLD, John	COFFMAN, Mrs. Catherine	9/25/1838
	S: George L. Rogers	
ARNOLD, John	THORP, Fanny	9/15/1846
	S: Jno. C.C. Thompson	
ARNOLD, John F: Henry	MONIN, Lavina(Lavine) F: Larkin S.	12/ 2/1846
ARNOLD, Wm. Daniel	STRICKLER, Elizabeth Jane F: Geo. W.	12/29/1847
ARNOLD, John	JOURDAN, Elizabeth F: Wm. JOURDAN S: Lewis Jourdan	9/ 5/1814
ARNOLD, John	JOURDAN, Elizabeth	9/ 5/1814
ARTMAN, Jacob	KENNEDY, Mrs. Phebe	1/18/1819
	S: Jacob Enlow	
ARVIN, Joseph S.	HAYDEN, Rosa Ann F: William	11/ 5/1844
ASHCRAFT, Jediah	MILLER, Barbary F: Abraham	10/15/1832
ASHCRAFT, Absolom	ALLEN, Delila F: Benj. ALLEN S: John Stith Jr.	8/ 6/1818
ASHCRAFT, Absalom	WIMP, Harriett F: John WIMP S: John Jenkins	12/11/1815
ASHCROFT, Absolom	WIMP, Harriett F: John S: John Jenkins	12/11/1815
ASH, Charles	ALLY, Nancy F: Ralph ALLY S: Wm. Ash M: Mary ALLY	8/18/1819
ASH, Isaac	DENNIS, Susanna S: Hugh Cole	9/ 6/1817
ASH, Reuben	BROWN, Mrs. Mary S: James Daugherty	7/ 4/1835
ASH, Samuel	STATER, Sally F: John S: J. Stater	12/12/1827
ASH, Henry	CARRICO, Nancy S: C. J. Coomes	7/24/1846
ASHLEY, John	FLOYD, Sarah M: Jane S: J. Floyd	8/15/1829
ASTER, John	HENDERSON, Margaret A. F: John S: James Haycroft	7/13/1832
ATCHER, Cornelius	BERRY, Martha F: John	12/15/1835
ATCHER, Cornelius	OLIVER, Mary S. M: Patsy	11/ 7/1848
ATHERTON, Joshua F: William	RAY, Hetta	12/18/1834

GROOM	BRIDE	DATE
ATHERTON, William	COYLE, Sarah	1/21/1846
		S: R. L. Thruman
ATON, Isaac	SNELLING, Hannah	8/23/1824
		S: Josiah G. Yager
ATTERBURY, Jesse	ATTERBURY, Levisa (?)	3/12/1814
	F: Thomas ATTERBURY	
ATTERBURY, Miahael	KESSINGER, Elizabeth	12/12/1816
	F: Joseph	S: Edw. Atterberry
ATTERBERRY, Hardin	SMITH, Frances	12/ 8/1847
	F: Rufus	
ATWELL, Charles	SHANKLIM, Jaines	11/29/1828
	F: Geo. NORCUT	
ATWOOD, George	BRIAN, Mary	10/23/1813
		S: Barton Rubey
ATWOOD, Josiah	COY, Margaret	8/26/1822
	F: Daniel COY	S: Coonrod Coy
	M: Elizabeth COY	
ATWOOD, John W.	VETTREES, Rebecca	12/29/1819
		S: Samuel Martin
		S: John Vertreese
AUBERRY, Samuel	LEGRAND, Sibbil	12/30/1834
		S: David G. Hoskinson
AUBERRY, Isiah	CARTER, Elizabeth A.	6/21/1834
	F: Benjamin	S: David G. Hoskinson
AUBREY, Joseph	PREWIT, Mary	7/14/1823
	Green B. Williams Bonds-	
	Turner, Matthew man says	
	she is 21.	
AUBREY, Ben	GOODMEN, Rebecca	12/18/1845
F: George	F: Daniel	
AUBRY, Philip	EVANS, Labina Patterson	2/24/1829
	M: Mary	S: Mary Evans
AURBRAY, Thomas	ANDERSON, Betsey	8/26/1831
F: Cravin		
AVIT, John R.	VANMETRE, Frances N.	12/ 8/1847
	M: Abisha	
BACON, John	ROGERS, Cynthia	5/23/1836
	F: Charles	
BACON, Jesse	LUCAS, Elizabeth	8/19/1823
		S: Stiles, Parker
BAILEY, Albert	ARVIN, Elizabeth Jane	10/31/1849
	Arvin, Edward H.	S: Jacob Rogers
	swore girl 21.	
BAILEY, Lewis	HOVEY, Mary	10/18/1820
	F: Joseph HOVEY	S: Wm. Tarpley
		S: Joseph Hovey
BAILEY, Littleton	PAWLEY, Margaret	12/15/1845
	F: Stephen	
BAIRD, James	EDLIN, Elizabeth	6/ 3/1817
	F: James EDLIN	S: James Edlin
BAIRD, Ralph	EDEN, Jane	10/ 2/1820
	F: James EDLEN	S: Isaac Coy

5

HARDIN COUNTY, KENTUCKY MARRIAGE RECORDS

GROOM	BRIDE	DATE
BAILEY, Richard H.	YAGER, Leatitia S.H.	11/19/1823
F: Richard R. BAILEY	F: Josiah H. YAGER	
	proven by Howel C. Cose	
BAILEY, Walter	PURDY, Polly	12/20/1825
	F: Edmond	
BAILEY, Willis	EMRY, Mary	8/20/1836
		S: Colmore Lovelace
BAIRD,? Ralph	EDLIN, Jane	11/ 2/1820
BAKER, Matthias C.	KIRTTON, B. E.	3/12/1846
BAKER, William	USTERBACK, Caroline	7/21/1834
	F: Benjamin	S: David Wright
BALL, Daniel	COY, Jane	9/ 1/1834
F: James	F: Amos	
BALLANGER, Mathew	ATHERTON, Lucinda	7/13/1830
	F: William	S: William Atherton
BALLENGER, William	DEAVER, Nancy	10/31/1830
F: Thomas	F: Stephen	
BALLINGER, Bryan	BROWN, Susan	12/ 6/1848
	F: Fred	
BALLINGER, Jonathan	HUFFMAN, Mary	11/15/1843
	Jas. Ballinger swore	S: Colmore Lovelace
	girl 21.	
BARBER, Amos M.	BROWN, Omimdia	1/ 9/1823
		S: Samuel Robinson
BARBER, Samuel	MURLIN, Hannah	7/ 9/1825
M: Margaret BARBER	M: Sarah MURLIN	
BARD, Abraham S.	PARKS, Margaret	2/28/1822
		S: Geo. L. Rogers
BARD, Samuel	SAND, Catherine	7/11/1836
	F: John	S: J. Band
BARLOW, Charles	BLAND, Sarah	4/ 8/1833
	F: Daniel	
BARLOW, Christ	LANG, Rebecca	1/23/1813
		S: Michael Hargon
BARNES, Abel	DEAVER, Mary	4/23/1835
	F: Stephen	
BARNES, James	TURNER, Susan	10/ 2/1824
	F: Zebediah TURNER	
BARNES, Reason	DUNN, Phebe	12/ 7/1839
	M: Elizabeth	
BARNES, William	DUNN, Lydia	3/25/1829
	M: Elizabeth	S: E. Dunn
BARNS, Josiah	KEESHEE, Elizabeth	11/ 4/1822
F: James BARNS	M: Elizabeth	S: James Barnes
		S: James Cunningham
BARR, Abraham S.	PARKS, Margaret	2/28/1822
		S: Wm. Farleigh
BARRET, John	JOHNSON, Mary M.	11/21/1844
	SF: John PARKS	S: Samuel Williams
BARRON, John Jr.	TREDWELL, Sally	9/18/1820
	F: Nathan TUCKER	S: John Bayran
	M: Marah TUCKER	

GROOM	BRIDE	DATE
BARRY, Josiah	HURCHAM, Margaret	3/ 2/1831
BAYNE, Jesse	HITTSON, Alice	9/24/1816
	F: Alexander S: Charles Middleton	
BAYNE, Thomas	SMITH, Amanda	9/20/1831
	F: Aaron	
BAYS, John W.	PEARMAN,	5/31/1827
BAYSINGER, Peter	RICE, Elizabeth	3/14/1832
or RAYSINGER, Peter	F: Elias	
BEARD, John R.	BEARD, Willimina	2/10/1816
of Washifo Ky.	F: John S: Nath Brown	
BEASLEY, John	PRICE, Elizabeth	10/20/1830
	F: John	
BEATLY, Joseph	AKERS, Sarah	1/28/1846
	F: Josiah	
BEAVERS, William	BRANDENBURG, Nancy	2/20/1821
	F: Henry S: Henry Brandenburg	
BECK, Nicholas R.	FOWLER, Calosta	8/ 3/1825
	F: Henry KEITH	
BEDFORD, William H.	STUART, Mary E.	9/17/1846
	F: Daniel J.	
BEELER, Christopher Jr.	MCGALLION, Martha Ann	12/ 5/1849
Both of Age.	S: R. S. Thurman	
BEELER, Jefferson	BOON, Nancy	9/22/1831
	F: Charles	
BENHAM, Peter	CRABLE, Elizabeth	9/ 4/1820
	F: Jonathan S: Shadrack, Brown	
BENNETT, John	CECIL, Lucinda	10/ 3/1850
M: Mary	M: Susan	
	certs. proven by Michael Bennett	
	and Jas. A. Cecil	
BENNETT, John	DUNCAN, Agnes F.	3/14/1850
	F: Thos. H.	
BENNETT, John H.	WELLER, Fanny	12/24/1842
Gdn: WILLS, C.O.	M: Mary	
BENNETT, Michael	DOWNS, Malinda	4/ 4/1850
	B.R. Young swore	
	girl 21.	
BELL, Isaac	CARLEY, Margaret	10/31/1828
	F: Jesse S: Thomas Carley	
BELL, John	YOUNG, Rebecca	11/28/1832
	M: Elizabeth	
BELL, John	MEEK, Levicy	4/21/1817
	B: Geo. McClean	
BELL, Nathaniel	THOMPKINS, Mary	12/28/1833
	S: James Haycroft	
BELL, William	DUNN, Nancy	7/23/1835
	F: John	
BELL, William P.	BUSAN, Katherine	6/23/1824
	S: Thos. J. Chilton	
BELLER, Richard	CASTLEMAN, Margaret	1/ 5/1835
	F: James	

HARDIN COUNTY, KENTUCKY MARRIAGE RECORDS

GROOM	BRIDE	DATE
BELLER, Thomas	WHITEHEAD, Dicey J.	10/12/1829
	S: Isaac Taylor	
BELT, Carlton	BURCH, Mrs. Dorcas	9/28/1825
	S: Wm. Tarpley	
BELT, Lee	HARNED, Elizabeth	3/8 /1831
	F: William S: Benjamin Keith	
BERRY, Green B.	SMITH, Susan Jane	1/ 4/1845
	F: William	
BERRY, Morris	SCIFRES, Martha Ann	10/ 8/1849
	S: Milton Stith	
BEST, Josiah E.	SMOOT, Emily	6/ 9/1847
	F: Elijah	
BETHEL, William	THOMAS, Kitty Ann	11/14/1846
	G. W. Taylor, pr.	
BETHEL, William	MILLER, Gilly G.	9/15/1829
	M: Mary S: M. Miller	
BEWLEY, Elijah H.	HALDRON, Mary Jane	1/14/1850
	F: Bartholemew	
BEWLEY, Kimble	LAWSON, Susan	10/ 6/1832
	F: Henry	
BICKETT, Hiram J.	MCVEY, Cynthia Ann	6/22/1835
	M: Elizabeth S: Robert Byron	
BIDDLETON, Daniel	PAWLEY, Sarah	7/31/1822
	F: John PAWLEY S: Wm. Tarpley	
BIDDLETON, Daniel	NEFF, Mary	4/10/1819
	S: James Cunningham	
BIGELOW, Alfred	MURLIN, Susannah	11/12/1820
	S: Stiles Parker	
BIGELOW, David E.	HUMPHREY, Mary E.	3/ 6/1849
	Deganquier, Aug. pr.	
BIRD, George	HAGAN, Julia Ann	3/ 2/1848
	Walker, Paul swore girl 21. R. L. Thurman, pr.	
BIRD, Henry M: Margaret BIRD	PARKER, Mary	8/ 7/1824
BIRD, Jacob	CREAGER, Mary Ann	3/22/1849
	F: Christopher	
BIRD, John	CREGER, Margaret	5/12/1823
	F: Daniel CREGER	
BIRD, Joseph M: Margaret BIRD	CREGER, Rachael F: Daniel CREGER	2/ 5/1825
BLACK, James	OSBURN, Susanna	8/23/1817
	F: Daniel Certificate by Wm. Brown	
BLACKWELL, Arthur M.	WILLIAMS, Mary M.	5/ 7/1827
	F: Thomas S: T. Williams	
BLANCET, Elijah	GREENWALT, Rebecca	9/30/1824
	F: Isaac GREENWALT S: James Haycraft	
BLANCET, Silas SF: Saul CARTER	HARRIS, Nancy M: Nancy HARRIS proven by David Parker	7/20/1822

8

GROOM	BRIDE	DATE
BLAND, Benj. (Black)	GRAYHAM, Susan (Black)	12/11/1819
BLAND, Harry	HARDING, Alice V.	4/21/1835
	S: Colmore Lovelace	
BLAND, Henry	ENGLISH Mariah	8/ 3/1829
M: Susan	M: Nancy	
BLAND, John H.	CRIGGER, Polly Mary	1/ 4/1820
	S: James Haycraft	
BLAND, Jesse	SPURRIER, Eliza	6/ 4/1827
	S: Samuel Brown	
BLAND, Samuel	HASKETT, Frances	3/19/1830
F: Daniel		
BLAND, Thomas O.	BLAND, Augustian	2/ 8/1834
	F: William S: H. C. Waggoner	
BLAND, Thomas R.	ROBINSON, Sarah	11/ 7/1846
Dougherty proved	Alexander Guston, pr.	
mother's cert.		
BLAND, William	ENGLISH, Adaline	5/11/1835
	M: Nancy S: Colmore Lovelace	
BLANDFREE, Ben	GRAYHAM, Susan	1819
(Colored)	girl of colour	
BLANTON, Richard H.	ENGLISH, Adah Ann	8/ 5/1844
	G: Hayden E. ENGLISH S: Willard Presburg	
BLEAKLEY, William	WITHERS, Martha F.	2/23/1846
	Wm. C. Myrtle swore S: Jacob Rogers	
	girl 21.	
BLEDSOE, Anthony	BUNGER, Nancy	8/15/1831
	F: Philip	
BLEDSOE, Benjamin	VERNON, Elizabeth	4/12/1828
	F: Anthony S: A. Vernon	
BLISSIT, Jacob	BROWN, Sally	8/17/1835
F: George J.	F: William	
BLOXON, William	CLARK, Elizabeth	9/ 7/1822
	S: Thomas Clark	
	S: John Stith Jr.	
BOARD, Buckner	THORPE, Mary	12/ 1/1846
	S: Wm. S. Evans	
BODINE, John	CHENOWITH, Rebecca	7/ 6/1839
	F: Isaac S: I. Chenowith	
BOGARD, Eli	ALLSTON, Lucinda	4/16/1833
	F: Jeremiah	
BOGARD, Jacob	JOHNSON, Ellen	9/12/1829
	F: John S: J. Johnson	
BOGUE, Elias	HANDLEY, Celia Ann	6/ 2/1849
SF: Edward CROGHAN	M: Julia Ann Cert. proven	
	by Henry Bradley	
BOGUE, John	BENNET, Judah	11/27/1826
	F: George B. S: G. Bennet	
BOHN, Wiley	HENDLEY, Sally	12/12/1827
	F: Archibald S: A. Hundley	
BOMAR, James A.	HANDLEY, Laura Ann	2/ 7/1850
	F: A. HANDLEY	

9

HARDIN COUNTY, KENTUCKY MARRIAGE RECORDS

GROOM	BRIDE	DATE
BOND, Granville	GRISTY, Elizabeth	9/13/1826
	F: Ben S: B. Gristy	
BOOGE, Elihue	FLANDERS, Arvilla	1/ 1/1821
	F: Jacob S: George Flanders	
	George flanders says S: Parker, Silas	
	girl was of age.	
BOOTHE, Athanasius	PAGOT, Susannah	10/13/1845
	F: John	
BOOTHE, William	FRENCH, Catherine	1/21/1850
F: Uthanasius	Valentine French swore	
	girl 21.	
BOUGER, James	BENNETT, Mavinda	11/19/1832
	G: Wm. E. WILSON S: H. C. Ulen	
BOWLES, John	ROOF, Rebecca	1/18/1836
G: ROOF, John		
BOWLES, Vardman	DUVALL, Ann	8/ 1/1831
	F: Thomas S: T. Duvall	
BOYCE, Richard	MCDOWELL, Mary	8/25/1835
	S: Pleasant Alverson	
BOYD, Jefferson	TABB, Susan E.	10/18/1850
	James J. Tabb swore S: Geo. W. Crumbough	
	girl 21.	
BRADBERRY, Hezikiah	SHREWSBURRY, Mary D.	9/ 6/1832
	F: Drewny	
BRADDOCK, Genl. (Col)	DAISEY, Cassandra, (Col)	8/15/1825
BRADLEY, Elisha	LASH, Elizabeth M.	7/25/1818
BRADLEY, James	KELLEN, Elizabeth	1/ 6/1823
	certificate of Joseph	
	LAFELETT, Gdn: of bride.	
BRADLEY, John	COOMB, Rebecca	9/10/1831
	S: S.C. Coomes	
BRADLEY, Samuel	LOGADON, Nancy	11/ 3/1828
BRACKETT, Benjamin C.	BOYD, Matilda	6/18/1846
	F: James	
BRANDENBURG, John F.	VERTREES, Elizabeth	5/14/1825
	F: William VERTREES	
	Isaac Vertrees says girl	
	is 21.	
BRANHAM, William H.	HAYS, America	10/31/1831
	F: Hercules	
BRASHEAR, Charles	YOUNG, Sarah Elenor	3/30/1831
	F: John S: J. Young	
BRASHEAR, Edwin	WATKINS, Nancy	10/ 2/1833
	M: Catherine	
BRASHEAR, James	TABB, Jane A.	4/ 6/1833
	F: Edmond C.	
BRASHEAR, Jonathan	SULLIVAN, Suthia	12/27/1833
	F: Price ; S: David Wright	
BRASHEAR, Linzey	STOVALL, Patsey	11/ 9/1829
	F: Hezekiah S: R. Stovall	
BRASHEAR, Samuel	MATHER,	12/31/1824
M: Maria M.	M: Mary MATHER	

GROOM	BRIDE	DATE
BRASHER, William	BRASHEAR, Amanda	1/10/1832
F: Edin	F: John HUSS	
BRATCHER, David	SELF, Lydia	12/30/1816
		S: Edw. Self
BRAY, Henry	MARTIN, Sarah	7/ 9/1833
BRECKETT, Benjamin W.	UTTERBACK, Ann Jane	3/26/1844
	F: Ben UTTERBACK	
	Thos. D. Utterback swore	
	girl 21.	
BREWER, Benjamin	HOWELL, Mary	8/12/1818
	cert. proven by S: John Baird	
	Thos. Price.	
	F: John HOWELL	
BREWER, John	WISE, Matilda	7/25/1818
		S: oath of Henry Wise
BREWER, Michael	MILLENDER, Martha	8/25/1816
	M: Cert. from Martha S: Geo. Sipes	
	MILLENDER	
BREWER, Uriah	HAGAN, Elizabeth	8/25/1848
	Chas. Brian swore S: C. J. Coomes	
	girl 21.	
BREWER, William	HATFIELD, Mary	11/12/1846
	Helen Hatfield swore girl 21.	
BREWER, William	FRENCH, Eleanor	5/30/1817
		S: Stephen French
BRIAN, Benjamin	BOLD, Tresy	10/25/1822
SF: Cert. Geo. WOOD,	F: William BOLD cert. of	
boy's. SF: proven by	Mr. Bold says age proven	
Thos. Wise	by Thos. Wise.	
BRIANT, Daniel	DISMORE, Sally	8/30/1822
BRICKEY, Christ	MINGES, Catherine	3/21/1818
		S: Peter
BRIDGEWATERS, Daniel	ENLOWS, Sally	7/24/1816
BRIDWELL, Haydon	LARUE, Martha S.	9/ 9/1835
	F: Squire	
BRIGHT, Lewis	JENKINS, Elizabeth	8/20/1819
	F: Ingatias JENKINS	
BRIN, William	POKE, Mariah	5/17/1838
	F: James S: J. Poke	
BRISCOE, John H.	VANMATRE, Mahalia	2/14/1827
	F: Joseph S: Joseph Vanmatre	
BRISCOE, Walter D.	WAGGONER, Eliza Ann	11/26/1829
F: Walter	F: Herbert	
BRISCOE, William C.	STAIGHTER, Amanda	9/22/1832
	F: Robert C.	
BRISTOW, Francis M.	HALM, Emily E.	3/ 3/1831
		S: John Stith
BROWN, Asa	PARTLOW, Katherine	4/30/1819
	F: Saml PARTLOW S: John Stith Jr.	
BROWN, Benjamin	ARNOLD, Elizabeth	4/ 1/1820
		S: Jonh Arnold
		S: Samuel Martin

HARDIN COUNTY, KENTUCKY MARRIAGE RECORDS

GROOM	BRIDE	DATE
BROWNFIELD, Calvin	WILLIAMS, Mary Jane F: Daniel	8/12/1833
BROWN, Charles	WILSON, Mary Jane M: Martha S: A. Abell	12/13/1846
BROWN, Daniel	THOMAS, Nancy F: Joseph S: James Daugherty	1/13/1830
BROWN, Edward	BOMAR, Katherine F: William BOMAR	3/21/1825
BROWN, Elijah	VANDERGRAFT, Catherine F: Samuel S: James Haycraft	1/14/1834
BROWN, Frederick	ROBINSON, Sarah S: James Daugherty	5/31/1827
BROWN, Frederick	HARRIS, Martha S: George H. Rogers	11/ 9/1826
BROWN, George	BUSH, Juliet Ann F: William	2/11/1836
BROWN, George	YOUNG, Ruth	9/16/1830
BROWN, George P.	CHILTON, Margaret Ann F: Thomas	5/23/1833
BROWN, James SF: Reubin ASH	GOODIN, M. Nancy S: James Daugherty	8/24/1850
BROWN, James B. F: Daniel	FUNK, Elizabeth Ann F: Alexander	2/15/1836
BROWN, James E. A.W. King proved cert. from mother	VESSELS, Lucinda F: James VESSELS	11/16/1846
BROWN, James, Jr. F: James BROWN, Sr.	REED, Rachael M: Charlotte REED	2/ 6/1826
BROWN, James Jr.	ASH, Nancy S: Henry Ash	4/20/1815
BROWN, John F: Joshua	READ, Lucretia F: Hensley READ S: Joshua Brown	11/21/1817
BROWN, John H.	WRIGHT, Laury F: James	8/ 8/1831
BROWN, John Oliver	CASAWAY, Sarah F: Samuel	3/13/1848
BROWN, Josedon	ALEXANDER, Lydia F: Andrew S: A. Alexander	2/ 2/1829
BROWN, Joseph	SOIFREE, Sarah Ann Isaac Soifres swore S: Colmore Lovelace girl 21.	11/26/1850
BROWN, Joseph	READ, Eliza S: James Smith	9/15/1827
BROWN, Joseph F: Isaac	WOOLDRIDGE, Harriet C. F: Daniel	12/10/1831
BROWN, Joshua	HARRIS, Catherine M: Mary HARRIS	2/24/1824
BROWN, Isaac	CARTER, Anna F: Samuel CARTER S: John Baird	3/10/1824
BROWN, Isaac	GILMORE, Jane S: Colmore Lovelace	10/ 1/1835

12

GROOM	BRIDE	DATE
BROWN, Isaac	SMOOT, Suckey	1/ 4/1813
	F: John	
BROWN, Lewis	CASTLEMAN, Matilda	7/19/1825
	B: John HODGE	
BROWN, Martin	WRIGHT, Martha	1/18/1828
F: Frederick	F: William	
BROWN, Nathaniel	BAIRD, Mary	2/ 4/1814
	F: John BAIRD S: Wm. Read	
BROWN, Patrick H.	LARUE, Mary	12/21/1830
	F: Squire S: David Thurman	
BROWN, Patrick M.	ENLOUIS, Louisa Ann	1/18/1836
	F: Abraham	
BROWN, Richard H.	JENKINS, Rebecca A.	5/23/1849
	cert. of Eliz. Jenkins	
	proved by R.P. Jenkins	
BROWN, Samuel	HANAN, Mary	2/ 1/1826
	D. Chas. Hanan says she is	
	of age.	
BROWN, Stephen F.	BROWN, Ignatia	1/ 5/1844
Gdn: Chas. CECIL	James Vessels Jr. S: C. J. Coomes	
BROWN, Wm.	BUNTON, Elizabeth	3/25/1813
	S: Mark Marshall	
BROWN, William	DORSAY, Harriet Ann	11/11/1844
	F: Amos	
BROWN, William	DEWITT, Minerva	12/ 9/1846
	Robert Hall swore S: James Daugherty	
	girl 21.	
BROWN, William	TWEEDELL, Nancy Mr.	11/ 2/1833
F: Frederick	S: Colmore Lovelace	
BROWN, William	COOK, Margaret	12/11/1818
BROWN, William E.	WILLIAMS, Elizabeth	8/25/1831
	F: Daniel M. S: D. M. Williams	
BROWN, William M.	VESSELS, Eliza J.	3/21/1845
	F: James Jr.	
BROWN, William S.	JOHNSON, Ann Mariah	12/17/1845
	Thos. W. Shackleford S: Colmore Lovelace	
	swore girl 21.	
BROWN, Zadock	GRADY, Polly	12/11/1828
	F: David S: D. Grady	
BROWNFIELD, George	WALSH, Nancy	5/15/1826
	S: David Thurman	
BROWNFIELD, James	BARLOW, Frances	11/29/1820
	S: Joseph Ryan(Binlow)	
BROWNFIELD, John	TEDLOCK, Sarah	2/21/1816
BRUMFIELD, James	DOUGHERTY, Hannah	12/26/1823
	Wm. F. Dougherty S: Jacob Enlow	
	says is 21.	
BRUMFIELD, James	DAUGHERTY, Abigail	2/12/1833
	F: Richard	
BRUMFIELD, Samuel H.	WOOLDRIDGE, Mary	8/20/1827
	G: Jesse S: Richard Brumfield	

GROOM	BRIDE	DATE
BRUNER, Geo. L.	VANMETRE, Susan Ann F: John	3/17/1846
BRUNK, John	BURKART, Polly F: Genrse S: Henry Burkart M: Barbara	2/ 1/1817
BRYANT, Alvas S.	CRAIG, Jane F: Samuel CRAIG S: Samuel Craig	9/28/1830
BRYANT, Daniel	DISMORE, Sallu cert. Wm. WHITE girl's S: John Stith Jr. guardian	6/20/1826
BRYANT, Y. Goodin	EDLIN, Ellen F: John	4/28/1849
BUCKANAN, David E.	WHEATLEY, Lucretia F: John	10/ 6/1834
BUCKLES, Aaron	FRIEND, Mary S: George L. Rogers	12/ 6/1830
BUCKLES, Alfred	BOARMAN, Susan Elizabeth F: Sylvester	2/ 2/1846
BUCKLES, Henry	GREENAULT, Mary Ann F: John	3/15/1832
BUCKLES, Jacob	COOK, Mary Ann S: Hugh Cole	7/25/1828
BUCKLES, John Jr. F: John Sr.	HART, Belinda M: Rachael HART, cert. proven by John Buckles Sr. who also gave consent for son's marriage.	8/27/1822
BUCKLES, Robert F: John	HART, Milly F: Aaron	11/ 5/1832
BUCKLES, William	WATSON, Jane S: H. G. Waggoner	12/21/1831
BUCKNER, Harry W.	BOMAR, Polly F: John BOMAR S: David Ferguson S: Daniel Whitman	8/ 3/1814
BUCKNER, Horrace	PURDY, Nancy cert. James Grigsby M: Sally PURDY	10/10/1818
BUCKY, Christopher	MINGIS, Catherine S: Wm. Downs	3/22/1818
BULER, Charles	FREEN, Juliet S: John Beatly	11/28/1835
BULHAM, Chas. S.	RAGLAND, Lucy B: Gidson, Ragland	3/23/1817
BUNCH, Jacob	HORNBACK, Phebe F: Daniel S: D. Hornback	2/15/1830
BUNGER, Fielden	TILL, Elizabeth cert. Davis GILMORE, S: Geo. L. Rogers girl's SF: proven by Alex Gilmore	8/ 1/1822
BUNGER, Henry	HOWEY, Lucinda F: James	1/ 3/1850

GROOM	BRIDE	DATE
BUNGER, William	NEFF, Elizabeth F: George NEFF B: Geo. NEFF	12/ 9/1825
BENNEL, Benjamin	BUMMEL, Mary F: William	9/13/1831
BUNNEL, William Jr.	NEWMAN, Elizabeth George NEWMAN her father	2/ 4/1824
BUNNELL, Samuel W. F: Archibald A.	LOVELACE, Catherine F: Colmore	12/15/1850
BUNNELL, William M.	WARREN, Tresa E. F: James Sinus (bro)	11/23/1850
BURBA, Henry	BOGUE? Deborah F: John BOGUE cert. proven by Peter Burba	7/11/1825
BURBA, John	BOAG, Rebecca F: Samuel S: H. G. Wagginer	12/10/1829
BURBA, Miles P.	BURBA, Azuba Nicholas Burba S: Silas Lee swore girl 21.	9/ 8/1846
BURBA, Nicholas	CARDIN, Elizabeth F: Archibald	4/ 9/1850
BURBA, Ralph	SMITH, Betsy cert. girl's father S: Stiles Parker F: John SMITH M: Jane SMITH	10/15/1819
BURBA, Willam	MURLIN, Jane F: John	11/ 9/1819
BURBE, Peter	FOSTER, Minerva Henry Burba says S: Stiles Parker bride is 21.	8/ 4/1823
BURCH, Alexander of Nelson Co., Jy.	CISSELL, Ellenor F: Ellider CISSELL	11/ 7/1814
BURCH, Drury	ARMOUR, Nancy F: David	10/ 7/1835

BURCH, Leonard	OVERALL, Mrs. Dorcas
	                 S: John Stith Jr.
	                 S: James Crutcher
		7/13/1829

BURCH, Joseph	BOARMAN, Susannah F: Thomas, cert. Thos. BOARMAN prven by Silvester Boarman.	1/15/1822
BURCH, Walter	CHASTAIN, Ann F: Elijah S: E. Chastain	4/16/1827
BURCHAM, Henry	HAYS, Mary S: Randal P. Hays	3/ 8/1815
BURDINE, John	EDLIN, Elizabeth S: J. P. Lancaster	6/19/1835
BURGE, William A.	FUNK, Therissa S. F: Alexander	5/30/1850
BURKHEART, Andrew	GRAHAM, Mrs. Susan S: John Hodgen	4/25/1823

15

GROOM	BRIDE	DATE
BURKHEART, Henry	DECOURD, Marian	1/14/1814
		S: John Rouse
BURK, James	RILEY, Mary Ann	4/13/1826
	F: Michael	S: Joseph Riley
BURKES, Samuel	SPURRIER, Corilla	4/15/1828
	F: Joseph	
BURKS, William	WYLEY, Sarah	4/ 5/1829
	G: PRICE, Sullivan	S: Blacher C. Wood
BURLER, William	LEE, Elizabeth	12/17/1816
	F: Emud bee	
BURRIS, Tobias	SCOTT, Mahalia	1/30/1833
	F: John	
BURRIS, William	SNELLING, Nancy	2/ 9/1825
F: Charles	F: Enoch	
BUSH, Christ	GOODWIN, Polly	4/ 1/1815
		S: Isaac Goodwin
BUSH, John	COFER, Sarah Ann	6/ 7/1824
	F: Thomas COFER	
	girl's father gave cert.	
BUSH, John	GLENN, Peggy	6/16/1813
		S: Christ Bush
BUSH, John M.	STADER, Catherine A.	10/21/1849
	F: Peter	
BUSH, Samuel	GARNER, Debby	12/30/1835
		S: Colmore Lovelace
BUSH, William Jr.	COFER, Matilda	4/17/1832
	F: Thomas	
BUSKITT, David	CHASTAIN, Nancy	12/28/1824
		S: Geo. L. Rogers
BUSAN, Jacob	MCDANIEL, Nancy	1/13/1826
	F: John St.	
BUTLER, Henry	MEEK, Elizabeth	9/14/1814
BUTLER, William	CAMAHORN? SEAMAHORN, Margaret	1/21/1818
	F: Nathaniel	S: Nathaniel Camahorn
BUZEN, William	PRICE, Polly	8/12/1822
	cert. Robert MCLURE	S: John Hodgen
	guardian of girl.	
BYERS, Philip	LACEFIELD, Mrs. Elizabeth	8/26/1835
		S: William H. Potter
CAIN, Edwin	MYRICKS, Elizabeth	10/15/1832
		S: Charles J. Cecil
CAIN, John	YATES, Rhoda	9/27/1844
F: James	F: James	
CALHOUN, Samuel	THURMOND, Elizabeth	8/31/1847
		S: Ezre Ward
CALLEN, Thomas	TABER, Sarah Ann	8/ 2/1849
	John Cullen proved	S: C.T. Meedor
	cert.	
CALVERT, Rolla	TURNER, Malvina	4/18/1825
	M: Sarah TURNER	
CALVIN, John	VAN METRE, Elizabeth	1/11/1826
	F: Jacob C. VAN METRE	
	Cert. girl's father.	

GROOM	BRIDE	DATE
CALVIN, John	DORSEY, Gilley F: Beal DORSEY	3/20/1820
CALVIN, Luther G.	VANMETRE, Martha Jane	12/14/1847 S: Jacob Rogers
CAMBRON, Benedict	ASHBOUGH, Sally	1/ 9/1832 S: Charles G. Cecil
CANDIFF, James R. or CUNDRIFF	HILTON, Ellen Ann M: Sarah A.	2/ 3/1848 S: Ezre Ward
CANN, James	MYERS, Nancy	3/23/1816 S: John Myers
CANN, John	GARDNER, Jincy	5/13/1814 S: James Miller
CANN, William B.	GOODMAN, Frances F: Jacob	3/10/1828 S: J. Goodman
CANN, William	CORNETT, Susan F: Lidwell	6/29/1848
CANTER, Samuel	PRICE, Amelia F: Halton PRICE	12/20/1816 S: Aden Clark
CARBY, Henry	CARBY, Mary Margaret F: Zachariah	5/ 5/1849
CARBY, William	NICHOLS, Margaret swore both to be age 21.	9/19/1822 S: Jesse Carby
CARDIN, Philip Jr.	PATTERSON, Sarah Ann F: George	4/ 3/1850
CARLINGHOUSE, Geo.	DRURY, Eley F: Timonth DRURY	12/29/1824 S: Stiles Parker
CARLISLE, John	NORRIS, Martha F: William	3/23/1849
CARLISLE, William	WISE, Rozella F: Garbriel	8/17/1846
CARLISLE, Walter	WISE, Julia Ann F: Thos. H.	1/24/1844 S: C. J. Comes
CARLISLE, Wm.	SLACK, Penelope	2/17/1814 S: Wm. Slack S: John Crutcher
CARLTON, Henry	WILLIAMS, Martha F: Green B.	9/ 6/1828 S: David Thurman
CARLTON, Hiram	HARTLEY, Rachael Jonathan Hartley says girl is age 21.	11/22/1823
CARLTON, John F: James SPILMAN		1/23/1826
CARMEN, Joseph	DUNCAN, Martha F: Sharack	2/ 2/1822
CARR, John	DODSON, Rhoda	2/31/1816 S: James How
CARRICO, George	CARRICO, Theresa M: Eleanor	5/ 9/1835 S: C. J. Coomes
CARRICO, Isaac	PRESTON, Amelia	6/25/1846 S: Colmon Lovelace

GROOM	BRIDE	DATE
CARROLL, David R.	SIMS, Elizabeth	2/ 1/1821
	F: Benjamin SIMS S: Lewis Carroll	
	M: Elizabeth	
CARROLL, James	DULEY, Sarah	7/26/1815
CARTE, Aaron	HARRIS, Hannah	2/ 7/1825
	S: James Haycraft	
CARTER, Benjamin Jr.	MOBERLEY, Elizabeth	10/16/1829
F: Benjamin Sr.	F: William	
CARTER, Jacob	SCOTT, Louisa	3/29/1848
F: James	F: John	
CARTER, Jacob	DAWNS, Sarah	8/24/1827
	S: Hugh Cole	
CARTER, James	HUNDLEY, Jane	12/ 4/1826
	F: Arch S: Arch Hundley	
CARTER, John	LILES, Matilda	9/26/1848
	Wm. Liles swore	
	girl 21.	
CARTER, Joseph	HORNBACK, Elizabeth	12/30/1850
	Jackson M. Percefull S: James Daugherty	
	swore girl 21.	
CARTER, Littleberry	JOHNSON, Harriet W.	4/30/1835
CARTER, Samuel	PRICE, Amelia	12/20/1816
	F: Hatton PRICE	
CARTER, Seman	KILLEN, Sarah	4/19/1834
	G: William	
CARVER, Jesse	ANBERRY, Eliza	9/ 1/1827
F: Pleasant	F: Craver	
CARVEY, John C.	SHEETS, Mary	7/16/1833
	S: Colmore Lovelace	
CASE, Jonathan	ANDERSON, Mrs. Eliza	1/ 7/1819
CASE, Josiah	MORRISON, Ruthy	3/21/1816
	S: James Morsison	
CASE, Abraham	GLOVER, Deborah	9/18/1820
	S: Bernet Straughan	
	S: James Haycraft	
CASH, Arch	ENLOW, Betsy	1/22/1813
	S: Thomas Duly	
CASH, James	CASH, Angeline	3/27/1846
	Claibourn Cash gave cert.	
	proven by Warren Cash.	
CASH, John	KEITH, Elizabeth	11/ 7/1817
	S: Enoch KEITH says S: Warren Cash	
	parents consent.	
	F: Alexander KEITH	
CASH, John	DUVAL, Lydia	7/15/1825
F: Clarborne	consent of boy's father	
CASH, Lewis L.	WILLIAMS, Julia P.	12/ 4/1845
F: Claibourn	Ira. Williams swore	
	girl 21.	
CASH, Warren	DUVALL, Kitty	10/28/1822
	cert. of both fathers S: Warren Cash	
	S: Thom. Duvall	

HARDIN COUNTY, KENTUCKY MARRIAGE RECORDS

GROOM	BRIDE	DATE
CASH, Warren	LOVE, Sarah E.	1/18/1848
	Jonathan C. COCHE Gdn.S: Benjamin Keith	
CASLEY, Zachariah	HENDERSON, Phebe	3/25/1828
	F: Freelove S: F. Henderson	
CASSWELL, Elias	FERLEY, Elizabeth	9/23/1844
	F: John	
CASWELL, John	BRACKETT, Sarah E.	9/25/1846
F: William	F: D. L. BRACKETT	
CASSWEL, John	SMITH, Katherine	2/ 9/1828
	F: John S: J. Smith	
CASTEEL, Abraham	SMITH, Letticia	10/11/1828
F: Zachariah	F: John	
CASTEEL, Jesse	SMITH, Mary	9/ 7/1831
F: Zachariah		
CASTLEMAN, Coward	WADLEY, Anna	2/13/1833
	F: William	
CASTLEMAN, David	THOMAS, Elinor	7/ 8/1833
	F: Moses	
CASTLEMAN, Lewis	LARUS, Sarah	8/30/1823
	cert. girl's mother S: John Hodgen	
	proven by Morgan Larue	
CASTLEMAN, Stephen	FREDERICK, Elizabeth	7/15/1828
	G: John ARNOLD S: George L. Rogers	
CASTLEMAN, Toliver	LARUE, Sarah H.	7/ 3/1833
	S: Colmore Lovelace	
CASTLEMAN, William	KING, Ann	10/24/1848
	Gdn: James Marshall S: R. L. Thurman	
CATLETT, Isaac	WALTERS, Mary	3/16/1825
	F: Conrod WALTERS	
	cert. girl's father	
CAULFELD, John H.	RILEY, Sophia	1/26/1833
	S: H. C. Ulen	
CAVAN, Samuel R.	DECOUR, Harriet	7/11/1817
F: John CAVAN of	Henry Burkhart, proved S: Henry Burkhart	
Warrance Ky.	cert.	
	M: Nancy ROUX	
CECIL, Joseph	KERFOOT, Celia	3/25/1848
	F: Geo. W.	
CEISSELL, Henry	KERFOOT, Julia Ann	5/ 3/1846
	F: Geo. W.	
CERBY? Thomas	NICHOLAS, Elizabeth	12/27/1819
CESSNA, Joanthan F.	MILLER, Nancy	2/11/1832
	F: Abraham	
CHALFIN, Archibald	MCGEE, Eliza J.	10/10/1835
	S: Jacob Rogers	
CHALFIN, Joseph	COUN, Mary Ann	6/30/1820
	cert. girl's father S: Shadrack Brown	
	S: John B. Helm	
CHALFAN, Joseph	PAUL, Mary	2/11/1823
	cert. of Thos. S: Buchanan, Simon	
	PEARMAN, SF. of girl	

GROOM	BRIDE	DATE
CHALFRON, Hiram	PEARMAN, Elizabeth	3/21/1830
	M: Mary S: H. Pearman	
CHAMBERS, Anthony	BLUE, Nancy	4/ 8/1819
	S. Cert. Mark Marshall S: Go. L. Rogers	
	F: Garrett BLUE	
CHAMBERS, Giles	DAVIS, Mrs. Ruth	9/ 6/1817
CHAMBERS, Henry V.	PRICE, Sarah E.	9/ 3/1844
	F: Samuel	
CHAMBERS, Isaac	GOODIN, Mabetable	10/14/1816
	S: Thos. Miller	
CHAMPLELAIN, Thomas	ALLEN, Mary	9/18/1835
	S: Colmore Lovelace	
CHANDLER, Hartwell	SHEETS, Elizabeth	10/ 2/1850
CHARLTON, John J.	BURRIS, Elizabeth Jane	1/29/1849
	F: Seth	
CHASTAIN, Stephen D.	MILLER, Rebecca	6/ 2/1834
	M: Elizabeth S: David Thurman	
CHENAULT, John B.	SMITH, Mary	9/ 5/1846
	S: R. L. Thurman	
CHENAULT, John C.	PETERS, Polly	8/10/1831
	F: Thomas	
CHENAULT, Thomas	MARLOW, Lucinda	1/ 3/1848
	F: Dary	
CHANOWITH, Hardin L.	HART, Nancy	1/ 9/1823
	S: Geo. L. Rogers	
CHENOWITH, John P.	HOWARD, Mary Elizabeth	9/26/1845
	S: C. J. Coomes	
CHESNUT, James	JONES, Sally	8/ 6/1816
	F: Olvier JONES S: James Jones	
CHILDERS, Jackson	REESOR, Martha	3/12/1845
	F: Peter	
CHILDRESS, John W.	HARE, Mary	1/28/1331
	F: Thomas S: Robert Byrn	
CHISMS, Robert	CHISMS, Lydia	9/17/1832
	S: Martin Utterback	
CHURCHILL, Andrew	MCELROY, Easter	2/ 2/1818
	cert. John H. Geoghegan	
	Guard-Robt. Dorsey	
CHURCHILL, Armstead H.	CRUTCHER, Elizabeth	5/ 7/1818
	F: James CRUTCHER S: James Crutcher	
CHURCHILL, Armistead S.	BROWN, Mary T. S.	8/15/1826
	M: Hannah S: H. Brown	
CHURCHILL, Charles T.	PAYNE, Susan C.	3/21/1850
	S: James Ovark	
CHURCHILL, George B.	SLAUGHTER, Elizabeth	1/26/1835
	F: Robert C.	
CHURCHILL, John	PERCEFULL, Eliza	12/24/1818
	S: Alex. McDougal	
CHURCHILL, Richard H.	BROWN, Sarah A.	7/12/1825
	F: Wm. BROWN Jr. cert.	
	proven by Wm. E. Brown	

GROOM	BRIDE	DATE
CISSEL, Charles F: Matthew	GEORGHAGAN, Rebecca F: D.	10/28/1828
CISSEL, Pine I. A.	REDMAN, Elizabeth F: John	11/ 5/1835
CLARK, Aden	PRICE, Elizabeth S: Hatten Price	12/11/1817
CLARK, Anthony	SITTLE, Debby M: Sarah S: Marshall Scott	11/20/1833
CLARK, Benjamin	MARKEY, Elizabeth S: J. W. Larue S: Geo. L. Rogers	5/25/1822
CLARK, David	OWSLEY, Patsey F: Thomas T. S: T.T. Owsley	2/ 8/1831
CLARK, John	PARKER, Elen (Parker) F: David	12/21/1846
CLARK, Joseph	OAKES, Polly S: David	1/19/1813
CLARK, Moses	WILKINSON, Ann F: Robert WILKINSON S: Robert Wilkinson	10/26/1818
CLATER, Presley C.	CUNDIFF, Mary Jane Chris Cundiff cert. proven by Pleasant R. Cundiff.	3/12/1848
CLAXTON, David	COGDAL, Levina S: Thos. Whitman	8/26/1817
CLEAVER, Benjamin	THOMPKINS, Rachael F: Robert, cert. proven by Benjamin Tompkins	12/ 9/1824
CLEAVER, Edmund P. F: Samuel	LUCAS, Louisa Jane F: Thomas	3/20/1850
CLEMENTS, Thomas	TWEEDLE, Drcey cert. of James TWEEDLE S: Geo. L. Rogers Step-father	8/ 2/1822
CLEMMENS, Wm.	GOLDSMITH, Sally S: David Swank	11/20/1815
CLEMMONS, Isaac	TEDLOCK, Franky S: James Simons swore girl 21	7/ 4/1821
CLINGLESMITH, Lewis P.	FRENCH, Elizabeth M: Margaret S.	12/10/1844
CLINGLESMITH, Noah	HICKS, Nancy F: John	1/ 2/1836
CLINGINSMITH, John	NEILL, Eliza Jane S: George L. Rogers	10/13/1829
CLUB, Pleasant C.	MILLER, Sarzh F: John	7/ 9/1833
COCKE, John	LOVE, Sarah G. F: William	10/23/1836
COCKRELL, Johnston	RAINE, Lucy L. F: William	8/22/1828
COFER, John	MACGILL, Mary Elenor M: Helen MCGILL cert. Helen McGill	11/27/1825

GROOM	BRIDE	DATE
COFER, Lawrence	MALLORY, Mrs. Lucy	6/ 7/1817
	S: Samuel Anderson	
	S: Jacob Strigler	
COFER, Thomas	HARDIN, Mary	2/14/1831
	F: Martin	S: M. Hardin
COFER, Thomas	SLACK, E. Letitia	11/10/1824
	S: Geo. L. Rogers	
COFER, Wesley	MARSHALL, Rebecca	8/ 3/1835
	F: John	
COFFMAN, Alfred T.	WOODRING, Susan Catherine	4/27/1846
	F: John Sr.	
COFFMAN, Henry	HUNDLEY, Sarah	1/21/1850
Gdn: Holland WILLIAM	F: Thomas	
COFFMAN, Henry	BEWLEY, Esther	12/15/1818
	S: John Stith Jr.	
COFFMAN, Moses	HOBBS, Nancy	5/26/1831
	S: Colmore Lovelace	
COFFMAN, Aaron	PENDLETON, Mamainne	3/16/1830
F: Abraham	F: Henry	
COFMAN, Harmon	MILLER, Elender	5/ 5/1823
	F: Wm. MILLER, proved S: David Thurman	
	father's conset	
COLE, Harkin	JONES, Orphy	6/10/1814
	S: Jasper Terry	
COLE, Harkin	DAVIS, Rebecca	3/ 7/1815
	S: Jacob Van Metre	
COLE, James	SLACK, Catherine	10/ 8/1848
	Robert Huff swore	
	girl 21.	
COLE, Jesse W.	BURKHEAD, Eleanor	11/20/1835
F: Francis	F: Thomas	
COLE, Joel	GIVENS, Ann	9/24/1831
F: Francis	M: Sally	
COLE, John H.	DUFNER, Mary	9/23/1820
	F: Jacob DUFER S: Jacob Dufer	
COLE, Thomas	BRYON, Mary Ellen	11/16/1850
	Wm. Bryon swore S: C. J. Coomes	
	girl 21.	
COLE, William	THORNBURY, Mary	11/ 2/1821
	also given written S: Barry Thornburry	
	plian also Mary Thomas	
	is plainly written as the	
	name of the bride. Robert	
	Abell pr.	
COLEMAN, Benjamin	LAMBERT, Hannah	10/10/1820
	S: Abraham Lambert	
COLEMAN, Chenault	BUNNELL, Martha	7/ 3/1830
F: Thomas	F: William	
COLEMNA, Benjamin	LAMBERT, Hannha	10/10/1820
	S: Alex. McDougal	
COLGEN, Jesse	MOORE, Margaret	1/19/1846
	S: C. J. Coomes	

GROOM	BRIDE	DATE
COLLARD, Elijah	JOHNSON, Elizabeth F: William S: William Johnson	2/ 8/1831
COLLINS, James W.	PITMAN, Elenor A. F: K. James	5/26/1837
COLLINS, William M: Mariah MERRIFIELD	WRIGHT, Nancy F: Laban	3/22/1837
COLVIN, John Jr.	GOODMAN, Vian cert. of Thos Geoghegan S: Milton Stith proven by J. B. Goodman	2/26/1849
COLVIN, William	CLINGLESMITH, Nancy S: Ezra Ware	2/ 9/1846
COMBS, Samuel H.	WILLIAMS, Susan father's cert. proven S: Thos. J. Chilton John C. Williams	3/15/1823
CONAWAY, John B.	ROGERS, Frances C. W.C. Wilson swore S: Jas. H. Jenkins girl 21.	8/ 9/1849
CONHEAD, James M.	MCMAHON, Purmelia S: Colmore Lovelace	6/ 5/1834
CONN or CANN, James	MYERS, Nancy	3/23/1816
CONNER, John	EVENS, Mrs. Eliza S: John Jenkins says Warren Cash Eliza has his consent widow of Tom Evens	10/23/1820
CONOUR, William	BOWLING, Rebecca F: William S: William Bowling	11/18/1828
CONWAY, William	HACKLEY, Frances Maria James Crutcher with who she lived	7/17/1823
COOGLE, John	GOODMAN, Kate F: Jacob S: J. Goodman	7/15/1838
COOK, George	HOWARD, Cynthianna cert. girl's father	10/29/1823
COOK, Richard	BUCKLES, Elizabeth F: John	10/20/1832
COOK, William	PRICE, Elizabeth F: John	11/15/1831
COOK, William	ROBERTSON, Mary M: Nancy	3/30/1835
COOK, William	HOWARD, Louisianna F: George H. S: George Howard	1/22/1828
COOK, William T.	SLY, Live Anne F: Benjamin SLY cert. Mr. Sly	3/ 3/1823
COOLEY, John Jr.	DOUGHERTY, Susan Wm. W. Dougherty S: A. L. Alderman swore girl 21.	4/11/1845
COOLEY, Lawson	RAIZOR, Rachel	12/31/1835
COOMBS, Greenberry	WILSON, Susan Warren Cash swore S: Ezra Ward girl 21.	10/ 1/1846

GROOM	BRIDE	DATE
COOMBS, Huston	HICKMAN, Polly	9/18/1817
		S: Warren Cash
COOMBS, Thomas	COOMBS, Elizabeth	1/18/1817
	F: Adin COOMBS	S: Jesiah E. Best
COOMES, James	BURNET, Susanna	9/20/1848
		S: Ezra Ward
COOMS, Fielding	COOMBS, Velinda	2/ 4/1820
	F: Adin COOMBS	S: Martin Utterback
		S: Thos. Coombs
COONROOD, Gideon	VEUS, Susanah	1/27/1831
F: George	F: Nathan	
COONROD, Stephen	LES, Candia	2/24/1819
	Guard: Green LEE	S: Martin Utterback
		S: Henry Leaser
COONROD, Thomas	JONES, Ann Colson	4/ 9/1816
F: George	F: William JONES	S: Barabas Cuarter
COOPER, Robert	COOPER, Treasy	11/14/1818
		S: N. F. Hall
CORN, Edward	FOWLER, Sally	5/ 3/1827
	F: James	
COSTLER, William	MCCANDESS, Nancy Ann	12/11/1845
		S: Warren Cash
COTRELL, Henry	THOMPSON, Elizabeth	2/17/1845
	F: William THOMPSON	
COTTON, Isaac	HARNED, Patsy	12/22/1834
	F: Eli	
COWHERED, Ezekiel H.	PENDLETON, Joanna S.	10/ 8/1849
	John P. Baker proved	S: Geo. H. Hicks
	cert. of father	
COWLEY, John	OWEN, Hester	1/11/1825
	consent of girl's	S: Jacob Enlow
	father	
COWLEY, John	BURCHAN, Sarah	2/20/1835
	F: David	
COWLEY, Thomas	SPENCER, Martha	11/20/1848
F: Colbert	Gdn: WILLIAMS, Samuel	
COWLEY, William G.	VIERS, Mary Ann	5/ 1/1848
	Elisha A. Viers swore	S: Jacob Rogers
	girl 21.	
COX, Jonathan	ANDERSON, Mrs. Eliza	1/17/1819
		S: John Cox
COX, Richard	KINGLESMITH, Sarah	2/18/1846
		S: Green B. Williams
COYLE, Robert	DAUGHERTY, Malvila	2/25/1848
	Elder James Daugherty's	
	cert proven by John M. Coyle	
COY, Amos D.	COY, Nancy	1/ 3/1824
	F: Debry COY says girl's	S: S. Martin
	age 21.	
COY, Daniel	TUCKER, Mrs. Mary	8/22/1835
		S: James Daugherty

HARDIN COUNTY, KENTUCKY MARRIAGE RECORDS

GROOM	BRIDE	DATE
COY, Wm.	ROBERTSON, Sarah	1/20/1814
		S: Samuel Robertson
CRADDOCK, James	GARDNER, Nancy	11/13/1815
	F: Wm. GARDNER	S: John Gardner
		S: Robert Miller
CRADDOCK, Jesse	COX, Drusilla	4/14/1813
	F: Henry COX	S: Gambriel Cox
CRADDOCK, William	GARDNER, Ann	10/15/1818
	S: John CANN	
CRADY, David Jr.	COY, Nancy	12/29/1817
John Crady witness,	F: Daniel COY	S: David Crady Sr.
brother	M: Elizabeth COY	
CRADY, Ebenezer	LEAMAN, Sarah E.	9/ 8/1848
	F: Samuel	
CRADY, James	COY, Polly	8/22/1826
	G: James HANCOCK	
CRADY, John	COY, Elizabeth	5/ 4/1818
	F & M: Daniel & Elizaley	
CRADY, Sharp	ATHERTON, Letticia	12/18/1834
	F: William	
CRADY, Thomas	COY, Margaret	11/16/1815
	F/M: John and Comfort COY	
CRADY, William	TUCKER, Ketruah	1/31/1821
	F: Nathan TUCKER	S: N. Tucker
	s: cert of Thomas	
	Tucker	
CRADY, William	DEWITT, Nancy	5/22/1829
	F: Solomon	S: James Daugherty
CRAHORN, John	MELTON, Lucy	11/ 6/1817
F: Thomas	F: Anderson MELTON	
CRAIG. Samuel	HOLSTON, Sally	3/15/1832
M: Elizabeth	F: William	
CRAIG, Thomas	FORD, Almira	10/ 2/1828
F: Elis	F: Moses	
CRAIG, William	MEDHAM, Abilgail	3/ 6/1828
	F: Timothy	S: T. Needham
CRAIL, Philip	BURKAHRT(?), Cath.	10/ 5/1814
		S: Henry Burkhart
CRAIN, William S.	PERRY, Mary E.	3/18/1845
	F: David	
CRALLEY, Samuel S.	SOUTH, Hannah Mrs.	2/17/1845
		S: Mo. D. Abell
CROMWELL, Levi	GRABLE, Sarah	12/23/1814
	F: Joseph GRABLE	S: Nicholas Ke-ly
CRANELL, Joseph	WELL, Mary Ellen	12/21/1849
	F: Martin	
CRASS, Henry	KINDLE, Elizabeth	12/17/1816
		S: Saml Hackley
CRAWFORD, James	FLORENCE, Elizabeth	11/ 1/1848
		S: James Daugherty
CRAWFORD, James	IRWIN, Marian	1/27/1847
		S: R. L. Thurman

25

GROOM	BRIDE	DATE
CRAWFORD, John	COFER, Mrs. Nancy	4/15/1819
	S: Geo. L. Rogers	
	S: Elijah Griffin	
CREAGER, John C.	CREAGER, Leodica	8/ 7/1848
	F: C. CREAGER	
CREAGER, Joshua L.	SWAN, Charlotte C.	7/12/1849
	F: Julius	
CREAGER, Valentine	GLOVER, Urith	1/ 5/1816
	S: Joshua Glover	
CREAL, Armistead R.	STARK, Margaret M.	7/31/1832
	F: James	
CREECH, William	STOVALL, Permelia	12/30/1829
	F: Hezekiah	
CREEWELL, Matthew	GREENWELL, Mary Amelia	1/30/1816
	F: James GREENWELL S: Stephen Greenwell	
CREGER, Chrisham	BIRD, Sally	12/19/1821
	F: Jacob BIRD. cert of	
	J. Bird swore by Adam	
	Bird	
CREW, Thomas	SHELTON, Ann	3/10/1834
	F: John J.	
CROOK, John	DAWSON, Nancy	10/12/1814
	F: John DAWSON S: Aaron H. McCarty	
	M: Hannah DAWSON	
CROW, William	BALLINGER, Elizabeth	9/22/1846
	Jas. Ballinger swore	
	girl 21.	
CRUTCHER, James M.	WINTERSMITH, Mary S.	4/12/1847
	S: Wm. B. Evans	
CRUTCHER, James	SWANK, Sarah	2/ 6/1832
	F: Jacob	
CRUTCHER, James	WOOLFOLK, Mrs. Susan	3/ 7/1825
	S: John Stith Jr.	
CRUTCHER, John	MCDOWELL, Kitty	12/15/1824
	F: John FORLINE S: John Stith	
	proved cert.	
CRUTCHER, John	SUMMER, Sally	7/10/1845
	S: Jacob Rogers	
CRUTCHER, Stephen W.	MCDOWELL, Mary S.	9/ 3/1833
	F: John	
CRUTCHER, Thomas A.	BRESHEAR, Elizabeth A.	4/ 2/1849
	G: Hezekiah C. STOVALL S: Jacob Rogers	
CRUTCHER, Willia	MCDOWELL, Margaret	1/ 8/1828
	F: John	
CRUMBAUGH, Geo. W.	CRANDELL, Sophrina	2/24/1848
	F: Lemuel	
CRUME, James	POPHAM, Sarah	1/13/1834
	F: Job	
CRUME, William W.	MOBLEY, Matilda Jane	12/19/1833
	F: William MOBLY	
CRUMES, William	HOSKINSON, Susannah	2/ 7/1825

GROOM	BRIDE	DATE
CRUTHER, Richard	MUDD, Frances Mrs.	7/20/1847
	S: Geo. H. Hicks	
CULBERTSON, Robert B.	COOK, Elizabeth	2/11/1819
	S: Warren Cash	
	S: Sam'l Haycraft Jr.	
CULLY, Don Carlee	MATTHIS, Mary Jane	8/ 2/1849
	John H. Arnold swore S: Geo. M. Crumbaugh	
	girl 21.	
CULLY, James	BUCKNER, Lauretta	12/16/1834
	F: Horace	
CULLY, Mathew	BURK, Elizabeth	6/29/1831
	S: Colmore Lovelace	
CULLY, Robert	CULLY, Elizabeth	4/27/1825
	S: John Hodgen	
CULLY, Thomas	GEORGE, Sarah	2/15/1821
	W. H. Porter says S: Colemore Lovelace	
	she is 21.	
CULVER, Daniel	COY, Susannah	10/13/1813
	S: Moses & Wm. Coy	
CUNDRIFF, James R.	HILTON, Ellen Ann	2/ 3/1848
or CANDIFF	M: Sarah A. S: Ezre Ward	
CUNDIFF, Shadrick	STILLWELL, Sally	9/24/1822
F: Marshall CUNDIFF	cert. of father S: J. A. Cundiff	
	proven by and S:	
	Stephen Stillwell	
	F: Isaac	
	M: Elizabeth	
CUNNINGHAM, Aaron	DAVIS, Mrs. Jane	12/19/1831
	S: Isaac Taylor	
CUNNINGHAM, Anthony C.	WINTERSMITH, Mary C.	5/ 1/1832
	F: H. G.	
CUMMINGS, Arthur	KELING? Susan	9/11/1824
PAYNE, Adam step-father	S: Wm. Tarpley	
CUTRIGHT, Con W.	CUTRIGHT, Abagial	12/20/1847
	Wm. Carr swore S: J. M. Yager	
	girl 21.	
CUTSINGER, George	WARMAN, Darky	2/12/1824
DALE, Abraham	FLETCHER, Effy	8/22/1814
	S: James Fletcher	
DALTON, Alexander W.	OVERTON, Nancy B.	1/17/1824
	F: George OVERTON consent	
	of Geo. Overton.	
DANIEL, John S.	VITTLOE, Mary Jane	1/17/1845
	Andrew S. Miller S: Jacob Rogers	
	swore girl 21.	
DANIEL, Richard S.	ROBINSON, Angeline S.	12/27/1844
	S: Jacob Rogers	
DARLING, Henry	MCGEEHEE, Louisa	3/27/1817
	S: Wm. L. McGeeHee	
DAUGHERTY, Benjamin	HAYWOOD, Susan	4/10/1820
	S: Wm. Haywood	

GROOM	BRIDE	DATE
DAUGHERTY, Canison	RICHARDSON, Eliza	12/ 9/1833
	F: Amos	
DAUGHERTY, Charles	STADER, Betsy	6/ 5/1816
		S: John Daugherty
		S: John Stader
DAUGHERTY, Christopher	HAYCRAFT, Lettice	2/ 8/1827
		S: James Daugherty
DAUGHERTY, Cornelius	HUNDLEY, Nancy	9/ 5/1817
M: Martha DAUGHERTY	F: Arch HUNDLEY cert.	
	of both parents.	
DAUGHERTY, Isaac	GREGORY, Sarah Ann	
M: Martha	F: Christopher	
DAUGHERTY, Jesse	HARNED, Sally	5/18/1816
DAUGHERTY, Jonathan	HOOKER, Ihrena	1/12/1828
M: Nancy	F: William	
DAUGHERTY, Lodowick M.	THOMAS, Letticia E.	9/ 1/1834
	M: Sarah BLAND	
DAUGHERTY, Miles	CARTWRIGHT, Mary	11/27/1829
F: James		S: James Daugherty
DAUGHERTY, Samuel	LANCASTER, Rebecca	5/ 4/1832
SF: William YOUNG		
DAUGHERTY, Samuel	STADER, Anna	6/ 7/1817
	Ann Stader swore both	
	of age.	
DAUGHERTY, William	RUST, Mary	3/29/1821
	Joseph Hargen cert.	S: Joseph Hargan
	girl age.	S: Jacob Enlow
DAUGHERTY, William	HARD, Susan	12/ 5/1845
		S: J. C. C. Thompson
DAVIS, Isaac	LESHLY, Many	4/ 3/1813
		S: Wm. Riley
DAVID, John	HARRIS, Sarah	11/ 5/1823
DAVIS, John R.	GREENAULT, Mary	10/14/1843
	James H. Friend	S: Isaac Hart
	swore girl 21.	
DAVID, Joshua	JACKSON, Mary	8/17/1832
	F: William	
DAVIT, Jacob	JOSEPH, Mary Ann	12/13/1820
		S: Wm. Downs
DAVIS, Jesse	MAYSON, Nancy	12/19/1815
	M: Hannah MAYSON	S: John J. Shelton
DAVIS, Moses S.	MCINTIRE, Sarah E.	12/28/1820
		S: David Thurman
		S: Henry P. Helms
DAVIS, Rice	CASTLEMAN, Peggy Ann	1/10/1829
	F: Benjamin	
DAVIS, Robert	SMITH, Martha Ann	5/16/1831
	F: Noah	S: N. Smith
DAVIS, Robert	BRYANT, Joysey	2/18/1829
	M: Mary ROGERS	S: Mary Rogers

GROOM	BRIDE	DATE
DAVIS, Robert S.	MCGRAN, Mrs. Mary	3/16/1831
		S: Georges L. Rogers
DAVIS, Smither H.	MOREMAN, Rhoda Jane	4/10/1846
	Jesse P. MOREMAN F:	S: Jan. P. Moreman
DAVIS, Wlisa	CRANDELL, Elizabeth	6/20/1846
	S.W. Crandell swore	S: J.C.C. Thompson
	girl 21.	
DAWSON, Middleton	MCCARTY, Nancy	11/13/1817
	F: Cornelius MCCARTY	S: Enos McCarty
	M: Susannah MCCARTY	
DEAR, Thomas	WARD, Thoda	10/18/1823
		S: Wn. Tarpley
DEAVER, Aaron	CRADY, Sarah	7/18/1835
		S: James Daugherty
DEAVER, Thompson	ATHERTON, Elizabeth	10/ 6/1830
F: Stephen	F: William	
DEAVORS, Miles	WISEHART, Lettice	/28/1819
		S: Thos. Deauer
DECKER, William	SMALLWOOD, Lidia	2/14/1821
		S: Michael Smallwood
DELANY, Joseph R.	MCDOWELL, Nancy	7/15/1817
		S: James McDowell
DENBO, Jesse	VANDEGRIFT, Nancy	11/27/1819
		S: Samuel Vandegrift
DENBO, Joseph	SUMMERS, Polly	9/11/1813
	F: Solomon SUMMERS	S: James Dooley
DENLE, James	VANDERGRAFT, Nancy	11/27/1819
or DENBE	F: Samuel VANDERGRAFT	
DERRITT, John	HANKINS, Mary Jane	12/25/1843
	F: Hardin	
DESARIEST, Chas. W.	MORRISON, Susan	8/20/1844
	James Buck swore	S: Ezre Ward
	girl 21.	
DEVEES, Joseph	LAWSON, Mary Rosina	11/ 5/1849
	F: Henry	
DEWIT, Soloman	FOWLER, Nancy	6/ 4/1822
		S: James Fowler
DEWITT, James	BEIGLER, Elizabeth	3/21/1831
GDN: Daniel CRUMP		S: Thomas Gibbons
DEWITT, James D.	DORSEY, Rachael	8/15/1849
		S: J. H. Yager
DICHEY, John Jackson	BALDWIN, Susanna A. Mrs.	10/ 9/1845
		S: Morgan J. Larue
DILLARD, James	HAYWOOD, Cynitha	8/22/1814
		S: Nicholas Miller
DILLARD, John	DITTO, Elizabeth	2/ 3/1835
	F: Hardin	S: Jacob Rogers
DILLIARD, John	DITTO, Nancy	1/29/1828
	F: Henry Jr.	S: Henry Ditto, Jr.
DILLARD, Samuel	ROBINSON, Mary	3/12/1846
	F: Andrew	

HARDIN COUNTY, KENTUCKY MARRIAGE RECORDS

GROOM	BRIDE	DATE
DILLINER, Henry	HARVEY, Mrs. Sarah	9/20/1830
		S: James Daugherty
DILLINGHAM, Joseph R.	LARUE, Lucinda	8/10/1829
	SF: Martin ROOF	S: H. G. Wagginer
DINWIDDIE,	MCLURE, Mariah	10/ 4/1815
	F: Wm. MCLURE	S: Robert Mclure
DITTO, Alfred G.	BROOKS, Jane	8/28/1834
	GDN: Thomas	S: John Rich
DITTO, Franklin	WITHERS, Narcissa E.	9/28/1846
	F: John	
DITTON, Hardin	ROSEBERRY, Frances	2/12/1836
	F: Charles	
DITTO, James C.	YOUNG, Ellen V.	12/29/1828
		S: Simeon Buchanan
DITTO, John Sr.	NORCUTT, Martha	10/ 9/1843
	Martin Nall swore	S: Jacob Rogers
	girl 21.	
DITTO, William	WITHERS, Margaret	11/ 3/1817
		S: Wm. Withers Jr.
DODGE, Charles	KENNEDY, Elizabeth	10/31/1825
	M: Phene ARTMAN cert.	S: Jacob Artman
	of girl's step father	
DODGE, Josiah	HENDRICKS, Drewsilla	9/ 8/1813
		S: Samuel Peacefull
DODGE, Josiah	COX, Mrs. Ann	7/19/1825
		S: Geo. L. Rogers
DODGE, Martin B.	BACON, Elizabeth N.	2/25/1846
	David Stamp swore	S: Alexander Guston
	girl 21.	
DODSON, John B.	AMENT, Cahanice	4/25/1833
F: Joseph H.	F: John	
DONAN, Jeremiah C.	HARRINGTON, Samira	5/16/1846
	F: John	
DONHAM, William R.	BENNETT, Nancy G.	2/ 2/1850
	Andrew Bennett swore	
	girl 21.	
DOOLY, Samuel	ENLOW, Polly	8/ 2/1819
Simon Guard		
DOOLY, Solomon	GARNER, Susan	2/15/1823
	cert. girl's mother	S: Geo. L. Rogers
	proven by Wm. Garner	
DOOLY, Thomas	STADER, Hannah	3/18/1819
		S: Thos. Coper
		S: Jacob Enlow
DOOIT, Jacob	JOSEPH, Mary Ann	12/12/1820
	M: Sarah JOSEPH	S: Thomas Gallaher
DORSEY, Anderson J.	DORSEY, Sarah	1/14/1836
	F: Richard	
DORSEY, Anderson J.	WILLIAMS, Polly	4/22/1847
	James B. Willet	S: Alexander Guston
	swore girl 21.	

GROOM	BRIDE		DATE
DORSEY, Eli D.	ENGLISH, Susan		10/12/1831
F: Richard	F: Noah		
DORSEY, Joshua F.	HILTON, Angeline		6/17/1834
	F: Wiliam F.	S: G. H. Wagginer	
DORSON, Middleton	MCCARTY, Nancy		11/13/1817
DAWSON?	F: Enos		
DORRIS, William	ARNOLD, Lydia		8/17/1825
	M: Mary ARNOLD swore girl 21.		
DORSEY, William	CANDA, Irena		12/23/1849
	B.C. Yager swore girl 21.	S: Alexander Guston	
DOUGHERTY, David	CHESIRE, Nancy		11/13/1815
		S: John Dougherty	
DOUGHERTY, James	HICKMAN, Elizabeth		1/ 1/1834
	F: Benjamin		
DOUGHERTY, Jesse	HARNED, Sally		5/18/1816
		S: Enos Harned	
DOUGHERTY, John	MALONE, Nancy		9/ 2/1815
		S: Wm. C. Morrison	
DOUGHERTY, John	HOOVER, Elizabeth		12/19/1826
DOUGHERTY, Richard	FERREE, Matilda		12/ 4/1834
	F: Cornelius		
DOUGHERTY, Samuel	STRADER, Anna		6/ 7/1817
		S: John	
DOWDALL, H. B.	BROWN, Elizabeth		1/19/1846
		S: Colmore Lovelace	
DOWEL, George	WYMP, Mary		9/ 6/1813
	F: John WYMP		
DOWELL, Elijah	HAYDEN, Mary		5/26/1823
	F: Daniel Hayden cert.	S: Daniel Hayde	
DOWELL, James	SHACKLETT, Barbara		2/ 8/1813
		S: Benjamin Shacklett	
DOWNS, William	BEARD, Sarah		3/ 7/1846
	M: Ann DONHAM cert. proven by Chas. Heard	S: Jacob Rogers	
DOYEL, Isaac	COPELAND, Polly		10/26/1816
F: Samuel	F: Charles COPELAND	S: Zachariah Copeland	
DRAKE, Alfred	REED, Catherine		12/23/1847
F: Francis	W. W. Reed swore girl 21.		
DRAKE, Johnson	OSBOURN, Susan A.		9/16/1850
	Nancy Osbourn certs. proven by Abram Drake		
DRAKE, Ruford	AUBREY, Sally R.		1/29/1850
	F: George		
DRAKE, Wm.	WALKER, Eleanor		9/27/1814
		S: Daniel	

GROOM	BRIDE	DATE
DRAKE, William	PAUL, Mary Ann	10/12/1843
	Walker swore girl 21.S: W. B. Maxey	
DRANE, Thomas Jefferson	KEITH, Susannah	2/ 6/1831
F: George	F: Benjamin	
DRANE, Thomas	CRUME, Mary	11/ 5/1831
	Gdn: William W.	
DRURY, Christopher	LOVEBERRY, Sophia	11/24/1831
	G: Samuel HAYDEN S: Charles J. Cecil	
DRURY, Elias	MATTINGLY, Ann	2/ 3/1834
	S: Edward A. Clarke	
DRURY, James	MULIN, Cybbiel	9/11/1820
	cert. by girl's S: George Mulin	
	father	
DURBIN, Edward	DURBIN, Emily	7/12/1828
G: Samuel ABLE	G: Thos. FAIRLEIGH S: Robert Byrn	
DURBIN, James	SHACKLEFORD, Sarah	1/18/1836
	F: John Sr. S: Ed. A. Clarke	
DURBIN, Joshua	WHITE, Mary	11/25/1828
	F: Arnold S: A. White	
DUCKWORTH, George	DUNCAN, Cynthia	12/15/1813
	M: Mary? DUNCAN S: Silas Eugert	
DUCKWORTH, John	WILLIAMS, Mary Quinn	10/21/1825
F: William	Gdn: Elijah DUCKWORTH	
DUCKWORTH, Nathan	BUCKHEART, Polly	12/ 2/1823
	F: George, cert. of	
	Geo. BUCKHEART	
DUFFY, Alvan	MARTIN, Jane	12/23/1833
	F: Moab	
DUFIELD, Benjamin	LEWIS, Mary Elizabeth	2/17/1848
	M: Winnefred	
DUGAN, Charles	JOHNSON, Harriet	8/ 1/1829
	F: John S: J. Johnson	
DUGAN, James	HOWLES, Mary	5/21/1825
	F: Wm. Dugan swore	
	girl is 21.	
DUGAN, William	SUTES, Elizabeth	10/30/1828
DUKE, Amos	DUNN, Rosanna	10/ 4/1825
	M: Elizabeth DUNN cert.	
	of girl's mother	
DUKE, John L.	MONEY, Sarah Elizabeth	10/24/1848
	Joseph Money swore S: R. L. Thurman	
	girl 21.	
DULY, Philip	PIGG, Maria	10/26/1818
	cert. Mrs. Sally S: Geo. L. Rogers	
	Scott and boy's father	
DULY, Philip	PIGG, Mona	10/26/1819
	S: Wm. Duly	
DUNCAN, James A.	DAUGHERTY, Kitty Ann	11/26/1846
F: Nathaniel J.	F: John	

GROOM	BRIDE	DATE
DUNCAN, John	CARMAN, Anne	10/29/1823
	Cert. boy's father proven by J. McDowell consent of girl's father.	
DUNCAN, John H. F: John Sr.	MORRISON, Mary H. F: Thomas	2/27/1833
DUNCAN, Johnson F.	LAWSON, Sarah E. F: John	1/27/1845
DUNCAN, Shadrick	KEITH, Priscilla	9/22/1820
		S: Thos. L. Chilton
		S: Wm. Cessna
DUNCAN, Thomas H.	BEIGLER, Lucretia G: Bennet DEWITT	2/21/1831 S: Colmore Lovelace
DUNCAN, William T. F: Nathaniel J.	KERFOOT, Eveline F: Samuel	8/ 7/1844
DUNN, James	LOGSDON, Elizabeth	7/20/1834
		S: James Haycraft
DUNN, William M: Elizabeth	ARNOLD, Julian F: John	12/ 3/1827
DUNNAVAN, William M.	MCELROY, Mary cert. Robert DORSEY Gdn:	12/ 7/1824 S: Geo. L. Rogers
DUNVAN, Samuel W.	OLLEAF, McDowell F: John	7/27/1832
DUNY, Henry	DAVID, Susannah F: Richard	2/ 8/1827
DURSE, George	IRWIN, Eliza	1/19/1846
		S: Colmore Lovelace
DURSE, Jacob	GOODMAN, Kesiah F: Isaac GOODMAN	12/15/1823
DURSEY, Peter	GOODIN, Rebecca	4/18/1818
		S: Isaac Goodwin
		S: James Dures
DURBIN, Christopher	BROWN, Margaret F: Calbe BROWN	11/12/1823
DURBIN, Elisha	LOGSDON, Polly	2/10/1821
		S: James
DURBIN, John Jr.	DURBIN, Mary	11/ 2/1821
		S: Robt. Abell
		S: John Durbin
DURBIN, Joseph	NORRIS, Dorithy cert. of both fathers	6/26/1822 S: John Durbin
DUVAL, Alexander	HINTON, Nancy	9/28/1818
		S: John Stith Jr.
		S: John Hinton
DUVALL, Benjamin	SHAWLER, Elizabeth cert. John Sharler	10/ 6/1824
DYE, Isaac	CHASTAIN, Wilmoth B. B: Wm. Redman	11/25/1823 S: John Hodgen
DYE, James R.	GRAY, Jane W.C. Gray swore girl 21.	10/11/1847 S: Silas Lee

33

HARDIN COUNTY, KENTUCKY MARRIAGE RECORDS

GROOM	BRIDE	DATE
DYER, Benjamin F.	BOOKER, Margaret E.	7/ 5/1845
	F: J. BOOKER	
EASTHAM, James	DORSEY, Elizabeth	5/10/1830
	F: Richard S: R. Dorsey	
EASTER, Jacob	TROTTER, Nancy Mrs.	6/27/1818
	S: Martin Roof	
EASTER, John	PRICE, Patsy	10/ 8/1813
	S: John Price	
EASTIN, Thomas N.	CHURCHILL, Penelope	5/ 3/1845
EDLEN, William	DUNN, Elizabeth	10/17/1825
F: William Sr.	F: Robert DUNN	
EDLIN, John	COY, Eliza	4/18/1831
Gdn: John EDLIN	Gdn: Amos	
EDLIN, John	WADLEY, Jane	9/22/1827
	F: William	
EDLIN, Richard	PARISH, Margaret	4/30/1826
	Gdn: Thos. J. Chilton S: Thos. J. Chilton	
EDLIN, Richard	CRADY, Kiziah	1/11/1832
	F: David	
EDLIN, Richard	METCALF, Elizabeth	5/27/1845
	F: Vincent	
EDLIN, Silas	COY, Unis	3/ 3/1834
	Gdn: James Hancock	
EDLIN, William	WELLER, Sarah	2/28/1848
	F: Thomas	
EDSALL, Benjamin	BUSH, Elizabeth	2/ 2/1819
	bondsman, cert. Jacob S: Thos Whitman	
	Bumgardner	
	F: Thos. BUSH	
EDSON, Daniel	NEEDHAM, Rachel	5/26/1824
	F: Elias NEEDHAM	
EDWARDS, John	MCDOWELL, Suan	3/23/1826
	F: John	
EGGIN, Tunis V.	COWHERD, Nancy P.	10/28/1850
	Ezekiel Cowherd swore	
	girl 21.	
EIDSON, H. P.	ROBISON, Martha	2/11/1845
	Thos. Ribison swore	
	girl 21.	
ELIET, Saunders	MILLER, Margaret	10/27/1832
	F: James S: H. C. Ullen	
ELIOT, Stephen V.R.	SWAN, Martha	1/27/1835
	F: Thomas	
ELKIN, Samuel H.	HOWELL, Martha Ann	4/11/1825
	F: John HOWELL consent of	
	John Howell	
ELLIOT, Richard	WILSON, Ruth Elizabeth	1/15/1844
	F: Jonathan Jr.	
ELLIOTT, Newton	KENDALL, Mabala	4/ 3/1829
F: Benjamin	S: Elliot, B.	

GROOM	BRIDE	DATE
ELLISON, David	CARR, Sarah	11/24/1846
	F: David	
ELLIT, Jacob	JACKSON, Mary	12/26/1827
	F: Alexander	
ELLIT, William	MILLER, Synthia Ann	6/ 4/1825
	F: Abraham MILLER	
ELLITT, John	OWENS, Elizabeth	10/11/1820
M & F: Wm. & Susanna	M: Elizabeth OWENS S: John Baird	
EMERY, Isaac	MCMAHAN, Susan	7/ 5/1830
	G: Wm. Shelton S: Colmore Lovelace	
EMLY, Isaac	BERRYMAN, Louise	8/26/1814
	Sister: Hetty BERRYMAN S: Robert Miller	
EMORY, Joseph	WOOLF, Ester	10/13/1819
	cert. girl's father S: Jacob Enlow	
	F: Peter WOOLF	
ENGLISH, Charles	ROSS, Frankey	9/28/1814
	S: John Ross	
ENGLISH, Daniel	PEARMAN, Judeth Ann	12/ 9/1835
	M: Nancy	
ENGLISH, Haydon E.	WINTERSMITH, Sarah E.	8/17/1835
M: Nancy	G: Samuel S. HODGEN	
ENGLISH, Hiram B.	YAGER, Elizabeth F.	11/19/1823
F: Robert ENGLISH	F: Joshia YAGER, consent	
	girl's father cert. Mr.	
	English proven by Noah	
	English	
ENGLISH, James M.	WILLYARD, Malvina	5/30/1849
	F: Samuel	
ENGLISH, John	BLAND, Mary A.	1/18/1836
	M: Susan S: James Noll	
ENGLISH, Lemuel	MCENTIRE, Eliza	4/10/1828
	F: Aaron	
ENGLISH, Lemuel	BRISCOE, Sally	12/22/1813
	F: Robert ENGLISH S: John Shachkleford	
	F: Walter BRISCOE	
ENGLISH, Noah Jr.	JOHNSON, Margaret Ann	8/ 3/1829
	F: John	
ENGLISH, Robert B.	FOUSHEE, Melvina	8/12/1847
	F: John S.	
ENGLISH, Siles	MILLER, Elizabeth	6/23/1819
	F: James MILLER S: Samuel Martin	
ENGLISH, William	VANMETER, Susan	2/14/1825
	consent of Wm. Bush S: John Stith	
ENGLISH, William W.	HOWARD, Sarah	7/17/1850
	Priscilla cert. proven	
	by P. T. Howard	
ENLOW, Jacob	AUCHER, Margaret	5/16/1831
	F: Christopher S: C. Atcher	
ENLOW, John	FORLINE, Malinda	12/22/1828
	SF: Cha. TURNER S: John Stith	

GROOM	BRIDE	DATE
ENLOW,	ENLOW,	5/ 1/1828
Hackley Lynch	Alias, Berry Malinda S: P. Enlow	
	M: Polly ENLOW	
ENLOWS, Henry	HAWKINS, Nancy	3/16/1816
	cert. Joseph Enlow	
ENLOW, Thomas B.	MCLURE, Ann M.	9/ 9/1822
	S: Alexander McDougal	
ESSEX, Issaac	NEFF, Susanna	10/14/1833
F: John	F: Samuel	
ESSEX, Thomas	EDLIN, Carziah	5/28/1819
	F: James EDLIN	
ESSEX, Warren	DAVIS, Ann	11/ 5/1845
	S: James Daugherty	
EVANS, David	PENNEL, Elizabeth	1/ 4/1826
	F: John Pennel	
EVARTS, Uriah B.	HARDING, Sarah	3/23/1844
	Henry Bladn swore S: C. H. Hicks	
	girl 21.	
FAITH, William	COOK, Elizabeth	9/23/1820
	F: Windle COOK, cert. S: Asa Rogers	
	by Windle Cook	
FAIRLEIGH, George	QUINN, Elizabeth	6/28/1833
	M: Sally	
FAIRLEIGH, Thomas	ABELL, Rebecca	3/24/1824
	S: Colmore Lovelace	
FAIRLEIGH, William	ENLOWS, Elizabeth	11/ 4/1819
	S: Thos. B.	
FALLON, Geo. M.	ARNOLD, Nancy	10/ 1/1825
M: Rosanna FALLON	F: John ARNOLD	
FARMER, James	SEDLEY, Mary Jane	5/ 5/1847
	Gdn: ALLEN, Jeptha S: James Daugherty	
FARMER, Jonathan	ASH, Hellon	10/28/1822
	S: John Hodgen	
FARMER, Leonard D.	BLAND, Jane	8/ 3/1829
	M: Susan S: S. Bland	
FARMER, Thomas	STEPHENS, Matilda	9/30/1850
	F: Beed	
FARMLEY, Alexander	STOUT, Rebecca	10/31/1823
	F: David STOUT	
	cert. David Stout	
FARRAND, Jordan	MCMILLEN, Eliza Ann	5/21/1849
	F: John	
FARRANT? or TARRANT	DODGE, Diademia	2/27/1822
	M: Sophia DODGE	
	John Mills swore mother	
	said girl 21.	
FELIX, William	GRAYHAM, Mary Ann	7/19/1821
	cert. girl's mother S: James Haycraft	
	proven by Wm. Harvey	
	M: Susannah GRAYHAM	

36

GROOM	BRIDE		DATE
FERGUSON, Jackson B.	MORRISON, Sarah C.		7/18/1849
	Thos. Morrison	S: Morgan L. Larue	
	swore girl 21.		
FERRISS, Jesse	WATKINS, Aley		12/13/1816
		S: James Watkins	
FIELDS, James	CROWN, Mary		9/16/1844
	John Stader swore	S: C. L. Coomes	
	girl 21.		
FIGG, James	ATHERTON, Margaret		12/ 4/1848
	F: William		
FIGG, Nicholas	CUTRIGHT, Mandeline		11/21/1815
	Samuel C. Cutright		
	swore girl 21.		
FINDLEY, James W.	LARUE, Louisa M.		11/23/1825
	F: Samuel LARUE		
	consent S. Larue		
FISHBACK, Charles	OVERTON, Elizabeth		1/ 1/1821
	F: George OVERTON		
	cert. by Geo. Overton		
FITZGERALD, Andrew	MORRISON, Anna		8/ 9/1822
	M: Mary MORRISON, Cert.	S: Elijah Ashcraft	
	Mary Morrison proved by		
	Elijah Ashcraft		
FITZHUGH, George	ROUNDTREE, Betsy		12/16/1826
	F: Dudley R. ROUNDTREE		
FLANDERS, Benjamin	DEWIT, Sally		3/ 8/1821
	M: Nancy DEWIT	S: Stiler Parker	
FLANDERS, Elisha	FLANDERS, Jacob		9/24/1824
	M: Elizabeth HATCH		
	Jacob Hatch		
FLACK, Hiram	DRAKE, Elizabeth		9/ 7/1822
	cert. girl's father	S: John Stith Jr.	
	proven by Wm. Drake		
	F: Breckston DRAKE		
FLANDERS, Jacob G.	RICE, Mary		7/13/1830
		S: Blatchly C. Wood	
FLANDERS, Solomon	WOOD, Trifman		11/27/1846
F: Elisha	F: Ezra Sr.		
FLENERY, John	FRANCE, Sarah D.		11/22/1818
		S: Shadrack Brown	
FLETCHER, James	KINKADE, Sarah		10/10/1829
	F: Robert	S: R. Kinkade	
FLETCHER, James	LINDSAY, Mrs. Lucy A.		8/23/1832
		S: Colmore Lovelace	
FLETCHER, Robert Jr.	MILES, Ruth		3/19/1847
	M: Nancy	S: Jacob Rogers	
FLETCHER, Robert	WITHERS, Marthy		10/28/1818
	by consent of Gdn:	S: Frederick Brown	
	Shadruck BROWN		
FLORENCE, John	KING, Rebecca		8/ 8/1832
	F: John		

GROOM	BRIDE	DATE
FLORENCE, Obid	WOLF, Polly	9/21/1820
	S: Samuel Martin	
FLORENCE, Thomas	LARKIN, Cinderilla	8/13/1831
	SF: John YORK	
FLOYD, Alexander	HART, Polly	10/31/1820
	F: Aaron HART S: Hugh Cole	
	cert. girl's father	
FLOYD, Edward	GOFORTH, Elizabeth	10/13/1820
	Amos VERTREES, Gdn: S: S. Martin	
FLOYD, Edward	KENNEDY, Sarah	3/ 6/1848
M: Mary CLADRIDGE	F: Samuel	
FLOYD, Mark	HUFFMAN, Lucy	12/17/1834
	S: Hart, Isaac	
FLOYD, Robert	HUFFMAN, Mary	3/29/1828
	F: Benjamin S: B. Huffman	
FLOYD, William	JENKINS, Charlotte	2/ 5/1818
	S: Ezekiel Jenkins	
FORD, Clement	LEWIS? Lucas Ammy	8/ 6/1821
F: John	cert. of J. Ford proven	
	by W. Walters who also	
	proved girl's age of 21.	
FORD, David	JACKSON, Matilda	7/18/1833
	F: John	
FORD, Mordecai	DAWSON, Jane	5/14/1845
FORD, Moses	MILBOURN, Rachel	4/20/1835
	F: Robert	
FORD, Joseph L.	ANDERSON, Jane	2/28/1820
	F: Wm. ANDERSON	
FORD, Joseph L.	WILKERSON, Elizabeth	3/18/1816
F: Moses FORD	cert. from each father	
	F: James	
FORD, Simeon	MOORE, Sarah	7/18/1825
	M: Mary MOORE	
FOGLE, Wm. McKelvey	MILLER, Elizabeth	11/20/1822
	F: Wm. MILLER, cert. Wm.	
	Miller proven by A. Miller	
FORLINE, John	ALLEN, Martha A.	2/ 2/1831
	S: George L. Rogers	
FOREST, John	VERTREES, Julian	9/28/1818
	F: Wm. VERTRESS S: Shadrack Brown	
	S: Solomon Branden-	
	burg	
FOSTER, Thomas	JOHNSTON, Mary	1/19/1822
	F: Thomas	
FOSTER, Thomas	JOHNSON, Mary	6/30/1825
	Jacob Dufner swore S: Thos. Butler	
	girl was age 21.	
FOSTER, William	GREEN, Minerva	4/16/1819
	F: John GREEN S: Stiles Parker	
FOUSHEE, William T.	WOOLFOLK, Elizabeth B.	2/ 1/1819
	F: Joseph T. WOOLFOLK S: Warren Cash	

HARDIN COUNTY, KENTUCKY MARRIAGE RECORDS

GROOM	BRIDE	DATE
FOWLER, Burnit	DUFNER, Ann consent Jacob Dufner	9/23/1825
FOWLER, James Jr. F: James FOWLER Sr.	TAYLOR, Elizabeth consent J. Fowler Sr.	1/12/1825
FOWLER, Mathew	BUSH, Lydia oath made by Henry Bush that John BUSH father of bride had no objections	9/28/1818
FRANKLIN, Daniel	PEARSON, Columbia John Pearson sent cert. proven by John R. Pearson	11/13/1848
FRANKLIN, Henry F: John	STANDIFORD, Mary	9/3/1835
FRANS, Tazwell F: John	BROWN, Sally G: Shadrack BROWN cert. from father proven by Peter Franc	7/21/1821
FREMAN, Abraham	MINOR, Hannah Mrs. S: Matthew Rust	11/7/1816
FREEMAN, George	FREEMAN, Nancy S: Henry Couts	4/8/1816
FREEMAN, Philip	COATS, Susanna S: Henry Coats	7/23/1814
FRENCH, Charles	SLACK, Susan F: Randolph	12/19/1844
FRENCH, Elisha	PAYNE, Mary S: Robert A. Abell S: Wm. Brewer	1/7/1822
FRENCH, George	VEITREES, Margaret A. Mrs. S: Thomas Hulter	4/30/1827
FRENCH, Henry	SLACK, Penelope	8/23/1834
FRENCH, John S.	GOODMAN, Irene F: James	6/13/1844
FRENCH, Leo	BRYAN, Mary F: Charles S: C. Bryan	4/23/1828
FRENCH, Martin	WISE, Elizabeth S: Henry Wise	10/20/1815
FRENCH, Raymond	RYAN, Martha F: Joseph	7/20/1836
FRITZ, George	ARNOLD, Mary Ann Both of age S: H. S. Thurman	11/29/1849
FRITZ, Michael	MILLER, Susan S: Colmore Lovelace	8/11/1846
FRIEND, Isaac	RUDE, Susannah S: John Merrifield	1/19/1813
FRIEND, James H.	GREENSULT, Katherine F: John	2/18/1834
FRIEND, James	GITTINGS, Ann M: Casandra S: C. Gittings	9/7/1829
FRIEND, Jesse	SCOTT, Mary S: Alexander McDougal S: Joseph Bates	10/31/1821

GROOM	BRIDE	DATE
FRIEND, Joshua	CALDWELL, Enode	1/21/1828
	M: Elizabeth S: R. Caldwell	
FRIEND, William	CHISMS, Elizabeth	10/ 8/1832
	F-in-L: Robert	
FROMAN, Bales	ALLSTIEN, Polly	8/28/1831
F: Abraham	F: Jeremiah	
FRYREAR, Charles	STANDAFORD, Hannah	2/23/1828
F: Jeremiah	F: John W.	
FRYREAR, Francis	AUBRY, Nancy	4/15/1820
Aged 45 years	F: Francis AUBRY S: James Haycraft	
	S: John Noafus	
FRYEAR, Harrison	FEDGETT, Elizabeth M.	9/ 6/1847
	S: Colmore Lovelace	
FRYREAR, Washington	CRUTCHER, Amanda	10/ 1/1832
F: Jeremiah		
FULKERSON, Bird	DENNIS, Amanda	9/31/1847
	Joseph DENNIS, Grandfather	
FULKERSON, James	HORNBACK, Margaret	10/26/1822
	F: James cert. proven by Abraham	
	Hornback	
FUNK, Alexander	WALTERS, Sarah	4/5//1819
	F: Conrad WALTERS	
FURGUSON, James	LONG, Lucinda	3/10/1832
	F: Andrew	
FURGUSON, Thomas J.	KEY, Sarah	3/14/1833
	S: H. C. Ullen	
GABLE, Benj.	STRAGE or SHAZE? Mrs. Cath.	5/15/1821
	S: Wm. Brownfield	
GAITHER, Greenbury	PERCEFULL, Caroline	11/25/1822
	S: James Percefull	
GAITHER, John Richard	BLAND, Anna Eliza	11/23/1849
	F: Henry	
GALLIHER, Joseph B.	HORNBACH, Marian	4/21/1813
	S: Isaac Hornbach	
GARDNER, Elisha	WATKINS, Hannah	11/13/1815
	F: James WATKINS S: John Watkins	
GARDNER, John	WELLS, Levisey	1/13/1819
	F: Lewis WELLS S: Thomas Wells	
GARDNER, Joseph	HICKS, Mary Ann	5/ 9/1849
	F: Thomas C. Hicks	
GARDNER, Madison H.	ROBERTS, Julia Ann	12/ 9/1843
	F: Shedrick	
GARDNER, William	ELMORE, Nancy	3/ 9/1819
	S: Thornton Elmore	
GARNER, Jacob	KNIGHTON, Margaret	4/22/1829
SF: Joseph HUMPHRIES	S: William Potter	
GARNER, Vincent	CASTEEL, Mrs. Leticia	5/24/1834
F-in-L: John HUMPHRIES	S: E. A. Clarke	
GASWAY, John	BROWN, Rachel	10/20/1831
F: Samuel	F: Isaac	

GROOM	BRIDE	DATE
GATEWOOD, William	PHILLIPS, Nancy Jane	8/20/1849
	Philip P. Phillips	S: Alexander Guston
	swore girl 21.	
GATES, Leaonard	STRANGE, Nancy	8/10/1818
	M: Cath. STRANGE	S: James Padset
GAVIN, William R.	SCHULTZ, Darah W.	4/12/1850
	M: Charlotte C.	
GAYLE, William Jr.	BALLOW, Christena	8/19/1818
	cert. by North Todd &	
	Andrew Hunt, guard? Fletcher	
GEAMAN, Stephen M.	HELM, Luiretia	4/17/1827
	Gdn: John	S: George L. Rogers
GEOGHEGAN, Ambrose	RULER, Mary Ann	3/ 2/1835
	F: Dorsey	
GEOGHAGEN, Robert D.	PARK, Sarah Elizabeth	1/ 1/1845
	F: F.A. PARK	S: Hiram T. Downward
GEOGHEGAN, Thomas D.	YOUNG, Maria L.	12/ 4/1833
	F: James	S: Colmore Lovelace
GEOGHEGAN, Thomas S.	JOHNSON, Elizabeth	1/28/1834
F: Denton	F: Elisha	S: J. A. Reynolds
GEORGE, Charles	GARDNER, Sarah	6/15/1850
	F: James	
GEORGE, John	HAYWOOD, Sally	12/25/1820
		S: Geo. L. Rogers
		S: Benj. Daughtery
GERM, Jonathan	BIGGER, Mary	4/ 3/1817
		S: Jonathan Paddock
GETTINGS, Horace H.	CHURCHILL, Lucy C.	4/27/1845
	Wm. C. Moore swore	
	girl 21.	
GETTINGS, Horace W.	DICKERSON, Nancy J.	2/22/1849
		S: R. L. Thurman
GIBSON, John	JONES, Elizabeth	12/14/1824
	F: Wm. R. JONES	
GIBSON, Miles H.	JONES, Mary	7/ 7/1830
	F: Zachariah	S: George L. Rogers
GILBERT, James	PARKER, Pilotheta	3/13/1821
		S: Warren Cash
GILBERT, Phiheas	LION, Mrs. Elizabeth	1/30/1821
		S: Stiles Parker
		S: Vincent Hawley
GILBERT, Samuel	PARKER, Philothela	3/12/1821
		S: James Rhodes
GILBSON, Thomas	MARTIN, Polly	5/19/1821
	Cert. girl's father	S: Thos. Whitman
	F: Fred MARTIN	
GILEHIEST, David	HENDERSON, Margaret	1/15/1845
		S: A. L. Alderman
GILES, Grenville T.	DUNCAN, Rosannah	6/10/1845
	R. T. McMurty proved	S: Wm. M. Howsley
	cert. of girl's mother	

GROOM	BRIDE	DATE
GILKY, Charles	STITH, Elizabeth F: Benjamin	6/23/1835
GILLELAND, James	GREENAWALT, Mrs. Catherine S: James Daugherty	2/27/1832
GILLELAND, James	LAWSON, Mary S: Erza Ward	9/25/1847
GILMORE, Alexander	MUDD, Melly F: Walter S: W. Mudd	4/ 2/1827
GILLMORE, Alexander	ROUSE, Martha M. Wm. J. Rouse swore girl 21.	3/25/1845
GILMORE, Benjamin	WILLIAMS, Amelia S: Thomas Williams	6/18/1817
GILMORE, David	TILL or HILL, Mrs. Mahatable S: Thos. Williams	
GILMORE, James F: James Sr.	MUDD, Nancy F: Walter MUDD	10/22/1817
GILMORE, Smith	MUDD, Priscilla F: Walter MUDD	11/23/1825
GINGERY, Joseph	SHREWSBURG, Ann A. F: Dowry SHREWSBURG proven by W: Temple Foster	9/25/1821
GIVENS, Hiram	YOUNG, Nancy F: Samuel S: S. Young	7/20/1830
GIVENS, James	NEEDHAM, Mellona F: Timothy	10/ 2/1834
GLASS, James	KELLY, Tempy F: Joshua KELLY	10/28/1815
GLASS, Royall	MCLEAN, Mary S: Robt. Read	2/10/1820
GLENN, James	HARRIS, Lidia M: Rachel HARRIS cert proven by Stephen Harris	7/ 6/1822
GLOVER, Charles	BASKET, Susan S: Cert. Warren Cash S: Warren Cash with whom she lived.	10/20/1819
GLOVER, John	HASKETT, Kitty Charles Glover swore S: Warren Cash girl was age 21	5/25/1823
GOATLEY, Thomas	REESOR, Sally S: Wm. Goatley S: Wm. Vertrees	10/ 7/1815
GOBLE, Benjamin	STRANGE, Catherine	5/14/1821
GOFF, Edward	THERMON, Betsy S: Charles A. Middleton	4/ 1/1815
GOLDSMITH, David	NORCUT, Salva Mrs. S: James W. Hall	7/23/1844
GOLDSMITH, Jesse	RILEY, Louisa F: Lewis S: Lewis Riley	1/15/1828
GOLDSMITH, John	GREENWOOD, Ann S: Jacob Enlow S: Owen Greenwood S: Joseph Greenwood	2/15/1819

GROOM	BRIDE	DATE
GOLDSMITH, Owen	GREENWOOD, Polly	2/15/1819
	F: Joseph	S: Jacob Enlow
GOLDSMITH, Reubin	MORRISON, Anne	3/25/1818
F: Samuel		S: James Morrison
GOLDSMITH, Thomas	BOLIN, Jane	10/27/1825
F: Samuel	F: Thomas BOLIN	
GOLLAHER, Joel P.	LAFOLLETT, Elizabeth	2/ 2/1836
GOLLISHER, Austin	PRICE, Polly	5/19/1828
		S: George L. Rogers
GONTERMAN, Wm.	THOMPSON, Betsy	8/15/1818
	F: Henry	S: John Thompson
		S: James Thompson
GOODIN, Albert	VERNON, Fanny	7/28/1832
	F: Anthony	
GOODIN, Gerrard	SWANK, Lettuce	7/26/1819
	F: Jacob SWANK	
GOODIN, Isaac	HARRIS, Rachael	10/14/1823
		S: James Haycraft
GOODIN, Isaac	RAIN, Mrs. Katharine	9/16/1826
		S: George L. Rogers
GOODIN, James	ROSSON, Martha Ann	1/16/1850
	F: Lauson JOURDON	S: Colmore Lovelace
GOODIN, James	PAIRPOINT, Mary	12/11/1815
		S: Jeremiah Pairpoint
GOODIN, John	SWANK, Kitty Ann	10/20/1828
	F: Jacob	S: J. Swank
GOODIN, John	DAUGHERTY, Elizabeth	1/23/1835
	F-in-L: Wm. YOUNG	S: Colmore Lovelace
GOODIN, Samuel H.	ATHERTON, Nancy	6/21/1847
	F: William	
GOODIN, Samuel	EDLIN, Susan	4/17/1821
		S: Geo. L. Rogers
		S: Wm. Edlin
GOODEN, Thomas	EDLEN, Polly	4/23/1827
F: Isaac	F: William	
GOODIN, Thomas	THOMAS, Susanna	7/23/1822
	F: Hardin THOMAS	
GOODIN, William	LEEMAN, Charlotte	4/22/1849
	F: Samuel	
GOODMAN, David	VANDERGRAFT, Susan	1/15/1849
	M: Mary	S: Ezra Ward
GOODMAN, Daniel	CLINGINSMITH, Elizabeth	1/14/1821
	B: Solomon BRING?	S: Geo. L. Rogers
	F: Geo.	
GOODMAN, Elijah	REYNOLDS, Nancy	6/19/1817
	B: John DAVISON	
	F: Mathian REYNOLDS	
GOODMAN, Henry M.	LAMPTON, Sally E.	6/ 5/1849
	F: E.H.S. LAMPTON	
GOODMAN, James	HAYCRAFT, Palmira	7/26/1826
	Grandm: Judith CHALFON	

HARDIN COUNTY, KENTUCKY MARRIAGE RECORDS

GROOM	BRIDE	DATE
GOODMAN, John	HOWE, Helenor	5/30/1821
		S: David Thurman
		S: Abram Howe
GOODMAN, Thomas	CLINGLESMITH, Mary	5/ 8/1830
	F: George	S: G. Clinglesmith
GOODMAN, William	DUNDIFF, Sarah Ann	3/12/1848
	F: Chris	
GOODWIN, Abraham	KING, Mary	11/ 8/1828
	F: John	S: J. King
GORDAN or JORDAN, Richard S.		
	STITH, Katherine	5/12/1821
	F: Benjamin STITH	
GORDIN, Gerrard	SUANK, Lettice	7/26/1819
		S: Geo. L. Rogers
GORDON, Henry	DRURY, Catherine	5/18/1826
	F: Timonthy B.	S: John Hodgen
GORE, Clemmy	HART, Elizabeth	6/17/1815
		S: Aaron Terry
GORMAN, James	DRAKE, Mary Jane	9/20/1849
	F: William	
GOAR, John	ASHLEY, Polly	4/17/1838
F: Isaac		
GRABLE, Christopher	BEAVERS, Elizabeth	11/20/1820
	F: Wm. L. BEAVERS	
	cert. Wm. L. Beavers	
GRAYHAM, George	TERRY, Catherine	1/24/1833
		S: James Haycraft
GRAYHAM, Joseph	HOWEY, Polly	5/31/1822
	F: John HOWEY gave	S: Joseph C. Winders
	consent	
GRAYHAM, Merrit	DAVID, Rebecca	12/11/1817
	F: Dead	S: Joseph Pepper
		S: Richard David
GRAYHAM, Turner	HOWELL, Patsey	1/ 9/1830
	F: James	S: J. Howell
GRAY, Harrison	SPAULDINGS, Nancy	5/ 3/1834
	M: Mary	S: Jacob Rogers
GRAY, Jacob	LUCAS, Malissa	11/ 8/1834
F: Francis	F: Jesse BECON	
GRAY, James E.	PRICE, Kitty Ann	4/ 1/1845
	M: Elenor	S: James Daugherty
GRAY, James	HELM, Margaret	7/20/1824
	F: Benjamin HELM	
GRAY, John	SMITH, Sarah	5/13/1823
	B: William SMITH	S: G. L. Rogers
GRAY, Jonas	EDLIN, Sarah	12/24/1832
	F: James	S: Colmore Lovelace
GRAY, John	PEARL, Rebecca	7/23/1846
F: Patrick	F: James	
GRAY, Joseph A.	REDMAN, Lucretia W.	11/26/1847
		S: R. L. Thurman

GROOM	BRIDE	DATE
GRAY, Peter	MILBURN, Mary Ann M: Nancy	3/31/1832
GRAY, Reubin	MEEKS, Rebecca	3/25/1813 S: Humphrey Smoot
GRAY, Warren G.	RUNNER, Frances M: Sarah	11/ 6/1834
GRAVES, Elias	LOGADON, Elizabeth F: James B.	4/30/1827
GRAVET, Joseph	MATTINGLY, Phebe	1/12/1821 S: Rich. David
GREENAULT, John	SCOTT, Sally F: John	12/19/1844
GREENAWALT, David F: Joseph	HATFIELD, Labitha	2/ 6/1834 S: James Haycraft
GREENAWALT, Jacob	BRADLEY, Mary F: William	1/21/1828 S: William Bradley
GREENAWALT, Joseph F: John	LEWIS, Elizabeth F: Thomas	5/10/1835
GREENAWALT, Lewis	LEWIS, Sarah F: Thomas	9/15/1835
GREENAWALT, Noah B. F: David	HUDGENS, Sarah F: Robert	1/12/1844
GREENAWALT, William F: David	MCCULLUM, Elizabeth F-L: GOALSON, Hicks	6/12/1834 S: James Haycraft
GREEN, Henry M: Patience	ROSE, Mrs. Sarah	1/29/1831 S: P. Green
GREEN, Jesse	VANMETRE, Rebecca F: Jacob	4/ 3/1827
GREEN, John F: Luke	WARMAN, Margaret F: Thomas	8/22/1832
GREEN, Mathew	KINDLE, Eliz	12/17/1816
GREEN, Matthew	SMITH, Mrs. Anna	8/10/1822 S: Warren Cash S: Wm. Green
GREEN, Vincent M: Patience	ERRELS, Jane	10/11/1833 S: Elijah Jefferies
GREENWALT, Anthony	ROOF, Nancy M: Barbara ROOF	8/ 5/1817 S: Nich. A. Roof
GREENWALT, Isaac	HART, Charity S: Consent of Moses Hart Jasper Terry F: Thos HART	4/12/1819 S: Wm. Downs
GREENWALT, James	HOOVERM, Katherine	7/30/1821 S: James Haycraft S: Paulser? Hoover
GREENWALT, John	BEALL, Christena	10/30/1823 S: James Haycraft
GREENWELL, Benedict	ASH, Maria consent of boy's mother and James Brown girl's Gdn.	10/12/1822
GREENWELL, Stephen	CRADY, Catherine F: David CRADEY	7/17/1817

HARDIN COUNTY, KENTUCKY MARRIAGE RECORDS

GROOM	BRIDE	DATE
GREENWELL, Robert	FRAKES, Doras F & M: Nathan & S: Nathan Tucker Jr. Hannah TUCKER Sr.	8/18/1817
GREER, Lawrence	DEVOUR, Hester S: James Humphrey	4/ 3/1813
GREER, Lawrence	HUMPHREYS, Lydia S: William H. Potter	4/20/1830
GREER, William P.	LARUE, Sarah Elizabeth Morgan Larue J. sent cert. proven by Jacob Larue.	8/31/1848
GRIFFIN, Anthony	PAWSEY, Hester F: John	3/21/1837
GRIFFIN, Samuel	BARRON, Elizabeth F: John BARRON	8/ 1/1820
GRIGSBY, Redman F: James Sr. Bro: James Jr.	KELLING, Nancy F: Wm. KELLING S: John Stith Jr.	4/ 8/1819
GRISTY, Clement	BREWER, Matilda M: Jane	10/ 1/1828
GURANTUEY, John	BUCKNER, Elizabeth M: Nancy S: Colmore Lovelace	1/30/1845
GUSLER, John	SANDERS, Mrs. Nancy S: Stiles Parker S: Nich Howard	7/25/1821
GUM, Jonathan	BISSER, Polly	4/ 3/1817
GUM, Jehu	STEVENSON, Anna S: Jacob Gum	7/20/1813
GUM, Jesse	DILLS, Polly S: Thomas Dills	3/15/1813
GUNTERMAN, William	THOMPSON, Betsy	8/15/1818
GUSTER, John	BROOKS, Margaret S: William M. Brown	2/ 4/1834
GUSTINE, Wm. B.	LYONS?, Ann (name of bride S: Geo. L. Rogers not given) girl's age proven by Joseph Lyon Jr.	4/21/1821
GUNSAULERS, James G.M.	ATWELL, Jane S: John N. Pendegast	3/20/1847
GUYLER, William M.	ENGLISH, Lydia L. F: H. B. ENGLISH	11/27/1845
GWANTNEY, Ephraim	JENKINS, Jane S: Allison Jenkins	11/ 8/1817
HABACK, Valentine	CLARK, Nancy M: Amelia CLARK Adin Clark her brother	9/28/1820
HAGEN, George W.	BEELER, Margaret F: William	10/ 2/1835
HAGAR, Henry	YOUNG, Mary F: Sam	3/ 6/1850

HARDIN COUNTY, KENTUCKY MARRIAGE RECORDS

GROOM	BRIDE	DATE
HAGAN, Henry M.	GEOHEGAN, Margaret Ann	9/27/1847
	G: Chas. CISSELL S: Aug. Denganquier	
HAGEN, Ignatius S.	VITTITOE, Nancy	4/12/1847
	F: John	
HAGAN, Ignatius	HAGAN, Susan	12/23/1849
	F: James	
HAGAN, John B.	WISEMAN, Rosella	10/ 8/1849
	S: Aug. Degenquier	
HAGAN, Raymond	HAGAR, Monica	8/ 3/1846
	F: James	
HAGAE, Robert	YOUNG, Elizabeth Ann	1/23/1849
	F: Samuel	
HAGAN, Samuel B.	REYNOLDS, Lydia B.	4/ 7/1849
	F: Joseph B.	
HAGER, Lawrence	PAUL, Rebecca	1/ 7/1832
	F: Edmund S: James Daugherty	
HAHN, Christian	HUFF, Elizabeth	1/25/1834
	F: Joseph S: Ed. A. Clarke	
HALL, Isaiah	KEELING, Julia	6/ 8/1826
	M: Susanna	
HALL, Henry	WILKINS, Elizabeth	1/13/1834
	S: Thomas T. Chilton	
HALL, James W.	YOUNG, Nancy	4/ 7/1818
	F: James YOUNG	
HALL, James W. Jr.	NAYLOR, Matilda S.	6/16/1847
	F: James	
HALL, John W.	YOUNG, Eliza P.	11/ 4/1826
	S: John Stith Jr.	
HALL, Josias	MOTON, Laura Ann	6/15/1847
F: Caleb	F: John	
HALL, Micager	THOMAS, Nancy	4/27/1828
	M: Mahaly S: Mahaly Thomas	
HALL, Oscar F.	CULLY, Martha	8/25/1849
	F: John S.	
HALL, Phillip	WILKINS, Martha	3/23/1833
	F: Thomas	
HALL, William B.	STEPHENS, Margared	3/ 9/1819
	F: Vincent STEPHENS S: Wm. Hays	
	W: Joseph S: Amistead Churchill Jr.	
HAMPTON, James	CASTEEL, Elizabeth	3/10/1831
	F: A. Zach S: Zach. Casteel	
HAMILTON, John A.	SMITH, Frances	6/23/1835
	S: J. P. Lancaster	
HANDLEY, George	CHURCHILL, Judith	1/16/1819
	F: John S: Warren Cash	
HANEY, Henry	WOODRING, Lucinda	2/21/1831
	F: John S: J. Woodring	
HANNA, John	LEE, Allis	10/10/1820
	S: David Thurman	
HARDAWAY,_____?	MOORE, Hannah	10/ 8/1849
	S: Milton Stith	

GROOM	BRIDE	DATE
HARDWAY, Thos. P.	STITH, Nancy cert. of John Stith Jr.	2/19/1818
HARDAWAY, Thos. P.	STITH, Nancy F: Joseph STITH S: John Stith, Jr. W: Luch A. STITH	2/ 4/1818
HARDIN, James	DEWIT, Hannah M: Anne DEWIT	9/ 4/1821
HARDIN, Joseph	DAVIS, Elizabeth S: Wm. Davis	1/27/1815
HARDING, Henry W.	ENGLISH, Elizabeth F: Noah S: Colmore Lovelace	10/ 1/1834
HARDIN, William	HOWEY, Cynthiana F: Joseph HOWEY S: Joseph Howey	3/ 1/1821
HARDWOOD, Wm. McWilliams	WILLIS, Nancy S. S: John H. Geoghegan	6/29/1818
HARGIS, Abraham M: Mary ALLEN SF: David ALLEN	FARMER, Elizabeth F/M: John & Elizabeth FARMER	10/ 8/1822
HARGEN, Benjamon	ARNOLD, Katherine F: John ARNOLD consent of J. Arnold	8/ 1/1825
HARGAN, Daniel F: Michael HARGAN	CUNTRYMAN, Margaret M: Elizabeth COUNTRYMAN	3/31/1825
HARGEN, Geo. W. F: Daniel	DAUGHERTY, Sarah F: James	2/25/1849
HARGAN, Joseph	BAYNE, Elizabeth F: William	3/20/1826
HARGAN, Joseph Jr.	RUST, Margaret	11/14/1832
HARKNESS, John R.	WOOD, Unis F: Ezra	6/ 6/1835
HARKWELL, Billings	NEEDHAM, Priscilla 11/11/1823 cert. of girl's S: Samuel Martin father proven by W. Mattingly	
HARLE? Hippocrates?	CRUTCHER, Lucy S: John Sneed	11/16/1816
HARNED, David	MCGUFFIN, Aley F: Samuel	9/20/1831
HARNED, John W.	LEE, Catherine S: S. Williams	11/30/1850
HARNED, William	ROBINSON, Katherine 10/21/1843 John Morris swore S: Wm. Mod. Abbett girl 21.	
HARRIS, Benjamin	MCMAHON, Rachel S: John Stith	3/10/1833
HARRIS, David F: William HARRIS	HOOVER, Margaret 4/24/1824 cett. of Wm. Harris proven by John McDaniel who states girl was 21.	

GROOM	BRIDE	DATE
HARRIS, Edward	WELLS, Sarah	8/27/1821
	B: Samuel Martin S: Samuel Martin	
	F: Abraham WELLS	
HARRIS, Green T.	NORRIS, Emily	7/15/1848
	Isaac Radley swore S: Geo. W. Crunbaugh	
	girl 21.	
HARRIS, Hezekiah	DORSEY, Deborah	2/ 4/1814
	F: Greenberry DORSEY	
HARRIS, Jacob	SLACK, Eliza Jane	10/ 2/1833
	G: Thos. COFER S: Colmore Lovelace	
HARREL, James	ROGERS, Rebecca	9/27/1815
	S: Russ Cox	
HARRIS, John	DAVID, Elizabeth	12/14/1827
	F: Richard	
HARRIS, John H.	MORRISON, Mrs. Elizabeth	4/30/1824
	S: James Haycraft	
HARRIS, John H.	STANDIFORD, Nancy	3/15/1819
Aged 21	F: Israel STANDIFORD	
HARRIS, John R.	HOBBS, Elizabeth	12/ 2/1831
	M: Sarah	
HARRIS, John W.	MARLOW, Clarisa	4/16/1850
HARRIS, Michael	HARDIN, Betsy	7/21/1824
	F: William HARDIN	
HARRIS, Samuel	FULKERSON, Phebe	11/23/1816
	S: John Fulkerson	
HARRIS, Warren	CRAVEN, Cassey	8/29/1820
	cert. of S: John Baird	
	Alexander Jackson	
HARRIS, William	MURPHEY, Nancy	1/11/1824
	M: Ann MURPHEY	
	cert. of Ann Murphey	
HARRINGTON, John W.	MOORE, Mary	1/ 2/1847
	F: Mathew	
HARRINGTON, William	READ, Perlina	2/12/1831
F: David	F: Robert	
HARRISON, James	GLOVER, Rachel D.	1/ 6/1850
	F: John	
HART, Aaron	CARSON, Polley	11/29/1822
	S: J. H. Yager	
	S: Jacob W. Larue	
HART, Abraham	TERRY, Amelia	3/ 2/1817
	S: Urrah Hart	
HART, Hezekiah	GOFORTH, Jane	11/28/1814?
	M: Anna GOFORTH S: Matthias Grimes	
HART, Iredell	HART, Amelia	12/26/1820
	cert. Daniel Linder, S: Geo. L. Rogers	
	SF: of girl	
HART, Jacob	RICE, Susannah	3/23/1829
F: John	F: Elias	
HART, Jacob	GORE, Matilda	2/13/1822
F: Oliver HART	B: Anelam Terry	
	F: Israel GORE	

GROOM	BRIDE	DATE
HART, Josiah	PENCE, Mary	4/27/1835
F: Hezekiah	F: Jacob	
HART, Oliver	LAMPTON, Zodorado	8/13/1845
	A. E. Lampton S: Isaac Hart	
	proved cert. of both fathers	
HART, Silas	FIELD, Mary Ann	5/23/1845
	F: Ezekiel	
HARTLEY, Jonathan	SMITHERS, Elizabeth	10/25/1825
	F: John SMITHERS	
HARTLEY, John	DOUGHERTY, Nancy	3/18/1815?
HARTLEY, Joseph	SINGLETON, Polly	1/22/1821
	S: Geo. L. Rogers	
HARTLEY, Joseph	SINGLETON, Polly	1/22/1821
F: John HARTLEY, Sr.	F: Benjamin SINGLETON	
HAYNE, Walter	HARGAN, Prudence	3/28/1826
	F: Joseph	
HATFIELD, Alexander	MORRIS, Rebecca	7/10/1850
	Dempsy Morris cert.	
	proven by David Hatfield	
HATFIELD, David	MORRIS, Sarah	5/1/ 1850
	Dempsy Morris sent cert.	
	proven by John Morris	
HATFIELD, David	GRAY, Polly	2/ 2/1818
	F: Reubin GRAY	
HATFIELD, Malen	LAWSON, Viey	8/ 7/1847
	M: Polly	
HAWKINS, James	STEPHENS, America	8/11/1823
	cert. of Wm. Hawkins Gdn	
	of bride S: Simeon Buchanan	
HAWKINS, James M.	DEWITT, Angeline	2/ 4/1846
	John Dewitt swore	
	girl 21.	
HAWKINS, Jesse	VANVACTOR, Margaret	8/22/1825
	F: Ben VANVACTOR	
	consent of B. VanVactor	
HAWKINS, Vincent	SEIFRES, Barbara	6/ 9/1828
	F: Mathias S: M. Seifres	
HAWKINS, William	SHELTON, Susanna	8/11/1817
	S: Warren Cash	
	S: Henry Shelton	
HAWLETT, Harrison	FRENCH, Susan	3/29/1834
	F: Thomas S: E.A. Clarke	
HAWLEY, Vincent	LEE, Sally	11/ 1/1824
	F: John LEE	
HAYCRAFT, Daniel K.	MCMURTRY, Elizabeth	11/19/1829
	F: Joseph S: J. McMurtry	
HAYCRAFT, Edgar N.	PARK, Mary E.	10/29/1846
	F: John	
HAYCRAFT, Isaac	ABELL, Lucy	12/14/1829
	F: Samuel S: S. Abell	

GROOM	BRIDE	DATE
HAYCRAFT, John	PARKER, Hannah	12/23/1822
F: James HAYCRAFT	F: Benjamin PARKER	
	cert. by both father's	
HAYCRAFT, Presley N.	KENNEDY, Elizabeth	9/ 2/1818
	F: Samuel KENNEDY S: Warren Cash	
HAYDEN, Daniel	WALKER, Mary	2/15/1836
	G: John H. TAYLOR S: James Noll	
HAYDEN, Robert A. M.	ALVEY, Elizabeth	9/ 1/1847
	Lewis Alvey S: Aug. Deganquier	
	swore girl 21.	
HAYDEN, William F.	COLEMAN, Agatha A.	6/ 2/1845
	S: Aug. Deganquier	
HAYES, Evans R.	ASHCRAFT, Margaret	4/ 1/1830
	F: John S: J. Ashcraft	
HAYES, Green B.	ASHCRAFT, Julian	3/ 3/1831
F: John	F: John	
HAYES, Parker	BROWNFIELD, Nancy	11/21/1821
	F: Wm. cert. Wm. BROWNFIELD	
	proven by Bracket	
HAYES, Randel P.	CALVIN, Sarah	12/16/1822
	F: Luke CALVIN	
	cert. Luke Calvin proven	
	by J. Calvin	
HAYNE, Jackson	SMITH, Susan S.	12/ 9/1834
	F: Aaron	
HAYNE, Joshua	SMITH Susan S.	12/ 9/1834
	F: Aaron	
HAYWOOD, John	DURBIN, Mrs. Hannah	1/ 22/1833
	S: E. A. Clarke	
HAYWOOD, John	PAWLEY, Susannah	10/ 1/1849
	F: James	
HAYWOOD, Thomas	THOMAS, Barbery	10/ 2/1849
	E. R. Cowherd S: M. Stith	
	proved cert. of	
	parents of both	
HAYWOOD, William	WISEMAN, Nancy	8/ 5/1846
	F: Christian	
HAYWOOD, William	RAINE, Mary	10/15/1818
	consent of James Dillard	
	F: Thomas RAINE	
HAYS, John P.	DORSEY, Eveline	1/ 8/1833
	F: Nelson S: Colmore Lovelace	
HAYS, William H.	NEILL, Nancy	7/13/1835
	F: Roles D.	
HAZLE, W. Caleb	STEVENS, Mary Mrs.	10/12/1816
HAZLE, Joseph	BARNES, Nancy Ann	11/30/1848
	F: Archibald	
HAZLE, William	DEWITT, Phebe	12/25/1833
	F: Abraham	
HEADRICK, Daniel	HARRIS, Mrs. Mary	3/10/1824
M: Sary HEADRICK	her parents Sarah & John DAVID	

GROOM	BRIDE	DATE
HEIGHTEN, Josiah	ASHBY, Rachel	6/12/1813
	S: Aaron Berry	
HELLION, Elihu I.	DECKER, Sally	3/ 4/1819
	consent of girl's S: Geo. L. Rogers father.	
HELM, Samuel	HUDDLESTON, Mary	2/17/1819
	B: Samuel Martin S: Samuel Martin	
HENCELEY, Morris G.	LARUE, Lydia	11/27/1828
	G: John MORRISON S: George L. Rogers	
HENDERSON, Andrew	TYRE, Mrs. Elizabeth	7/ 5/1830
	S: Chas. Stuleville	
HENDERSON, Hilry H.C.	FRYREAR, Martha E.	7/ 7/1847
	James Riddl swore girl 21.	
HENDERSON, Sampson	TYREE, Mary	9/20/1845
	Jesse Carley grandfather sent cert. proved by Zachariah Carley S: Isaac Hart	
HENDRICKS, Andrew	CREAGER, Sarah E.	4/ 1/1850
	F: Christian	
HENDRICKS, Daniel	GARDNER?, Nancy	9/10/1813
	F/M: John and Mary GARDNER	
HENNA, William N.	RICHARDSON, Artemison	11/27/1849
	F: Richard	
HERNDON, David	MOREMAN, Polly	5/22/1816
	F: Jesse MOREMAN	
HEWITT, Thomas	READ, Mary	11/19/1832
	F: Robert	
HEWITT, Robert	CHASTAIN, Eliza A.	6/30/1830
	S: Thomas J. Chilton	
HIBBS, Isaac	HIBBS, Nancy	3/18/1813
	S: George Hargan?	
HIBBS, Jeremiah	HIBBS, Belinda	11/ 2/1846
	F: Jo.	
HIBBS, Joseph Jr.	HARGIN, Mary or Polly	3/27/1819
	consent of girl's S: Jacob Enlow father Michael HARGIN	
HIBBS, John	HIBBS, Sally	10/30/1813
	S: Isaac Hibbs	
HIBBS, Samuel	JARBER, Caty	11/15/1824
	Elizabeth Laswell S: Jacob Enlow swore girl was age 21.	
HICK, William W.	BACON, Rebecca	1/ 8/1820
	S: Warren Cash S: Geo. Throp	
HICKS, Amos	SINGLETON, Mahala	10/24/1833
F: John C.	F: Benjamin	
HICKS, Coalman	MCCULLUM, Mrs. Sally	8/10/1822
M: Sally HICKS	S: James Haycraft	

HARDIN COUNTY, KENTUCKY MARRIAGE RECORDS

GROOM	BRIDE	DATE
HICKS, Daniel	VANMETRE, Polly	5/21/1820
	S: James Haycraft	
	S: Joel C. Morrison	
HICKS, George H.	HARTLEY, Susan	3/ 9/1835
F: John	Gdn: Jacob	
HICK. Haden	POPHAM, Phebe Ann	9/18/1844
	F: Job	
HICKS, John C.	CANNAWAY, Martha	2/ 8/1831
	SF: Harvey GILES S: Benjamin Keith	
HICKS, John C.	COKE, Sarah G. Mrs.	10/ 9/1835
	S: G. C. Ulen	
HICKS, William	ALLEN, Susan	1/29/1835
M: Hester	F: David S: Alfred Hamilton	
HICKS, William W.	MASTERSON, Elizabeth	2/25/1850
	Both of Age S: Aug. Deganquier	
HICKS, William	WOODRING, Nancy	2/ 5/1849
	F: William	
HICKS, Wilson	ARMER, Ann Jane	8/22/1849
	Daniel G. Hicks S: E. Wane	
	swore girl 21.	
HICKS, Zachariah	GIBBS, Susan	11/ 8/1843
	M: Nancy S: Green B. Williams	
HIGHBOUGH, David	BROWN, Elizabeth C.	8/25/1830
	F: William M. S: W. H. Brown	
HIGDEN, Benjamin	SETZER, Louisa	6 /27/1848
F: Samuel cert. proven	F: Samuel	
by Andrew J. Higden		
HIGDON, Sugustus	RIBEY, Teresia	2/ 8/1828
	F: Barton S: B. Robey	
HIGHFIEL, Thomas	MILLER, Nancy	4/18/1821
	also of age S: Geo. L. Rogers	
	proven by	
	Thomas Miller	
HILL, James F.	GLINGLESMITH, Matilda	4/27/1835
F: John M.		
HILL, John C.	GRAY, Polly	2/15/1819
	F: Simeon GRAY	
	cert. by father's of	
	boy and girl	
HILL, John Jr.	THOMPSON,_____?	8/26/1823
F: HILL, John Sr.	F: James THOMPSON	
	cert. of both fathers.	
HILLS, Jonathan	LINCOLN, Lucy	10/11/1817
	consent of Jackson Hodges	
	with whom she resides, no	
	parent or Gdn.	
HILL, Robert	ANGEL, Elizabeth	12/29/1813
	S: John Angel	
HILLS, Thos. C.	GRAY, Polly	2/15/1819
	F: James	

GROOM	BRIDE	DATE
HILL, Wm.	STRADER, Elizabeth	12/ 4/1815
	S: Wm. Strader	
HILLIARD, Samuel	LESLYE, Elizabeth Mariah	12/ 7/1819
	cert of girl's S: John Stith Jr.	
	father	
	S: Seth W. Leslye	
HILSON, George W.	GEOGHAGEN, Sarah Elizabeth	3/ 6/1845
	F: John H.	
HILTON, Alexander	WISE, Sarah M. Mrs.	6/ 2/1819
	S: Geo. L. Rogers	
HINTON, Joseph	ALVEY, Nancy	10/5/ 1844
	F: Philip	
HINTON, Walter B.	COOLEY, Rebecca	5/17/1825
F: John C. HINTON	F: John COOLEY	
HOBACK, Valentine	CLARK, Nancy	9/27/1820
	M: Emiliah CLARK	
HOBBS, Greenburg D.	NOLL, Mrs. Lucy	12/26/1833
	S: H. C. Ulen	
HOBBS, Jesse	BOAG, Aseneth	6/ 6/1830
	S: Cash, Warren	
HOBBS, Joshua S.	NOLL, Fanny	12/ 2/1831
	F: William	
HOBBS, John J.	WILLIAMS, Nancy	4/12/1825
	M: Nancy WILLIAMS	
	Elisha Williams proved cert	
HOBBS, Martin L.	WILLIAMS, Elizabeth	10/ 9/1849
	Orwen Williams	
	swore girl 21.	
HODGEN, Jacob	BROWN, Frances B.	11/27/1818
HODGEN, Samuel	MONTAGUE, Lucy F.	7/ 3/1832
	S: David Thurman	
HODGES, John T.	CESSNA, Mary	9/ 9/1833
	S: Thomas J. Chilton	
HOEY, John H.	MATTINGLY, Susan	12/11/1848
	S: R. L. Thurman	
HOLBERT, Andrew J.	WILLIAMS, Susan Jane	2/11/1848
F: John	F: Green B.	
HOLDEN, Bartholamew	CARLTON, Elizabeth	2/ 1/1830
	F: John S: Benjamin Keith	
HOLDEN, Henry	LUCAS, Polly	9/19/1822
	F: Abraham LUCAS	
	Thomas Holden swore boy 21	
	and proved cert. of Abraham	
	Lucas	
HOLDREN, Jacob	MARTIN, Nancy	11/13/1845
	James Martin S: Green B. Williams	
	(Bro) swore girl 21.	
HOLDREM, Christopher	ROBERTS, Catherine	10/11/1834
HOLLAND, William	SHEARUM, Mary	1/ 1/1833
	Jno. K. Davis, sw. S: John Stith	
HOLLIS, John	SHOEMAKER, Nancy	4/15/1815
	S: John Montgomery	

HARDIN COUNTY, KENTUCKY MARRIAGE RECORDS

GROOM	BRIDE	DATE
HOLLOWAY, George	RICHARDSON, Mahala	8/27/1844
	S: Jacob W. Pence	
HOLLOWAY, Lewis	GREENAULT, Lewisa	4/ 1/1847
	F: David GREENAULT	
HOLMAN, Thomas J.	HARLEY, Lucy	6/28/1845
	S: Geo. G. Hicks	
HOLSCLAW, James	HISHFIELD, Polly	10/18/1817
HOLT, James T.	SLACK, Polly	3/11/1820
F: Isaac E. HOLT	cert. boy's father S: Geo. L. Rogers	
HOOKER, William	CLINKINGBARD, Mary	2/ 1/1828
	S: George L. Rogers	
HOOPER, Moses	COY, Mrs. Phebe	1/15/1824
	S: Samuel Martin	
HOOVER, Joseph	GREENWALT, Polly	6/ 4/1821
	S: David Greenwalt	
HOOVER, Moses	WOOLEY, Mrs. Lydia	2/28/1819
	S: David Thurman	
	S: Stephen Mattingly	
HOOVER, Paulser	BEAGLER, Polly	7/30/1821
	S: James Haycraft	
	S: John Bigler	
HOOVER, William	DEWITT, Permelia Elizabeth	1/18/1847
	F: John D.	
HORN, John	DISDEMEANY, Thomas	2/18/1828
	S: J. Thomas	
HORNBACK, Isaac	HORNBACK, Kitty	9/ 8/1814
	S: Daniel Hornbach	
HORNBACK, James	BROWN, Polly	11/21/1815
	S: Philip McLean	
HORNBACK, John	SCAMABORN, Keziah	3/22/1825
	F: Nathan SOAMAHORN consent of girl's father	
HORNBACK, William	GUSLER, Elizabeth	9/ 3/1821
	cert. of girl's S: John Gusler age proved by John Gusler	
HORNBACK, Daniel	MILLER, Peggy	10/14/1828
	S: David Thurman	
HORNBACK, Squire	KIRKPATRICK, Elizabeth	6/29/1832
	M: Roseana	
HORNBACK, Charles	LOGSDON, Mary	7/20/1835
	G: Chas. HORNBACK S: Thomas J. Chilton	
HORTON, Daniel	CLARK, Elizabeth	2/15/1817
	F: Thomas CLARK	
HORTON, Geo. W.	CLARK, Nancy	7/18/1825
	Chas. S. Dorsey says girl is 21.	
HORTON, George W.	NORRIS, Susan	1/30/1844
	Elijah Allen S: Jacob Rogers swore girl 21.	
HORTON, John F.	ALLEN, Sarah	10/17/1849
	F: Elijah	

55

HARDIN COUNTY, KENTUCKY MARRIAGE RECORDS

GROOM	BRIDE	DATE
HORTON, John N.	SHEETS, Providence Jane	7/24/1846
	Gdn: D. K. HAYCRAFT	
	S: Colmore Lovelace	
HOSKINS, George C.	HARNED, Nancy	9/24/1828
	S: Benjamin Stith	
HOSKINSON, John	BREWER, Catherine A.	4/20/1846
	Uriah Brewer S: C. J. Coomes	
	swore girl 21.	
HOUGH, William	SHEETS, Mrs. Rebecca	5/18/1846
HOUISTON, Isaac W.	NORRIS, Louisa	6/10/1830
	S: George L. Rogers	
HOUSTON, Isaac	WHITEHEAD, Susannah W.	8/13/1821
	cert. of girls S: Wm. Whitehead	
	father	
HOWARD, Geo. W.	COFER, Susan W.	1/18/1849
	Gdn: Letitia COFER	
HOWARD, James	ENGLISH, Mahala	9/22/1819
	cert. of R. English S: Rogeert English	
HOWARD, Philip B.	MERRIFIELD, Jemima	7/ 3/1834
	S: James Daugherty	
HOWARD, Thomas N.	ASHBROUGH, Martha	5/13/1833
	S: Colmore Lovelace	
HOWARD, Westley	MOORE, Mary	1/17/1825
F: James HOWARD	M: Margaret JOHNSON	
	cert. of both parents	
HOWARD, Wilson	READY, Martha	1/19/1835
	F: Richard	
HOWE, Abraham	PINDELL, Jane	2/17/1815
	S: Jacob	
HOWE, David	SOIFREE, Margaret	1/ 1/1827
	F: Mathias	
HOWE, Thomas H.	BROWN, Ellen	5/23/1829
	F: John C. S: J. C. Brown	
HOWEL, Charles	LANDNA? Rachel	10/21/1819
	S: John Baird	
HOWEL, James	BROWN, Sally	10/14/1816
	F: Jeremiah BROWN	
HOWEL, John	BRAW or BROWN, Rachael	3/22/1820
	S: John Jackson	
HOWELL, Amos	NEWSON, Elizabeth	1/14/1823
HOWELL, Jacob	MARSHALL, Mrs. Polly	10/12/1820
	S: John Baird	
HOWELL, Jacob	HOWELL, Mary	2/ 4/1834
	F: Nathaniel S: Marshall Scott	
HOWELL, James H.	PECK, Martha Jane	9/14/1846
F: C. HOWELL	F: Thomas	
HOWELL, Jesse	SMITH, America	3/30/1848
	F: William	
HOWELL, John	MCDANIEL, Mary	10/23/1827
	F: William	

GROOM	BRIDE		DATE
HOWELL, John Jr. F: Jno. HOWELL Sr.	CUNDIFF, Mary cert. boy's father and Joice Price girl's guardian		2/11/1824
HOWERTON, Thomas	ROLL, Lena F: Abraham	S: Colmore Lovelace	3/ 3/1827
HOWERY, Elijah	JENKINS, Louivoy F: Phillip	S: P. Jenkins	1/12/1828
HOWEY, James S.	BUNNEL, Sarah F: William	S: Colmore Lovelace	3/ 2/1834
HOWEY, Joseph Jr.	KEELING? _____ cert. girl's mother and boys father proven by Lewis Keeling	S: Wm. Tarpley	8/ 4/1823
HOWEY, William	COZART, Nancy cert. Robert H. MCLURE, girl's guardian	S: S. Martin	5/ 3/1824
HOWLETT, Isaac	GIST, Catherine	S: Jacob Enlow	4/20/1822
HOWSLEY, William M.	HARDIN, Ann	S: Colmore Lovelace	2/17/1831
HUBBAN,? Nathaniel	WOOD, Rebecca F: Thomas WOOD		3/11/1817
HUBBARD, Absolom P.	WOOD, Matilda	S: Isaac Hart	5/ 4/1847
HUBBARD, Theodorick I.	DAVIS, Nancy		2/14/1824
HUBBS, John W.	BOLIN, Mary F: William	S: William Bolin	5/22/1828
HUDDLESTON, John	DUNN, Nancy cert. of both fathers	S: G. L. Rogers	1/15/1823
HUDSPITH, Allen D.	MARTIN, Mary Jane M: Nancy		9/ 9/1834
HUDSPITH, Masbech F: John	MARTIN, Elizabeth M: Nancy	S: James Haycraft	7/ 8/1834
HUDSON, John H. F: John	ELLIT, Mariah F: John		4/ 9/1831
HUFF, James H. F: Joseph	DUGAN, Elizabeth F: William		7/12/1849
HUFFMAN, James	SMITH, Elizabeth	S: Noah Smith	4/24/1820
HUFFMAN, Peter	JONES, Cynthia cert. Solomon Welch		9/ 6/1827
HUFFMAN, William	GOFORTH, Peggy M: Anne GOFORTH	S: Arron Terry, Esq.	1/13/1817
HUGG, John F: Joseph	NORRIS, Eliza Jane F: William		12/27/1849
HUGHES, Francis	DUNCAN, Agnes R. F: Johnson		8/13/1850
HUGHES, Isaac	KASTER, Kitty Ann cert. father's proven by Frederick Kaster, girl 21.	S: Alexander McDougal	1/21/1817

HARDIN COUNTY, KENTUCKY MARRIAGE RECORDS

GROOM	BRIDE	DATE
HULCE, Thomas	KINNEY, Martha	2/10/1835
	M: Mary	
HULSINPILLER, Jacob	BUNGAR, Susannah	9/ 9/1822
	F: Jacob BUNGAR S: Jacob Bungar	
	cert. proven by	
	Aaron Prindle	
HUMBLE, Martin	BROWN, Nancy	4/11/1835
	F: Eli	
HUMPHREY, David	THOMAS, Mrs. Charlotte	3/19/1817
	S: Alex. McDougal	
	S: James L. Foster	
HUMPHREY, John	HUMPHREY, Susannah	3/31/1825
	F: John Larue S: Thos. J. Chilton	
	proved cert.	
HUMPHREY, Thomas	ROYALTY, Amanda	3/10/1847
M: Drucilla	M: Ann ABENY	
HUMPHREYS, James L.	BURKS, Mary Elizabeth	3/14/1846
	M: Mary Ann S: A. L. Aldersman	
HUMPHREYS, John	ALLEN, Susan	7/18/1826
F: Samuel	F: Elisha	
HUMPHREYS, Joseph	SELSON, Mrs. Rachel	8/11/1828
	S: S. Martin	
HUMPHREYS, Samuel	DODGE, Jane	7/30/1835
	F: Josiah	
HUMPHRIES, James	HILL, Sally	8/30/1825
M: Rebecca HUMPHRIES	F: John HILL	
HUNDLEY, Thomas	HOLLAND, Agens	12/27/1831
	F: John B.	
HUNDLEY, William J.	MILLER, Lucetia Ann	12/17/1844
	Clement Holland S: Green B. Williams	
	swore girl 21.	
HUNT, Silvester	ROGERS, Anna	9/ 2/1822
	cert. of girl's S: Stiles Parker	
	father S: Elias Rogers	
HUNT, Polemns	SHARPENSTEEN, Mary Ann	4/ 7/1828
	F: John H.	
HURD, Charles	DOWNS, Frances	9/ 6/1847
	F: Zachariah	
HURD, Justus	ROOT, Cynthia	8/5 /1822
	proved by Benj. S: John Stith Jr.	
	Sims	
	F: Saml. ROOT	
HURLEY, William	NEILL, Elizabeth Ann	7/11/1832
	F: Thomas	
HUSS, Charles F.	THOMAS, Ann W.	8/27/1835
F: John	F: Henry W.	
HUSTON, Amos	CLARK, Nancy	1/ 5/1836
HUTCHERSON, John	KING, Nancy	10/18/1831
	Jas. Johnson S: G. C. Ulen	
	she was of age.	

HARDIN COUNTY, KENTUCKY MARRIAGE RECORDS

GROOM	BRIDE	DATE
HUTCHESON, John M.	REDMAN, Alta	1/ 7/1835
	Nathaniel sw: S: Warren Cash	
HUTCHASON, William	RHODES, Rosanna	4/14/1826
	S: Stiles Parker	
HYNES, Abner	LINSEY, Lucinda	5/20/1824
	F: George LINDSEY	
	cert. of girl's father	
HYNES, Isaac L.	STITH, Patsey	7/23/1826
	F: Joseph STITH	
	cert. of Joseph Stith	
	proven by Wm. Hardeway	
HYNES, James	EDEN, Anny	2/ 9/1825
	M: Anny EDEN Sr. S: Vincent Smallwood	
HYNES, Joseph	SCIFES, Endamile	12/ 8/1850
	F: Joseph, David (Bro)	
INGNAM, Samuel	NEWBILL, Eliza	9/ 2/1829
	F: Thomas S: Thomas Newbill	
INMAN, Zekiel	SANDER, Sally	11/16/1824
	F: Wm. SOUTH S: James Haycraft	
	sates she is age 21.	
IRELAND, John	JOSEPH, Rutha	9/28/1829
	M: Sarah S: S. Joseph	
IRWIN, Hans	OVERALL, Sarah	1/10/1817
	M: Mary OVERALL S: Dennie Walker	
IRWIN, John	BUSH, Sarah R.	4/21/1849
	F: C. BUSH	
IRWIN, Lewis	STADER, Margaret	11/ 6/1822
	cert. boy's father S: Geo. L. Rogers	
	and girl's proven age	
	21 by John Stader	
	S: Isaac Irwin	
IRWIN, Solomon	SMITH, Lucretia	10/29/1832
	F: William	
ISAACS, Jesse	HUTSON, Martha	11/ 7/1847
	M: Mary S: Jacob Rogers	
ISBOURN, David	MILLER, Martha	6/29/1835
	F: Michael	
ISREAL, Richardson	DUNCAN, Amanda	3/30/1833
	F: Joseph	
IVOYSE, Tomson	GREEN, Peggy	8/20/1817
	F: Matthew	
	M: Patience GREEN	
JACKSON, Elijah	HART, Olive	4/10/1820
	S: Josiah Hart	
JACKSON, James	BROWN, Rebecca	6/ 5/1828
	Zadock sw: age S: James Daugherty	
JACKSON, James	ENLOW, Amy S.	3/20/1833
	Joseph Reed, sw: age S: William Tarpley	
JACKSON, John	PADGETT, Catherine	2/ 4/1846
	F: John PADGETT swore	
	girl 21.	

59

GROOM	BRIDE	DATE
JACKSON, John	PRICE, Sarah	12/19/1815
	F: Thomas	
JACKSON, Neely	NIX, Nancy	5/26/1827
	F: William CAYTON	
JACKSON, William Sr.	RAINE, Elizabeth	5/30/1849
	James H. Jenkins Pr.	
JAGGERS, Levi	WEST, Asa? Alsa	3/ 4/1813
	F: James WEST	
JAHAM, Didler	COTTERL, Adite Josephine	5/22/1850
	M: Catherine, F. George L.	
JAMES, Henry F.	DORSEY, Mary	2/15/1822
	F: Chas. DORSEY Jr.S: Thos. J. Chilton	
JEFFRIES, David	BOLDING, Elizabeth	2/16/1850
F: John	F: Wiley	
JEFFRIES, Elias	WILLETT, Mary	7/12/1834
F: James	F: James S: Thomas T. Chilton	
JEFFRIES, Henry	GREENAWALT, Rachel	5/ 7/1833
F: Isham	F: David	
JEFFRIES, Henry	CALVIND, Milly	11/11/1834
	F: James	
JEFFRIES, James M.	LIPSEY, Elizabeth	2/16/1850
	F: Mortimer	
JEFFRIES, John J.	WAGGONER, Nancy E.	9/16/1850
	S: James H. Jenkins	
JEFFRIES, John	PRICE, Eliza	8/ 4/1834
	F: Martin S: Elijah Jeffries	
JEFFRIES, William	WILLIAMS, Catherine Ann	2/15/1836
	F:1. Arch. S. FLETCHER	
	S: Thomas J. Chilton	
JENKINS, Austin	JENKINS, Megra Ann	12/ 6/1834
	S: E.R. Clarke	
JENKINS, Allison	GILBERT, Nancy	1/30/1815
	S: Jehu Jenkins	
JENKINS, Benjamin	GREEN, Perthena	1/19/1825
	F: John GREEN	
	cert. of John Green	
JENKINS, Elisha	ENGLISH, Malvina	10/ 8/1846
	F: Francis	
JENKINS, Ezekiel	SMALLWOOD, Harrietta	2/12/1818
	Gdn: Saml HAYCRAFT S: Shadrack Brown	
JENKINS, James	SCOTT, Virginia	6/27/1828
	Jonathan McCandless S: Thomas J.	
	sw. age. Chilton	
JENKINS, K. James	IRWIN, Malinda	2/20/1832
	F: Benjamin	
JENKINS, John	GILBERT, Alianor	11/23/1816
JENKINS, John	BURBA, Harriet	11/28/1843
	F: William	
JENKINS, Joseph	FARMER, Elizabeth	11/14/1827
	F: James Cert. James Farmer	

HARDIN COUNTY, KENTUCKY MARRIAGE RECORDS

GROOM	BRIDE	DATE
JENKINS, Lewis	JOHNSON, Ann	9/17/1819
	F: Martha JOHNSON S: Bro. James Johnson	
JENKINS, Lewis	SHACKLEFORD, Matilda	1/19/1849
Gdn: Elisha JENKINS	Gdn: Sam WOODRING S: J. H. Yager	
JENKINS, Phillip	SHAVER, Polly	1/31/1814
	F: Jacob	
JENKINS, Robert C.	LAWSON, Sarah H.	1/22/1822
	F: James LAWSON	
	age proven by	
	Asa Chambers	
JENKINS, Robert C.	CONN, Polly	3/18/1820
JENKINS, Samuel	LANDERS, Malinda	3/16/1833
F: Philip		
JENKINS, Thomas	BUCKLES, S. Emily	11/ 7/1849
	F: John	
JENKINS, William	DURBIN, Secilly	5/19/1834
	M: Margaret S: E. A. Clarke	
JENNINGS, David	LAWSON, Lilly Ann	2/26/1844
	F: William	
JENNINGS, John	GOFORTH, Mrs. Ann	7/ 5/1817
	S: Jonathan Paddock	
	S: Thos. Vetress	
JENNINGS, John W.	MARRIOTT, Martha Jane	1/20/1846
	Gdn: Thos W. VERTREES S: Ezra Ward	
JETT, Hugh	HILTON, Frances	2/ 3/1835
	M: Jane	
JEWELL, Joseph F.	PEAKE, Martha	12/27/1847
	S: Jacob Rogers	
JOHNS, Jacob	STEPHENS, Harriet	7/ 5/1823
	cert. girl's S: John Stith Jr.	
	mother swon by	
	Joseph Stephens	
JOHNS, Jeffries	GREENAWALT, Levina	5/10/1831
F: Isham	F: David	
JOHNS, William	BROWN, Nancy	3/ 3/1817
	B: J. Kelly S: Shadrack Brown	
	F: Shadrack BROWN	
JOHNSON, Henry B.	GILMORE, Lucinda	12/21/1836
	F: Mahetable S: Alfred Hamilton	
JOHNSON, Ignatius	JENKINS, Harriet	4/21/1827
	S: Robert Byrn	
JOHNSON, James	GOODMAN, Dlora	4/26/1832
	Young sw. age S: James Haycraft	
JOHNSON, James	DOUGHERTY, Matilda	12/15/1835
F: William	F: James	
JOHNSON, James	JENKINS, Mary	8/20/1819
	Geniel	
	S: Ignatries Jenkins	
JOHNSON, John	DRAKE, Kitty	1/ 5/1819
	proven by Richard Simons	
	F: Allan DRAKE	

61

GROOM	BRIDE	DATE
JOHNSON, Quincy	SWANK, Elizabeth F: John	6/ 9/1847
JOHNSON, Sylvester	BOON, Mildred F: Charles	8/ 6/1836
JOHNSON, Thomas	VITTETOE, Nancy F: Thomas S: Robert Byron	12/ 9/1833
JOHNSON, Thos. D.	MILLER, Martha F: William	5/ 4/1858
JOHNSON, Thomas F: John	MIDDLETON, Jane F: Micajah	7/29/1833
JOHNSON, William James Johnson proved cert.	JENKINS, Susannah B. Thos Butler	10/ 9/1824
JOHNSTON, Joseph	STEVENS, Nancy cert. Chas. Buan? F: James STEVENS	8/ 3/1816
JOHNSTON, Mathew	MILTON, Mrs. Marian S: Michael Milton	1/ 2/1815
JONES, George P: George JONES	DURKIN, Ruth M: Mary DURKIN	7/26/1813
JONES, John	WELSH, Polly S: Shadrack Brown S: Redmon Jones	4/21/1817
JONES, Thomas	REYNOLDS, Nancy F & M: John & Mary REYNOLDS	11/16/1816
JONES, Samuel H.	PENDLETON, Sarah E. F: James K.	2/14/1849
JONES, William	STITH, Polly W. F: Remy STITH S: John Stith Jr.	3/ 8/1817
JONES, Zachariah F: William JONES	OWENS, Amedia F: Timothy OWENS	2/25/1824
JORDAN, Richard Stith	SITTH, Katharine	5/13/1821
JOURDON, William	PEARPOINT, Mrs. Sarah S: Samuel Anderson	11/ 2/1817
KANBERRY, James	OWENS, Mary F: William S: William Owens	5/23/1836
KANNAHAM, William	TATE, Elizabeth F: Jesse M.	5/ 7/1832
KASEY, Alexander B.	LAWSON, Leeann F: Henry	12/ 3/1846
KASTER, Coonrod	COY, Ellen Coonrod, Coy S: James Daugherty sw. age	3/28/1829
KASTER, Frederick	CONN, Elizabeth F: Wm. CONN Sr. M: Mary CONN cert. of father proven by Wm. Conn Jr.	12/ 4/1820
KASTER, Miles	PAYTON, Sarah F: Gabriel S: G. Payton	2/23/1830

GROOM	BRIDE	DATE
KEATS, Henry Wm.	SKEENS, Lacinda	2/ 5/1845
	M: Nancy	
KEELING, Campbell	HOMES, Elizabeth	5/23/1832
	M: Isabella	
KEELING, Lewis	HOWEY, Lydia	7/16/1821
	S: Wm. Tarpley	
KEES, Samuel F.	KEY, Mary	7/24/1820
	S: Martin Key	
KEITH, William	BROWN, Patsey	10/25/1816
	F: Edward WILLSON	
KELLAM, Harrison	BUCKLES, Elizabeth	6/ 4/1850
	Jacob Buckles cert. proven	
	by Ephriam Buckles	
KELLEM, Charles	HINCH, Phoebe	4/18/1821
	ages cert. by S: Thos. J. Chilton	
	Jas. Duffey	
KELLEN, William	PICKEREL, Polly	7/31/1823
	cert. Samuel Puckerel proven	
	by David Pickerel	
KELLY, Richard	LONG, Nancy	5/17/1833
	M: Sally ARNOLD	
KEMP, Reubin	ROYALTY, Elizabeth	9/14/1825
	F: Thomas ROYALTY	
KEMP, William	REED, Hesther	1/12/1820
KEMP, William H.	JOHNSON, Ellen	2/24/1848
	F: John	
KENDALL, Enoch	HOLLOWAY, Elizabeth	8/25/1820
	S: Warren Cash	
	S: Thomas Williams	
KENDALL, Stephen	MILLER, Catherine	3/28/1827
	F: Adam S: Adam Miller	
KENDALL, William T.	COFFMAN, Lucretia	1/21/1832
	F: Abraham	
KENDIE, Augustus	SWAN, Mrs. Martha	1/23/1823
	S: Hugh Cole	
KENNARD, William L.	CASH, Elizabeth	2/17/1827
	F: William	
KENNEDY, Alfred H.	PARK, Caroline	6/13/1846
	S: S. Williams	
KENNEDY, John	CHENOWITH, Ruthy F.	12/ 4/1844
	F: Isaac C.	
KENNEDY, Stephen	KENNEDY, Elizabeth Jane	4/18/1849
KENDALL, Henry D.	HOSKINS, Rachael	8/26/1850
	S: D. C. Culley	
KENNEDY, Daniel	PARK, Rebecca	5/26/1828
	F: George S: George Park	
KENNEDY, Charles	PHILLIPS, Sarah	9/16/1833
	F: Ashel	
KENNEDY, Alfred	QUINN, Elivra	1/25/1836
	M: Sally S: Colmore Lovelace	

GROOM	BRIDE	DATE
KENNEDY, James	BLEDSOE, Sally	6/25/1829
	M: Milly S: H. Bledsoe	
KENNEDY, John	VERNON, Lucinda	9/19/1826
	F: Anthony S: A. Vernon	
KENNEDY, Luke	BLACKFORD, Jane	6/21/1830
	John King sw. age S: George L. Rogers	
KENNEDY, Robert	FARLEIGH, Mary	8/ 2/1831
	SF: James WILLIAMS S: George L. Rogers	
KENNEDY, Thos.	BUZAN,? Phebe	6/28/1815
	S: Wm. Buzan, Jr.	
KENNEDY, Samuel	HENDRICKS, Mitilda	3/ 2/1822
	F: Fabias HENDRICKS	
	cert. Fabias Hendrio proven	
	by Edward McGovern	
	F: Tobias HENDRICKS	
KENNEDY, Samuel	YOUNG, Susan	7/13/1818
	S: Shadrack Brown	
	S: Solomon Brandenburg	
KENNEDY, William	COFFMAN, Ann Eliza	5/24/1847
F: Samuel	F: Hermon	
KERFOOT, Geo. N.	WILLIAMS, Sarah Ann	11/20/1844
	F: John R.	
KERFOOT, John S.	WILLIAMS, Nancy	2/15/1850
	F: Samuel	
KERMICKLE, John	MCLURE, Cloa	2/26/1820
	M: Rachel MCCLURE S: David Thurman	
KERMICKLE, Samuel	TRAINER, Mary	11/26/1825
	F: Wm. TRAINER Sr.	
	cert. Wm. Trainer Sr.	
KERNES, James J.	ARTHUR, Ann H.	12/12/1850
	F: Meredith	
KERR, William	BUCKLES, Mrs. Nancy	3/ 3/1817
	F: John BUCKLES	
	Widow of John Buckles	
KEY, Crassy D.	RAWLINGS, Sarah	12/27/1814
	S: Stephen	
KEYES, John Y.	KESSINGER, Milly	2/14/1818
	cert. William Keys	
KEYS, John Jr.	WELLS, Margaret	4/ 9/1818
	S: Geo. McClean	
	S: Reavis Wells	
KILLEN, Robert	CARTER, Anna	2/30/1831
	F: Jacob	
KILLIAM, Charles	HENCK, Phebe	4/18/1821
	S: James Duffey	
KILLION, Elihu I.	DECKER, Sarah	3/ 4/1819
KIMBROUGH, Richard	MORRISON, Jane	4/24/1816
	F: James MORRISON	
KIMPEL, George	BARKER, Martha	10/ 3/1843
	F: Jesse	
KING, Greenup	DITTO, Hanna	1/28/1850
Both of age	S: Jacob Rogers	

GROOM	BRIDE	DATE
KING, George	PENCE, Nancy	2/10/1823
	John Pence swore	
	girl 21.	
KING, John	MARSHALL, Mrs. Lucy	10/ 3/1826
	S: S. Martin	
KING, Peter	PAYNE, Elizabeth	12/29/1819
	F: James PAYNE S: Cert. Lewis Payne	
KLINGLESMITH, Daniel	HUTCHASON, Nancy Jane	6/17/1848
	F: William W.	
KLINGLESMITH, Moses	WILYARD, Elizabeth	11/28/1835
	F: Henry	
KINNARD, Lemuel M.	HIBBS, Mary Ann	8/ 4/1849
	F: Joseph	
KINKADE, George	TRANER, Saley	9/ 3/1816
F: Robert		
KINKADE, John	OLDHAM, Malinda	2/25/1818
F: Robert	S: John Oldham S: Geo. McClean	
KINKADE, Robert	TRANER, Elizabeth	11/27/1815
	S: Wm. Traner	
KINKEAD, Addison	WAIDE, Evelyn	2/25/1833
	S: John Stith	
KINKAID, William S.	UPTON, Mary Margaret	9/29/1845
	Walter Murlin S: Silas Lee	
	proved father's cert.	
KIPER, Andrew	ALLEN, Elizabeth	1/29/1835
	F: David	
KIPER, Henry	YATES, Patience Mrs.	9/ 5/1846
	S: Isaac Hart	
KIPER, Henry	ALLEN, Ellis	10/ 8/1831
	F: Elisha	
KIPER, William	JOHNSON, Susan	3/23/1831
	F: William	
KIRKPATRICK, George	TRANER, Sally	9/ 3/1816
KIRKPATRICK, James	FRIEND, Elizabeth	9/ 6/1823
	cert. both fathers S: James Haycraft	
KIRKPATRICK, James	GUM, Sally	2/28/1822
	cert. proven by S: Thos. J. Chilton	
	Henry Morrison	
KIRKPATRICK, John	WALKER, Eliza or Nancy	6/18/1822
	M: Nancy WALKER proved	
	by Thomas Kennedy	
KIRKPATRICK, Joseph	PRICE, Polly	9/21/1822
	age 21 by S: John Hodgen	
	Marth Easter	
	S: John Easter	
KIRKPATRICK, Joseph	PRICE, Elizabeth	8/16/1832
	Jos. A. Young S: Thomas J. Chilton	
	sw. age	
KNOWLES, Joseph	POSTON, Leeann D.	8/ 1/1832
	F: Temple	

GROOM	BRIDE	DATE
KURNER, Robert	HOBBS, Mary F: Nicholas HOBBS	10/31/1825
KURTS, Jacob K.	COWLEY, Nancy F: John S: J. Cowley	12/14/1829
LACEFIELD, Wm.	ROBERTSON, Elizabeth S: Jesse Lucefield	10/17/1814
LAFOLLETT, George W.	ROBERTSON, Lucretia F: Carter T.	2/ 4/1833
LAFOLLETT, Isaac	DUVALL, Mrs. Nancy S: Benjamin Keith	7/15/1830
LAFOLLETT, Joseph	HENTON, Hetty cert. both S: Daniel Walker fathers proven by Jacob Keith	10/18/1821
LAFOLLETT, Robert G.	SWANK, Polly F: Jacob S: cert. Jacob Swank	5/30/1826
LAFOLLETT, Squire	THOMPSON, Mentilda F: J.	11/17/1835
LAIN, Elijah	HANKINS, Nancy S: John	1/12/1813
LAMBERT, Abraham	WILLIAMS, Delilah Gdn: John COFER S: Alexander Guston	12/ 7/1844
LAMBERT, Garrett	DUFFEY, Ruth Ann David Pickerel S: John Duffy	4/12/1816
LAMKIN, James	BAYNES, Sarah F: William BAYNES	2/ 7/1825
LAMKIN, Jeremiah	BOMAR, Sally F: John BOMAR S: Thos. Whitman cert. David Fergusin	1/25/1819
LAMPKIN, John	BROWN, Sarah H. S: Samuel S: William M. Brown	7/29/1834
LAMPKIN, Henry	DAVIS, Rachel S: James Haycraft	12/ 9/1834
LAMPKIN, Patrick	HELM, Mary Jane S: Jacob Rogers	12/7/ 1833
LAMPTON, Henry S.	UPTON, Maria F: Daniel	12/30/1831
LAMPTON, James M. M: Susan	HUNTER, Eliza Ann SF: Wm. J. SINGLETON	11/29/1832
LAMPTON, Marcellus A.	PATTERSON, Ruth F: Andrew K.	9/30/1846
LANE, Barney	DITTO, Malvina M: Elizabeth	11/ 3/1835
LANGDON, George Coles	HORN, Mary M: Priscilla HORN Daniel Hayden swore girl was 21.	3/ 4/1822
LANGFORD, Larkin	FOWLER, Elizabeth F: James S: J. Fowler	1/13/1829
LANGFORD, Walker	DODGE, Ireneigh M: Nancy S: N. Dodge	1/13/1830

GROOM	BRIDE	DATE
LANGLEY, Benedick	PENCE, Polly	1/15/1821
	cert. Thed. Pence C. Coomes	
LANGLEY, Randall H.	CALVIN, Susan E.	9/10/1849
	F: Luke D.	
LANSDALE, Samuel S.	DITTO, Elizabeth	6/26/1821
	F: Henry DITTO, cert. of	
	Henry Ditto proven by Levi Ditto	
LARKIN, George	ALLEN, Martha	3/11/1848
F: William	F: William	
LARKIN, John	THOMAS, Sally	5/21/1825
	F: Wm. PEAK S: Colmore Lovelace	
	swore girl was 21.	
LARKIN, William	MCMILLEN, Rebecca	9/12/1821
M: Amy WASHER	F: Wm. MCMILLEN proved cert.	
	of boy's mother and girl's	
	father	
LARKIN, William	CRUSE, Mary	8/ 6/1824
	M: Charecy CRUSE	
LARUE, Isaac	LARUE, Elizabeth	4/ 3/1821
	F: William LARUE	
LARUE, Jacob	WELSH, Mrs. Deborah	3/14/1826
	S: John Hodgen	
LARUE, Jacob Warren	HELM, Elizabeth C.	12/14/1820
	David Thurman	
	S: John T.S. Brown	
LARUE, Jacob H.	PARK, Sarah C.	3/26/1827
	John Hodgen	
LARUE, Jacob H.	THURMAN, Elizabeth	11/18/1835
	Thos. sw. age	
LARUE, Jesse V.	MORGAN, Mary	11/ 5/1831
	F: James	
LARUE, John H.C.	DORSEY, Branetta	8/13/1827
F: Squire	F: Richard	
LARUE, Morgan J.	CASTLEMAN, Maria	9/ 1/1824
	cert. both parents John Hodgen	
LARUE, William B.	MCDONALD, Mary	3/ 4/1822
	S: Samuel Hodgen Alexander McDougal	
	swore girl's age to	
	be 21.	
LARUE, Wm.	PRICE, Sally	8/ 2/1813
LASHLEY, Thomas M.	HARLAND, Elizabeth	7/10/1832
	Foster-M: Eliz. ENGLISH H.C. Ulen	
LASSWELL, Benjamin	MCWILLIAMS, Mary Jane	8/11/1846
	F: James	
LASSWELL, Charles	SHECKLES, Hester	9/24/1832
F: Jesse		
LASSWELL, Jesse	SPENCER, Eunice Mrs.	9/13/1849
	S. Williams	
LASSWELL, William	WILLIAMS, Saly	10/12/1829
F: Jesse	F: Charles	

GROOM	BRIDE	DATE
LASSWELL, Uriah	JACKSON, Ann	12/ 6/1824
	F: Wm. swore Jacob Enlow girl was 21.	
LAWRENCE, Charles	SMITH, Rachel R.	5/22/1827
	F: Aaron con. A. Smith	
LAWSON, Amos	NEFF, Nancy	2/24/1832
	M: Sarah James Haycraft	
LAWSON, David Jr.	MARTIN, Tabitha	2/15/1845
F: William	F: Moab	
LAWSON, Felix	MARTIN, Elizabeth	6/ 1/1850
	F: Moab	
LAWSON, George	HARTLEY, Elizabeth	12/ 5/1844
	Geo. O. Bannon	
LAWSON, Henry	HARNED, Amy	2/16/1814
LAWSON, Samuel	RICHARDSON, Polly	9/15/1824
	F: Amos RICHARDSON cert. Amos Richardson	
LAWSON, William	MARTIN, Nancy	2/15/1848
	Stephen D. Martin swore girl 21.	
LEASAR, Adin	RUTHERFORD, Mary	3/ 6/1833
	F: William	
LEASER, Starlin	DARAKE, Elizabeth	12/13/1833
F: Josiah	F: Lead	
LEASOR, Martin	CURTRIGHT, Fanny	6/ 6/1835
	F: Samuel	
LEASOR, Zachariah	RUTHERFORD, Malinda	12/19/1829
	F: William William Rutherford	
LEASTON, William H.	KENNEDY, Elizabeth	1/26/1832
	Thomas J. Chilton	
LEE, Green	LEE, Abigail	12/17/1812
LEE, Henry	PEARMAN, Elizabeth	7/ 2/1834
	M: Nancy Colmore Lovelace	
LEE, John	KELLER, Elizabeth	8/ 2/1834
	F: Frederick B. C. Wood	
LEE, Miles	MORGAN, Malvina	12/ 8/1834
	F: William	
LEE, Olvier	BEARD, Eliza A.	3/ 1/1830
	F: John J. Baird	
LEE, Silas	GARLINGHOUSE, Hannah	11/ 9/1819
	Stiles Parker S: James Garlinghouse	
LEE, Sylvester	ROBINSON, Cofrona	10/27/1847
	William Lee proved D. C. Shear cert. from both parents.	
LEE, Thomas	LEE, Annie	3/18/1818
	proven by Green Lee	
LEEMAN, Samuel	GOODIN, Nancy	10/ 2/1820
	M: Margaret GOODIN	
LEEMAN, Samuel	EDLEN, Sally	11/27/1822
	F: William EDLIN cert. William Edlin	

GROOM	BRIDE	DATE
LEET, Charles	THOMAS, Hulda	4/15/1826
	S. Martin	
LEFLER, William	MABIUS, Nicy Jane	7/20/1848
	F: D. H.	
LEFOLLETT, Joseph	HENTON, Hetty	10/18/1821
F: Oza.?	F: John C. HENTON	
LEGRAND, Edwain	FORD, Sibbel	11/14/1821
F: Wm.	cert. of both M. Cunningham	
	fathers proven by John Legrand	
	F: Moses	
LEGRAND, John	COX, Mrs. Nancy	1/18/1819
F: Wm.	cert. William Legrand	
LEMMONS, Abraham	MELTON, Sary	11/ 1/1815
	S: Jones Melton	
LEMMONS, Wm.	RUNNELLS, Polly	6/17/1815
LEMONS, Thomas	WINCHESTER, Elizabeth	3/ 9/1831
	Hordan sw. age Em. G. Brown	
LEPLEY, James	HICKS, Elizabeth	10/31/1850
F: John	F: Thos. G.	
LETCHER, Archibald S.	WILLIAMS, Mrs. Winefred	4/23/1825
	John Hodgen	
LETCHER, Thomas H.	ENLOW, Sally	con. Polly Enlow
	BERRY, alias	Gdn.
LETSON, George	GARNER, Rachael	3/21/1823
LEWIS, Abihag Jr.	WHITE, Joyce	12/14/1822
F: LEWIS,Abijah Sr.	F: Pence WHITE, cert Pence	
	White and Abijah Lewis, proved by	
	William White	
	M: Pearl WHITE	
LEWIS, Benjamin	HANNA, Elizabeth	2/29/1848
	F: John S.	
LEWIS, John A.	BERRY, Nancy S.	10/30/1848
	Morris Berry sent cert.	
	proven by Wm. T. Berry	
LEWIS, Joseph	PARKER, Polly	7/20/1822
	F: Benjamin PARKER	
	cert. Benjamin Parker	
LEWIS, Noah	MOSEBARGER, Elizabeth	1/12/1825
	F: Samuel MOSEBARGER	
	cert. Samuel Mosebarger	
LEWIS, Thomas	HARRISON, Mrs. Isabel	10/ 2/1828
	David Thurman	
LEWIS, William	VANMETRE, Mary Jane	1/14/1828
	F: Jacob J. Vanmetre	
LEWIS, William R.	GREEN, Trecy	2/ 2/1844
	Wm. Hayden swore D. J. Coomes	
	girl 21.	
LEWIS, Zealy	THORP, Cynthia M.	4/18/1850
	SF: John R. TRENCH Colmore Lovelace	
LINCOLN, Thomas	JOHNSON, Mrs. Sarah	12/ 2/1819
	Geo. L. Rogers	
	S: Clinst Bush	

HARDIN COUNTY, KENTUCKY MARRIAGE RECORDS

GROOM	BRIDE	DATE
LINCLAR, Samuel	BUNGER, Elizabeth	3/10/1821
	S: Jacob	
LINDER, Asher P.	STEVENSON, Lilly Ann	8/10/1830
	F: John A.	J. A. Stevenson
LINDER, Israel	BURKHART, Pheby	3/ 9/1816
	S: Thos. Burkhart	
LINDER, Squire D.	BLAND, Nancy	5/27/1827
SF: A. ASHBOUGH	John H. sw. age	S. Ashbough
LINDER, Thomas O.	FUNK, Nancy	12/16/1844
	F: William	
LINSEY, William A.	YEAGER, Sarah Jane	5/ 4/1830
	F: Josiah H.	J. Yeager
LIPSEY, John	HARRIS, Nancy	8/ 8/1825
	F: Samuel HARRIS	
LITSEY, John E.	MCCULLUM, Mary	10/10/1832
	SF: Goolson HICKS	William Bolding
LITTERAL, William	HAGAN, Mary Elizabeth	4/ 8/1847
	Samuel R. Hagen	Morgan L. Larue
	swore girl 21.	
LIVEZY, Seward, John	SHEETS, Sarah	10/28/1826
		John Hodgen
LOCK, John	SPENCER, Margaret	3/ 6/1824
	John Worman says	J. H. Yager
	girl was 21.	
LOCKE, Washington	HOBACK, Mariah	2/ 3/1823
	F: Isaac	
LOFTIN, Henry	COZART, Mrs. Mary	4/ 8/1819
	S: Samuel Martin	
LAGADON, Hiram	THORP, Editha	4/22/1817
	M: Jane THORP	Thos. Whitman
LOGSDON, James	MCCLURE, Sarah	11/ 3/1835
	F: William	
LOGADON, James	DURKIN, Margaret	9/23/1819
	F: Joseph DURKIN	Robert Abell
LOGSDON, James	JONES, Sally	3/19/1813
	S: Arthur Goodman	
LOGADON, Joseph	DURBIN, Hannah	11/ 7/1820
	F: Joseph DURBIN	Robert Abell
LOGSDON, Joshua	ROW, Elizabeth	1/18/1813
	M: Mary ROW S: Robert Row	
LOGSDON, Lewis	HARRIET, Elizabeth	5/ 3/1831
	Jacob Carter, sw	James Haycraft
	age	
LOGSDON, William	SIMON, Ann	7/26/1822
F: James	F: John SIMON	
	cert. of both fathers	
LONG, Daniel	WATSON, Anne	12/20/1827
	James sw. age	John Hodegen
LONG, Thomas C.	HARLE, Sarah Ann	12/16/1844
	Leander W. Harle	H. T. Downward
	(Bro)swore girl 21.	

GROOM	BRIDE	DATE
LONG, Tolover H.	YAGES, Martha	3/19/1849
	F: William	
LONG, Tolover,H.	NALL, Belinda	12/18/1843
	F: John	
LONG, William	CRUTCHER, Elizabeth Ann	11/23/1824
	M: Nancy CRUTCHER	
	consent of Nancy Crutcher	
LORD, Jesse	GADDIE, Rebecca	11/13/1817
LOVE, Charles P.	MORRISON, Lucinda	12/12/1835
M: Sally	F: John	
LOVE, Isaac	DEWITT, Nancy W.	2/28/1849
	G: James D. DEWITT	
LOVE, Philip L.	DILLARD, Mahala Ann	10/ 4/1830
F: William	F: James	
LOVELACE, Colman	IRWIN, Christina	6/19/1824
	F: Benjamin IRWIN	
	consent of girls father	
LOVELACE, Thomas	SHEILD, Eliza	11/ 1/1830
		Colmore Lovelace
LOWEREY, Winston	ROBERTS, Louisiana M.	10/26/1830
		John Stith Jr.
LOWRY, William B.	LONG, Elizabeth	1/30/1836
	F: Andrew	
LUCAS, Benedict	ROBERTSON, Sarah	3/ 7/1833
	F: Carter T.	
LUCAS, John	BRASHEAR, Milly	3/11/1835
	F: Edward	
LUCAS, Thomas	BRASHEAR, Mary	3/11/1833
	F: Edward	
LUCAS, William	WATKINS, Lucy	4/21/1826
	F: William	William Watkins
LUIKER, Hangton H.	WATKINS, Alcerty	5/11/1825
F: Ralph LUIKER	F: Wm. WATKINS	
LYNCH, Hardin	STEPHENS, Elizabeth	2/ 6/1834
	Jesse sw, age	William Tarpley
LYNCH, James	STANDAFORD, Cinderella	4/ 7/1829
F: Thomas	F: Isreal	
LYNCH, Jesse M.	RUST, Matilda	7/30/1834
		Edward Simmons
LYON, David	COOLEY, Elenor	1/19/1836
	John says sw. age	Colmore Lovelace
LYON, Elijah	GRAY, Sarah	4/19/1847
	F: John	
MADDOX, James	DUNCA, Klen	9/26/1849
	F: Johnson	
MAFUS, John	AMENT, Abigail	12/28/1825
	F: Anthony AMENT	
MALLORY, Moses	SHANKS, Susannah	12/ 6/1831
	F: Robert	
MALONE, Nathaniel	CARTER, Nancy	12/13/1849
	both of age	James Daugherty

HARDIN COUNTY, KENTUCKY MARRIAGE RECORDS

GROOM	BRIDE	DATE
MALONE, William	ABELL, William	6/ 1/1846
		Isaac Hart
MARKS, James	HOWEY, Jane	8/25/1828
SF: Wm MORRIS	James Howey	cert. Wm. Marks
MARK, John B.	MCMAHON, Rosannah	1/12/1832
	SF: Phillip BURKHEAD	
MARKS, Thomas	HOWEY, Lydia	9/17/1827
M: Anna HARRIS	G: James HOWEY	cert. K. Howey
MARKS, William	MCMAHON, Savina	3/17/1834
		H. C. Ulen
MARLOW, Jetson	GRAY, Hannah	4/ 7/1830
F: Dory	F: Jonas	
MARLOW, William	KELLER, Marietta	2/ 8/1836
	F: Frederick	
MARRIOTT, John S.	SMITH, Ellen	11/11/1847
	Wm. Showers swore	Samuel Williams
	girl 21.	
MARRIOTT, Henry D.	CASH, Lucretia W.	1/10/1848
	Gdn: Wm. D. DUVAL	Aug. Denganquier
MARSHALL, Benjamin	KENNEDY, Sally	2/24/1822
	F: Peter	cert. P. Kennedy
MARSHALL, James	CASTLEMAN, Grace Ann	11/26/1834
	F: James	
MARSHALL, John	HUGHES, Peggy	5/28/1814
		S: Abner Hughes
MARSHALL, Mark Jr.	WADLEY, Mary	5/11/1822
	cert. Wm. Wadley	S: William Wadley
MARSHALL, Martin	OVERALL, Dorcas	4/22/1829
	Thos. W. sw. age	Geo. L. Rogers
MARSHALL, William R.	CLEAVER, Sarah Ellen	4/22/1850
	F: Samuel	
MARTIN, Amos	SMITH, Mary	12/ 7/1829
	Thos. sw. age	James Daugherty
MARTIN, Charles	ROGERS, Rachel	1/20/1820
F: John MARTIN	M: Mary Rachel ROGERS	
		Geo. L. Rogers
	S: John Rogers	
MARTIN, Christopher	YATES, Jane	12/15/1834
F: Jonathan	F: Elias	
MARTIN, Daniel	YATES, Ann	8/ 2/1844
	F: Elias	
MARTIN, Daniel J.	MCGREW, Hannah E.	9/13/1847
	G: Parmenas R. MCGREW	
MARTIN, Gibson	HENRY, Martha Jane	5/15/1847
	Stephen Henry swore	Jacob Rogers
	girl 21.	
MARTIN, Jesse	GOODMAN, Polly	9/ 8/1846
		Jacob W. Pence
MARTIN, John	PETERS, Rebecca	8/22/1849
	Young, Goodman swore	Green B. William
	girl 21	

GROOM	BRIDE	DATE
MARTIN, John	FURGUSON, Malinda	2/ 3/1829
		George L. Rogers
MARTIN, John	BUSON, Mary	9/23/1826
		Thos. J. Chilton
MARTIN, Moab	UTERBACK, Vacinda	2/20/1827
F: David	F: Thompson	
MARTIN, Rall	BALL, Betsy	10/15/1827
	F: John	cert. J. Ball
MARTIN, Stephen D.	MILLS, Elizabeth	5/13/1848
	Geo. H. Vessels	Ezra Ward
	swore girl 21.	
MARTIN, William D.	COFER, Elivra A.	11/17/1845
	F: John	
MARVIN, Daniel	PEARPOINT, Mary	10/15/1817
MASDEN, Harden	MILTON, Charlotte	4/ 4/1845
	M: June	R.L. Thurman
MASON, Benjamin	LEASER, Polly	5/20/1829
	F: Henry	G. Leaser
MASON, James	LUCAS, Margaret	1/17/1831
	F: Alexander	A. Lucas
MASTERSON, Jacob	MASTERSON, Rachel	4/ 3/1835
	F: James	
MASTERSON, Jeremiah	MILLER, Jane	4/11/1831
	S: Pickerel sw. age	Marshall Scott
MATHER, Henry	WALTERS, Lucretia	1/27/1830
	F: Coonrod	G. Walters
MATHER, James C.	MCINTIRE, Nancy M.	3/14/1832
	Thos. sw. age	Wm. M. Brown
MATHER, John	DILLARD, Nancy	8/15/1821
		J. H. Yager
MATHIS, Ambrose	PIRTLE, Cebra Ann	1/ 4/1847
	F: Abner	
MATHIS, David	SMITH, Elizabeth	1/ 6/1836
	F: Washington	
MATHIS, John	DILLARD, Nancy	8/15/1821
		S: James Dillard
MATTERLY, Henry	MILLER, Malvina	9/ 6/1831
	F: Philip	
MATTINGLY, Benedict	BROWN, Matilda A.	9/28/1833
	Austin, sw. age	
MATTINGLY, Stephen	KERVAT or CAVAT, Eleanor	10/29/1816
		S: Uriah Mattingly
MATTINGLY, Uriah	DAVID, Nancy	9/20/1813
	F: John DAVID	
MAXFIELD, James	KERR, Ruth	1/ 6/1825
	Wm. Delley	Hugh Cole
	provered cert.	
MAY, John	PATTON, Lettitia Newland	3/20/1836
	F: Thomas	Colmore Lovelace
MAY, Richard	LINDER, Elizabeth	3/ 2/1816
	F: Jacob LINDER	

GROOM	BRIDE	DATE
MAY, Samuel	WILLIAMSON, Rosanna	2/15/1826
	Wm. Percefull says Geo. L. Rogers	
	girl is 21.	
MAY, Stephen	PARK, Louisa	2/24/1848
	Mariah Park cert. was	
	proven by Jas. D. Park	
MAY, William	MAY, Elizabeth E.	9/24/1844
	Garret Davis	
MAYFIELD, John	FRIEND, Harriet	12/ 7/1822
	cert. girl's father,David Thurman	
	proven by George Brownfield	
	F: Charles FRIEND	
MEADOR, Richard	TUCKER, Mary Ann	6/17/1834
	F: Jacob H.C. Ulen	
MECHAM, Parkman	SOUTH, Rebecca	12/15/1834
	F: Milburn	
MEDCALF, Andrew	SCIFRES, Mary Malvina	1/25/1848
	Matthias Scifres Colmore Lovelace	
	swore girl 21.	
MEDCALF, Ignatius	LEFFLER, Sarah	6/12/1847
	R. L. Thurman	
MEDCALFE, Joseph	EDLIN, Margaret	12/ 3/1849
	F: William	
MEDCALF, Samuel	WILLIAMS, Ann Eliza	8/ 2/1844
	F: John C.	
MEDCALF, Simis	JENKINS, Julia Ann	4/19/1834
F: Ignatius	F: John E. A. Clarke	
MEDCALF, Vincent	JENKINS, Mary Ann	5/27/1834
	John sw. age J. A. Reynolds	
MEDLEY, John B.	BRYAN, Ellenor	5/ 4/1821
	cert. Geo. Atwood	
	SF: of girl	
MEDLEY, Joseph F.	BRYAN, Ann	9/29/1832
F: John	F: Charles	
MEEKS, Silas	LOGADON, Phebe	11/26/1817
	cert. Humphrey Smoot	
	F: Wm. LOGADON	
MELTON, Calistees	NORRIS, Elizabeth	1/21/1822
	cert. Richard Norris	
	proven by S. Norris	
	F: Richard NORRIS	
MELTON, James	LEMMON, Sarah	11/ 5/1815
MERCER, F. George	RINGO, Catherine A.	8/ 4/1849
	Jacob Rogers	
MERRIFIELD, John	WELSH, Sarah	10/29/1816
	F: John WELSH	
	proven by A. Churchill	
MERRMER, Rene	CARRICOL, Barbara	6/29/1832
	John sw. age C. J. Coomes	
METCALF, Charels	CARRICA, Sarah	12/23/1834
	F: James	

GROOM	BRIDE	DATE
MILBOURN, Simeon E.	THOMPSON, Nancy M.	4/24/1847
	William Thompson (Bro)	
	swore girl 21.	
MILBURN, John	DRANE, Mary	12/30/1833
F: Robert	F: Walter	
MICHAELS, William	MCVEY, Mary	3/18/1820
	cert. boy's mother and	
	girl's father	
MICHAELS, Wm.	MCVEY, Mary	3/18/1820
M: Silvey MIKLES	S: James McVey	
MIDDLETON, Alexander	WALTERS, Elizabeth	7/18/1818
	F: Andrew WALTERS	
MIDDLETON, Andrew	LEE, Margaret	3/ 9/1846
	John M. Lee cert. proven	
	by William Lee.	
MIDDLETON, Charles W.	MCDOUGALL, Elizabeth	3/18/1820
	David Thurman	
MIDDLETON, James	BRISCOE, Mary Jane	4/ 8/1824
	F: Walter BRISCOE	
	cert. Walter Briscoe	
MIDDLETON, Preston S.	HARGAN, Sarah Ann	9/18/1849
	F: James	
MIDDLETON, Micajah	RHODE, Mrs.	6/15/1827
	John Hodgen	
MIDDLETON, Micajah	HIRCH, HINCH, Eveline	12/ 5/1814
MIDDLETON, Thomas C.	MANFIELD, Nelly	7/ 8/1824
	M: Margaret MANFIELD	
MIKIES, Joel	PICKRELL, Mary	4/ 2/1821
	F: Wm. PICRELL	
MILES, Joseph	CASTLEMAN, Evaline	12/ 5/1834
	F: Benjamin	
MILLER, Abraham Jr.	MCVAY, Rachael	1/ 8/1827
	M: Mary	
MILLER, Allen	AMENT, Mrs. Mary Ann	9/ 9/1847
	Green B. William	
MILLER, Andrew T.	TORRANCE, Susan Mary	1/17/1845
	F: Albert	
MILLER, Andrew	HOWARD, Martha Jane	12/26/1823
	F: Ricard HOWARD cert	
	girl's father	
MILLER, Barney	YOUNG, Polly	5/18/1815
MILLER, Benjamin	TABER, Elizabeth M.	10/20/1849
	Hiram M.	
MILLER, Francis	LASSWELL, Emily	10/29/1832
or MCMILLEN	F: Jesse	
MILES, George L.	SLAUGHTER, Abegail	2/18/1819
	cert. by fathers Warren Cash	
	F: Robert C.	
MILLER, Gerard	FRYREAR, Sarah	10/ 1/1832
F: Adam	F: Jeremiah	

GROOM	BRIDE	DATE
MILLER, Gerrard	PARK, Mary F: George	10/ 7/1833
MILLER, Greenberry	CALVIN, Elizabeth F: Luke	10/13/1831
MILLER, Henry	HORNBACK, Amy	10/ 9/1815
MILLER, Isaiah	HELM, Louisa M: Rebecca	1/12/1831
MILLER, Larkin	KENNEDY, Rosannah Colmore Lovelace	1/23/1833
MILLER, Leonard	NEWMAN, Mary Ann Colmore Lovelace	8/30/1847
MILLER, Phillip	JENKINS, Sarah F: John JENKINS	1/ 9/1817
MILLER, Jacob	TABB, Elizabeth James E. Tabb William Turner swore girl 21.	2/28/1848
MILLER, James	BLISSIT, Nancy S: Reason Blissit	12/30/1815
MILLIN, James	HABAXK, Nancy cert. by father John Baird	12/ 7/1818
MILLER, James F: Adam MILLER	CULLY, Mary Ann F: Thomas CULLY consent of both fathers	12/16/1824
MILLER, James	CASH, Susan M. M: Catherine Tabb Bailey	2/24/1849
MILLER, John	KEFMAN, Axsa F: Abraham KEFMAN cert. girl's father proven by Harmon Kofman	12/18/1822
MILLER, John	LYON, Phebe Joseph SW: age Colmore Lovelace	5/24/1826
MILLER, John	MCCARTY, Kissiah Thos. Kelly sw. age	9/ 3/1833
MILLER, John H.	SAMUELS, Mrs. Mary	10/16/1830
MILLER, John F.	DRAKE, Permelia F: Abraham	2/ 7/1850
MILLER, John R.	SMITH, Elizabeth F: Aaron	11/12/1832
MILLER, John S.	MILLER, Sally F: Mike	6/12/1846
MILLER, John William	LANE, Sophia	6/ 5/1849
MILLER, Joseph	HENDERSON, Alley F: Thomas HENDERSON	8/24/1822
MILLER, Robert	FERGUSON, Sally	4/18/1816
MILLER, Samuel	ROBERTSON, Lean M: Nancy	11/17/1834
MILLER, Samuel	ROOF, Rebecca M: Barbara ROOF cert. of Barbara Roof proven by Nicholas Rool	3/ 3/1821

HARDIN COUNTY, KENTUCKY MARRIAGE RECORDS

GROOM	BRIDE	DATE
MILLER, Samuel	BUNGER, Elizabeth cert. girls father James Haycraft	3/10/1821
MILLER, Samuel	WITHERS, Polly Geo. L. Rogers	9/11/1822
MILTON, Samuel R.	STATER, Lydia Ann F: Adam	1/ 5/1835
MILLER, Thomas	CULLY, Frances Greenbury Miller sw. age	10/20/1830
MILLER, Thomas H.	VERNON, Susan F: Richard	12/ 9/1844
MILLER, Wm.	HUTCHERSON, Melinda Elias Morris says Stiles Parker girl is 21.	3/14/1825
MILLER, William	HUGHES, Kitty Ann F: Isaac	9/19/1849
MILLER, William	TADE, Polly F: John H.	10/ 9/1850
MILLER, William L.	WILSON, Elizabeth L. George L. Rogers	4/ 4/1831
MILLER, William R.	MILLER, Sarah F: Philip MILLER consent of girl's father	2/17/1824
MILLS, Stephen	THOMPSON, Mary F: Ignatius I. Thompson	5/11/1828
MINGIS, George	COTTER, Elizabeth	12/21/1816
MINGIS, Isaac	TUCKER, Nancy F: Jacob	2/16/1845
MINTER, Merrit Jr.	MALIN, Elizabeth M. F: Thos. J.	12/ 3/1850
MITCHELL, Joseph W.	DAVIS, Ellen E. M. Davis proved H. T. Downward father's cert.	7/ 7/1845
MINTER, Willis	MILLER, Serena Allen Miller swore girl 21.	9/18/1847
MOBBERLEY, Loui J.	COLE, Mary F: Francis	6/ 9/1835
MOCK, Peter	SMITH, Martha Lemuel Smith says Geo. L. Rogers girl is 21.	1/10/1826
MONNIN, Joseph	LINDER, Abigail Geo. L. Rogers	3/17/1819
MONROE, Byrd	LINDER, Margaret F: Jacob J. Linder	6/ 3/1829
MONTGOMERY, Chas. M.	HAGAN, Henlen W. Catherine Auberry, mother cert. proven by Thos. L. Hagan	12/12/1844
MOORE, Alexander	DILLARD, Matilda D. L. Hodges	3/12/1846
MOORE, Archibald	LONG, Margaret F: Andrew LONG consent of girl's father	4/ 7/1825

GROOM	BRIDE	DATE
MOORE, Asa	PAWLEY, Sarah Ellen	9/ 9/1844
	F: James	
MOORE, Cadwallander W.	MERRIFIELD, Adaline	11/ 2/1833
	F: Alexander	Thomas J. Chilton
MOORE, Charles S.	BAIRD, Sarah	12/ 5/1820
	F: John BAIRD Sr.	
	cert. proven by John Baird Jr.	
MOORE, Cyrus H.	ELLIT, Mary	1/26/1848
	F: Thos. G.	
MOORE, James H.	SHACKLEFORD, Elizabeth	3/10/1846
		Colmore Lovelace
MOORE, James W.	MCNEALL, Lelvina	6/27/1848
	Gdn: John L. HELM	R. L. Thurman
MOORE, Thomas	STOVAL, Lucy	6/24/1818
	F: Hezekial STOVALL	
MOOR, Washington	DOWDALL, Rebecca B.	2/ 2/1829
	F: William	William Dowdall
MOORE, William	REDMAN, Mary R.	10/23/1845
	Geo. W. Howard	A.L. Alderman
	proved mothers cert.	
MOORE, William	GRIGSBY, Mrs. Sally	3/15/1828
MOORGAN, Jonas	MILLER, Mary	8/17/1848
	F: Isaiah	
MOORMAN, Jesse	MOORMAN, Mrs. Elizabeth	10/20/1835
		H. C. Ulen
MOON, Matthew H.	WARD, Irena	12/ 1/1835
	John sw. age	Colmore Lovelace
MORELAND, Joseph C.	MILLER, Elizabeth	8/22/1827
	F: Christopher	con, C. Miller
MOREMAN, Alanson	STITH, Rachel	3/ 5/1827
	F: Benjamin	con, Benjamin Stith
MORGAN, Charles	REDMAN, Nancy	5/26/1831
	George, sw. age	Thomas J. Chilton
MORGAN, Daniel	MCVEY, Nancy	3/15/1830
	M: Elizabeth	E. McVey
MORRIS, Demay	ASHBOUGH, Sophia	4/ 1/1822
	cert. girl's father.	James Haycraft
MORRIS, Elias	HUTCHESON, Nancy	8/10/1822
	F: Joseph HUTCHESON	
	James Mason says girl is 21.	
MORRIS, Elzy	PERCEFULL, Louisianna	12/ 2/1847
	M: Maria Jane	Jacob Rogers
MORGAN, James	REDMAN, Elizabeth	3/ 6/1835
	F: George	
MORRIS, John	LARUE, Molly	7/24/1816
	F: Jacob LARUE	
MORRIS, John	HATFIELD, Martha	5/ 1/1850
	David Hatfield	Ezra Ward
	swore girl 21.	
MORGAN, John B.	HICKS, Elizabeth	6/14/1834
		G. C. Ulen

GROOM	BRIDE	DATE
MORGAN, Merriman A.	ROBERTS, Mehala F: Shadrick	2/ 4/1832
MORGAN, Wm.	GRAY, Elizabeth	12/24/1815
	S: Wm. Lyon	
MORGAN, William	EDLIN, Sarah F: Thomas	11/ 4/1834
MORRIS, Cornelius	READ, Sally F: Hensley REED, Sr. cert. girl's father	6/ 6/1825
MORRISON, Andrew	BEIGLER, Agatha F: John	10/23/1830 J. Beigler
MORRISON, Andrew T.	RICE, Dunice Jane Wm. F. Wright swore girl 21.	11/15/1844 Alex. Guston
MORRISON, Elem	GOODMAN, Elizabeth Joseph Goodman says girl is 21.	4/12/1824 Thos. J. Chilton
MORRISON, Henry	HUMPHREY, P. Salley M: Betsy HUMPHREY	7/22/1824
MORRISON, James	REDDING, Elizabeth F: John REDDING	3/ 5/1817
MORRISON, Joel A. F: Jesse MORRISON	ROBINSON, Cynthia cert. Jesse Morrison	9/20/1824
MORRISON, John	KIRKPATRICK, Polly	4/22/1815
	S: Samuel Haycraft Jr.	
MORRISON, John R. F: Thomas	GREENWALT, Rebecca F: Luke	12/31/1834
MORRISON, Joseph	REDDING, Elizabeth F: John Bro: Wm. Redding	3/ 5/1817
MORRISON, Samuel F: Isaac	GILLELAND, Sally F: James	1/18/1834 James Haycraft
MORRISON, Thos. G.	WOODRING, Lucinda F: William	10/11/1847
MORRISON, Thos. W.	VANMETRE, Elizabeth Wm. B. Vanmetre swore girl 21.	2/ 8/1845
MORRISON, William	SANDERS, Nancy Samuel Sanders swore girl 21.	2/ 1/1845 Wm. M. Howlsey
MORRISON, William C.	DAUGHERTY, Elizabeth	5/13/1819 James Haycraft
MORTIMORE, Lipsey	PRIOR, Hannah SF: Isaac HART	1/ 1/1829 John Stith
MOSSBARGER, Jacob	BUNGER, Mary	4/14/1829 H. Bunger
MOUNT, M. William	BLAND, Katherine F: William	1/14/1833
MOURNING, Lewis	JONES, Anna M: Annice	11/ 2/1830 A. Jones

HARDIN COUNTY, KENTUCKY MARRIAGE RECORDS

GROOM	BRIDE	DATE
MUDD, Daniel	STEWART, Frances Mrs.	12/24/1833
		Joseph Armstrong
MUIER, Jasper	JOHNSON, Martha	6/ 3/1850
	Gdn: F. TROUTMAN	P. B. Samuels
MUILIN, Abraham	LEASAR, Elizabeth	10/11/1832
	F: Henry	
MULHALL, Thos. Jr.	BRADLEY, Susan	11/25/1844
	F: Elijah	
MUHHOLLAND, Hugh	CRUTCHER, Malvina	4/20/1826
		John Hodgen
MULHOLL, James P.	REDMAN, Hannah Ann	8/ 9/1850
	Job D. Redman swore	Isaac Hart
	girl 21.	
MULLEN, Joseph	HENDERSON, Ally	8/24/1822
	F: Thomas HENDERSON	
	cert. Thomas Henderson	
MUMFORD, Jirah	SMITH, Rebecca	10/16/1818
	F: Joseph SMITH	Jacob Enlow
MUNFORD, Joseph	GOODIN, Keziah	3/29/1846
	Joseph A. Smith	R. L. Thurman
	swore girl 21.	
MUNSON, Lewis S.	MULHOLL, L. Mary Ann	6/ 9/1850
	James P. Mulholl	Aug. Deganquier
	swore girl 21.	
MULVENS, Jacob	BROWN, Elizabeth	12/14/1850
	F: Elijah	
MURLIN, Daniel	BROWN, Sally	12/29/1819
	cert. girl's father	Warren Cash
	F: John W. BROWN	
MURPHY, Benjamin	CUNDIFF, Polly	8/21/1815
	F: Elisha	
MYRTLE, William G.	WITHERS, Mary	1/10/1846
	F: William B.	
MCABNEY, Robert	SMITH, Catherine	11/14/1831
	F: Aaron	
MCAFEE, Charles	LIVELY, Mary	1/27/1827
M: Polly RIMPLE	M: Katherine	
MCAFEE, Geo. L.	RICHARDS, Susan A.	10/22/1846
	F: Richard	
MCCANDLESS, Eli	KASTER, Sina	11/11/1828
	F: Coonrod	con, C. Kaster
MCCANDLESS, Jonathan	CARR, Elizabeth	10/14/1828
	Sml. Burks sw. age	Blately C. Wood
MCCANDLESS, Jonathan	WILLIAMS, Elizabeth	3/17/1821
	Brother: Joseph Williams	
MCCANDLESS, William	HUTCHERSON, Polly	11/13/1821
		Martin Utterback
		S: Geo. Helm
MCCANN, Talbot	FLETCHER, Jane	3/ 7/1832
	F: William	

HARDIN COUNTY, KENTUCKY MARRIAGE RECORDS

GROOM	BRIDE	DATE
MCCARTY, Aaron Hardwick	BEAVERS, Nancy	11/28/1814
	S: Wm. Beavers	
	S: Thomas McCarty	
MCCARTY, Enos	DAWSON, Antemca	7/16/1819
	S: Middleton Dawson	
	S: John Dawson	
MCCARTY, Thomas	JENKINS, Elizabeth	7/21/1822
	cert. of girl's father	
	proven by Elias Rogers	
MCCERTY, Enos or Easnas	DAWSON, Artimica	7/ 5/1819
	cert. girl's father	Daniel Walker
MCCHENEY, David	GADDIE, Ginsey	5/18/1818
	F: Wm. GADDIE	S: Jesse Gaddie
MCCLEAN, John	JONES, Arrena	2/ 8/1818
		Geo. McClen
	S: Wm. Jones	
MCCOY, Bernard	WITHERS, Ann Eliza	8/ 6/1846
	F: Gideon	
MCCULLUM, Marçum	MILLER, Sarah Jane	3/25/1835
	F: Adam	
MCCULLUM, William	OWEN, Sarah	9/ 1/1835
	F: William	
MCDANIEL, Baton	NEEDHAM, Nancy	8/18/1828
	F: Elias	cert.
		Parkman, Needham
MCDANIEL, Hatten	JEFFRIES, Selina	2/10/1846
F: John	John Jeffries swore	
	girl 21.	
MCDANIEL, John	PRICE, Nancy	2/23/1820
F: Wm. MCDANIEL	F: Hatten PRICE	
MCDANIEL, John	WARD, Maria	11/ 3/1823
MCDONALD, Clements	ALLEN, Patsey	8/14/1816
	F: William ALLEN	
MCDONALD, Hugh	SHEHI, Eliza	10/ 1/1830
	F: John	J. Shehi
MCDONALD, John	JOHNSON, Lucretia	10/21/1834
F: James	SF: Hawkins WOOD	Robert Byron
MCDOWEL, Allen	LUCAS, Mary	9/27/1823
	cert. girl's father.	David Thurman
MCDOWELL, Jesse	PHELPS, Elizabeth	5/ 9/1821
	F: Anathony PHELPS	David Thurman
	proven by Allen McDowel	
MCDOWEL, John	EDWARD, Elizabeth	1/ 7/1824
	F: William EDWARDS	
	cert. Wm. Edwards proven	
	by J. Edwards.	
MCDOWELL, John	TRAINER, Nancy	10/17/1821
	F: William TRAINER	
	cert. Wm. Trainer proven by	
	Swepson McDowell.	

81

HARDIN COUNTY, KENTUCKY MARRIAGE RECORDS

GROOM	BRIDE	DATE
MCDOWELL, John C.	PURCELL, Mary	2/ 1/1832
	Daniel sw. age	Benjamin Keith
MCDOWELL, Swepson	CARMAN, Elizabeth	1/ 7/1822
	F: Caleb CARMAN	
	cert. Caleb Carman	
MCGAMISH, James	SMALLWOOD, Elizabeth	2/ 6/1836
	F: Hezekiah	
MCGEE, Anderson	RUSH, Elizabeth	8/29/1820
	brother Thomas Rush	Shadrack Brown
MCGEHEE, John H.	FIELD, Maria	9/ 7/1832
	A. Chalfon, sw. age	John Stith
MCGELL, George H.	DUVALL, Sarah	10/12/1829
	F: Thomas	T. Duvall
MCGHEE, Thomas	DEWITT, Gatha	11/30/1836
		George L. Rogers
MCGILL, Charles R.	GEOGHEGAN, Susan R.	11/24/1836
	F: Denton	
MCGILL, James T.	COAL, Catherine	9/24/1834
	G: Thos. WATKINS	David G. Hoskinson
MCGILL, William S.	COALE, Harriet Ann	2/21/1831
	G: Lurine WATKINS	David G. Hoskinson
MCGILL, William S.	PERRY, Emily	4/ 3/1845
	Albert Kelly Pr.	
MCGINNIS, David	HUTCHER, Elizabeth	8/14/1827
		Thomas J. Chilton
MCGREW, James R.	KING, Susan	1/19/1846
	M: Hannah MCGREW	Jacob Pence
	sent cert. proven by	
	W.C. King	
MCHURNEY, James	HOWARD, Mary	6/ 4/1835
	F: Woolford	
MCINTIRE, Nicholas	LINDER, Sally	4/ 2/1819
	consent of girl's	Geo. L. Rogers
	father.	S: Jacob Linder Jr.
MCINTIRE, Patrick	BERRY, Elizabeth	8/ 6/1833
	John S. sw. age	Benjamin Stith
MCINTIRE, Robt. H.	ENLOW, Malvina	6/24/1824
	F: Ison ENLOW	John Hodgen
MCKAY, James H.	RAWLINGS, Lucy M.	11/14/1846
	M: Elizabeth	Abraham Quick
MCKENNEY, Thomas	CAWLEY, Polly	8/ 8/1831
	F: John	
MCKENSEY, James	HARRIS, Elizabeth	9/10/1824
	M: Mary Ann HARRIS	
	cert. Mary Ann Harris	
MCLURE, Enoch	CANN, Mary	8/10/1828
	F: William	William Cann
MCLURE, Lewis	TWEDLE, Martha	5/28/1835
	M: Martha	
MCLURE, Lewis	FARMER, Nancy	7/22/1831
	F: James	J. Farmer

HARDIN COUNTY, KENTUCKY MARRIAGE RECORDS

GROOM	BRIDE	DATE
MCLURE, Otha F. F: William	JENKINS, Elizabeth	7/ 7/1830 William McLure
MCLURE, Robert	ENLOW, Lydia F: Isom ENLOW	6/ 3/1816
MCMAHAN, Thomas	THOMAS, Lettitia	9/15/1831 H. C. Ulen
MCMANUS, Charles	ROBY, Marian	11/24/1817 S: Barton Roby
MCMILLAN, Andrew	MAHONEY, Letty	9/10/1814
MCMILLEN, Andrew J.	GOODIN, Sarah Bryant Y. Goodin swore girl 21.	4/24/1849
MCMILLEN, Benjamin	ROGERS, Mary F: John	4/ 8/1850
MCMILLEN, Francis or MILLER, Francis	LASSWELL, Emily F: Jesse	10/29/1832
MCMILLEN, Geo. Henry	THOMPSON, Mary Jane John Thompson (bro.) swore girl 21.	9/26/1847
MCMILLEN, John	MAHONEY, Tresy Gdn: Andrew MCMILLEN	9/ 1/1821
MCMILLEN, John	MCBRIDE, Loretia	11/29/1847 C. J. Coomes
MCMILLEN, Samuel	SHIECKLES, Fanny Thomas	4/16/1828 T. Shieckles
MCMILLEN, William	IRWIN, Margaret F: Benjamin IRWIN cert. girl's father	12/12/1824
MCMONEN, Rawleigh	UPTON, Emily F: Daniel	2/11/1830 D. Upton
MCMURTRY, Stephen	LUSK, Polly	2/10/1817 S: Hugh Lusk
MCMURTHY, Wm. T.	MCCARTY, Elizabeth F: James MCCARTY	4/15/1822
MCNEAL, Daniel	VANMETRE, Mary Mrs.	1/30/1825 Warren Cash
MCQUOWN, W. Richard	MORRISON, Mary Ann C.H. Wood swore girl 21.	10/17/1843 S.S. Deering
MCWILLIAMS, David F.	MCWILLIAMS, Martha F: James	12/ 9/1845
MCWILLIAMS, Hugh	KEELING, Thomas bondsman girl's mother gave consent	3/ 8/1824 Wm. Tarpleau
MCWILLIAMS, James M.	LASSWELL, Sibba Jane F: Jesse	8/21/1849
MCWILLIAMS, James	CALVERT, Conny F: James	7/29/1835
MCWILLIAMS, James Jr.	VISERS, Susan	6/ 2/1818 Jacob Enlow S: Elisha Viers

HARDIN COUNTY, KENTUCKY MARRIAGE RECORDS

GROOM	BRIDE	DATE
NAFUS, Cravan	PINDLE, Nancy M: Ann PINDLE cert. girl's mother	12/27/1825
NALL, Jacob	BLEVINS, Lydia F: Nathan	10/19/1850
NALL, James W.	THOMAS, Einnefred F: Thomas THOMAS cert. Thomas Thomas	3/22/1824
NALL, James	BOONE, Amanda F: Enoch BOONE cert. Enoch Boone proven by H.C. Boone	9/21/1822
NALL, John M.	STITH, Elizabeth B. Wm. Nall swore girl 21.	2/10/1845 A. L. Alderson
NALL, John S.	BUCKNER, Louisana M: Elizabeth	7/12/1830 E. Buckner
NALL, Joseph C.	ARNOLD, Mary E. F: George	9/28/1846
NALL, Larkin	LEWIS, Catherine A.	7/ 3/1848 Jacob Rogers
NALL, Nathaniel	NALL, Polly F: John	7/12/1830 J. Nall
NALL, Nathaniel	NEWMAN, Frances Mariah	7/27/1846 Geo. C. Hicks
NALL, Robert	COLEMAN, Elizabeth F: Daniel	2/18/1828 D. Coleman
NALL, Thomas B.	NALL, Sally F: John	11/21/1831
NALL, William	BRUMFIELD, Elizabeth F: Richard BRUMFIELD consent of girl's father	10/10/1825
NALL, William	SHANKS, Mary Jarret Smith swore girl 21.	6/25/1846 Colmore Lovelace
NEAFUS, Cornelius	WILMOTH, Amelia J. Strickler sw. age	3/22/1832 G. C. Ulen
NEAFUS, Highland	MOORE, Elizabeth M: Julia	3/29/1831 Julia Moore
NEEDHAM, Albert B.	FORD, Sarah Jane F: Simeon	12/10/1844
NEFF, Andrew	ATHERTON, Lydia F: William	8/ 4/1848
NEFF, George	SMITHER, Susan F: John	11/30/1826 cert. J. Smither
NEFF, Jacob	WHEATLEY, Rosannah F: John	12/ 8/1834
NEFF, John	EDLIN, Mary F: John	3/17/1834
NEFF, John	LINDER, Mrs. Nancy	9/27/1822 James Haycraft S: Don Richardson

84

GROOM	BRIDE	DATE
NEFF, William	HOWELL, Ruth	12/14/1819
	M: Amasa HOWELL	Geo. L. Rogers
		S: Clabourn Howell
NEIGHBOURS, Abraham Jr.	CARRICO, Susan	11/ 4/1844
	Gdn: Abraham NEIGHBOURS Sr.	
NEILL, James B.	HAYS, Mary F.	10/11/1849
	F: R. P. MAYS	
NELSON, George	HARRIS, Sally	7/28/1832
	F: William	
NELSON, John	STILWELL, Rachel	2/23/1825
M: Katherine NELSON	cert. boy's mother and girl's father.	
NEVILL, Samuel E.	FELTCHER, Ann Eliza	9/26/1843
		Jacob Rogers
NEVITT, John	KEZEE, Ann	8/ 2/1824
	cert. Benjamin Parker girl's Gdn.	Elisha Dobbin
NEWMAN, Jacob	BRADLY, Rebecca	4/10/1826
	Benj. Marshal sw. age.	Isaac Taylor
NEWMAN, John J.	HOWEY, Cinderilla	12/21/1849
	F: James	
NEWMAN, Jonathan	MILLER, Susan	3/ 6/1826
F: George NEWMAN	F: Thomas MILLER consent of parents	
NEWMAN, Hardin	NALL, Mana	7/20/1835
	F: John	
NEWTON, Isaac	WILLIS, Elizabeth	10/20/1848
	F: Bird T.	
NEWTON, Samuel	IVANS, Elizabeth	6/20/1822
	M: Ancny ROBANTSON	
NICHOLAS, Henry	CUTRIGHT, Sally	5/24/1816
		S: Richard Cutright
NICHOLS, Benjamin	PEARMAN, Polly	2/11/1815
		S: Cebert Pearman
NICHOLS, George	MCVEY, Betsey	10/11/1823
	F: James MCVEY cert. James McVey	
NICHOLS, Jabez	COCHE, Mary Jane	2/14/1848
	Gdn: Jno. C. HICKS	Benjamin Keith
NICHOLS, John	ELIOT, Ruth E.	4/ 2/1849
	John Wilson swore girl 21.	Creed T. Meador
NICHOLS, Lewis	GRACEY, Hetty Ann	7/15/1826
	John Henderson swore girl 21. or Hugh Cole bondsman.	
NOE, Robert	LAWSON, Mary	3/21/1850
	F: William	
NOISE, Thomas	GREEN, Peggy	8/21/1817
	cert. by Paul Ridgeway	
NORRIS, Charles	SPARKS, Polly	11/10/1827
		Robert Byrn

HARDIN COUNTY, KENTUCKY MARRIAGE RECORDS

GROOM	BRIDE	DATE
NORRIS, Dempsey	ASHBAUGH, Sophia	4/17/1822
	S: David Ashbaugh	
NORRIS, Ephriam	DAWSON, Lucinda	1/30/1845
	M: Jane	T. T. Williams
NORRIS, James H.	SPALDING, Mary Jane	12/15/1848
	F: John	
NORRIS, John	COY, Sarah	4/20/1827
NORRIS, Leo	KEEZEE, Jane	6/26/1830
	John Newit sw. age	
NORRIS, Samuel	PAIN, Margaret	3/ 7/1824
	F: Francis PAIN	
	cert. girl's father	
NORRIS, William	BRYANT, Elizabeth	8/24/1820
	cert. Geo. Atwood	Ganiel
NORTH, William	GUNDIFF, Permelia	6/17/1818
	F: Masha GUNDIFF	
NORTON, William	HILL, Martha	2/ 7/1816
	cert. from Daniel Whitemer	
	B. William Bomar	
	F: Eph. HILL	
NOTTINGHAM, Henry	STANDLY, Emily Jane	8/ 5/1845
	Pleasant Standly	C. Meador
	proved mother's cert.	
NUIEN, William	SWAN, Cloe	3/ 6/1824
	F: David C. SWAN	
	consent of David Swan	
OCCARMAN, Jacob	LINDER, Katherine	10/12/1824
	F: Jacob LINDER	
	consent of Jacob Linder	
O'CONNER, Michael	BROWN, Elizabeth	5/24/1815
O'DANIEL, James	HOWELL, Margaret	8/ 9/1830
	F: James	J. Howell
O'DANIEL, John	EMANNE, Charlotte	4/ 3/1830
	G: Robert JOHNSON	J. H. Yager
OLIVER, Robert	BOLIN, Mariah	1/17/1831
	F: William	William Bolin
OLIVER, William	DILLARD, Susan	3/22/1850
		Colmore Lovelace
ORRICK, Allen	HARDIN, Patsey	2/23/1819
	cert. by Joseph Hendrix	
	F: Wm. HARDIN	
ORRICK, Lewis	MERIDETH, Elizabeth	12/11/1815
	F: Jesse MERRADETH	
OWEN, Alfred	RINGEE, Matilda	11/19/1832
	F: Cornelius	
OWEN, William	MCCULLUM, Polly	3/23/1819
	consent of girl's father	S: James McCullum
OWENS, Samuel	SUMMERS, Pattsy	12/ 7/1823
	cert. girl's father proven	
	by John K. Owens.	

GROOM	BRIDE	DATE
OWSLEY, Hurr W.	MORRISON, Alice	10/14/1829
	F: William	William Morrison
PAGET, James B.	WHEATLEY, Mary Anne	1/10/1822
	F: Geo. WHEATLEY	
	cert. Geo. Wheatley proven	
	by Benson White	
PAGET, John	VANVACTOR, Mary Jane	10/14/1848
	Gdn: David B. CARR	
PAGET, John	SHERRARD, Ann	1/20/1845
	Adam Sherrard swore	C. J. Coomes
	girl 21.	
PAGET, John		8/30/1823
SF: Jacob DUFNER		Wm. P. O'Brian
Thos. Foster swore girl		
21, cert. boy's SF: proven		
by Sam Cofer		
PAGGET, Reubin	HAWKINS, Nancy	
	James Strugen swore	Wm. G.F. Hays
	girl 21.	
PAINTER, William	GARWOOD, Martha Jane	12/18/1850
	F: Samuel	
PALMER, Alexander	RIGGS, Kesiah	9/16/1850
PANE, James	RICE, Katherine	10/18/1828
	F: Elias	E. Rice
PARCELS, Thomas	NICHOLS, Kitty Ann	10/ 4/1827
	SF: Jacob STIGLER	George L. Rogers
PARENT, David	AUBERRY, Jane	11/ 6/1830
	F: John	J. Auberry
PARENT, William	MARTIN, Priscilla	7/14/1821
	cert. girl's father.	Chas. Fankesley
		S: Henry Martin
PAREPOINT, Jeremiah Jr.	HARRISON, Elizabeth	11/ 6/1826
		Chas. Parepoint
PARISH, Thomas W.	MILTON, Sally	10/23/1820
	S: Charles Milton	Geo. L. Rogers
PARK, Arthur	SHACKLEFORD, Mariah	1/17/1822
		S: Jeremiah Shackleford
PARK, James	MCINTIRE, Sarah C.	6/18/1821
	Sarah C. McElroy	
PARK, James	WILLIAMS, Nancy	8/10/1818
	F: James WILLIAMS	Warren Cash
PARK, James	MCELROY, Susan	6/18/1821
		Geo. L. Rogers
PARK, John	MATHIS, Katherine	8/23/1824
	F: George METHIS	
PARK, Joseph L.	MCDONALD, Mary	3/16/1833
	F: James	
PARKER, Asberry	RICHARDSON, Mary	11/ 1/1832
	F: Israel	James Haycraft

GROOM	BRIDE	DATE
PARKER, David	HARRIS, Susannah	7/20/1822
F: Benjamin PARKER	M: Nancy HARRIS	
	cert. Mr. Parker & Mrs. Harris	
PARKER, Joel	HAYCRAFT, Hiram	1/10/1826
F: David PARKER	F: James HAYCRAFT	
	cert. Parents	
PARKER, Leonard B.	FAIRLEIGH, Elizabeth	10/26/1820
	David Thurman	
	S: Wm. Fairleigh	
PATE, James	FLETCHER, Susannah	10/23/1830
	F: William	Wm. Fletcher
PATRIDGE, Richard	BROWN, Elsey W.	10/ 4/1828
	F: Samuel	S. Brown
PATTERSON, Alex	VEIRS, Lydia	1/ 7/1817
	S: Nathan Veirs	
PATTERSON, Andrew	BRASHEAR, Margaret	12/30/1816
	S: Edw. Brashear	
PATTERSON, Andrew K.	11/ 5/1848	
	Archibald sent cert.	
	proven by Leonard Cardin	
PATTERSON, Edward D.	LAMPTON, Sucky Ann	12/15/1845
	F: H. H. LAMPTON	
PATTERSON, George	VEIRS, Mary	2/28/1824
	F: Nathan VEIRS	
	consent of Nathan Veirs	
PATTERSON, Geo. W.	MUMFORD, Mary	7/16/1849
M: Christian PATTERSON	Joseph Mumford swore	
gave cert. proven by	girl 21.	
Wm. Patterson		
PATTERSON, Henry F.	SHALTON, Sally	9/21/1849
	S: William P.	
PATTERSON, John	SULLIVAN, Sally Ann	10/ 3/1843
	F: Henry	
PATTERSON, Kison	ALLEN, Patsey	10/18/1822
	F: William ALLEN	
	cert. Wm. A. Allen	
PATTERSON, William	BRUMFIELD, Joanna	11/30/1814
	S: Rich. Brumfield	
PATTON, Chas. M.	BUSH, Katherine E.	9/19/1844
	Thos. J. Duvall proved	L. Meador
	parents cert.	
PATTON, Miles G.	VERNON, Susan	9/ 3/1832
F: Thomas	F: Anthony	
PATTY, John	HODGES, Ann Elizabeth	10/29/1827
F: Gorton	F: Galen	
PAUL, George	PURCEL, Elizabeth	7/12/1817
	Samuel Anderson	
PAUL, Geo. P.	BEST, Elizabeth	11/12/1845
	Thos. J. Duvall	C. L. Meador
	proved parent cert.	

GROOM	BRIDE	DATE
PAUL, Walter	HAGAN, Bahenny	2/18/1836
M: Ellen	F: James	
PAWLEY, James	NALL, Mildred	2/13/1818
		John Stith Jr.
PAWLEY, James	SMITH, Nancy	2/ 4/1828
	F: James	J. Smith
PAWLEY, Lewis	AUBRY, Ellender	8/12/1834
	F: Samuel	
PAWLEY, Stephen	HOWELL, Susan	8/31/1819
	F: James H. HOWELL	John Stith Jr.
PAWLEY, Walter	BIDDLETCOME, Laura	1/22/1822
	S: Daniel Biddlesome proved	
	both of age.	
PAWLEY, William	DUMWIDDIE, Elizabeth	7/ 3/1816
PAYNE, Richard	SHAKLET, Sally	9/ 4/1822
	cert. girl's father proven	
	by Jesse Shacklet	
	F: Ben SHACKLET	
PAYNE, Thomas	SMITH, Mary	8/12/1819
		S: John Rush
PAYTON, Reuben	HUMPHREYS, Jemima	1/27/1832
	M: Elizabeth	
PEAK, George	YAGER, Lydia	11/30/1849
	Both of age.	G. W. Crumbaugh
PEARK, Theodore	SPINK, Eliza Jane	5/18/1845
	F: Henry	
PEARL, John M.	FRENCH, Nancy	5/23/1834
	F: Stephen	E. A. Clarke
PEARMAN, Elisha	PEARMAN, Sally	1/ 5/1819
		James Cunningham
		S: Wm. Pearman
PEARMAN, Enos K.	CECIL, Louisa Jane	1/ 6/1849
	G: Bryon R. YOUNG	Milton Stith
PEARMAN, Hardin	SEIFRES, Lucinda	6/19/1832
	F: Mathias	
PEARMAN, Hugh	WHALING, Nancy	1/ 1/1823
	cert. girl's mother	S. Buchannan
	proven by Samuel Pearman	
PEARMAN, John	LYONS, Salley	10/18/1814
		S: Joseph Lyons
PEARMAN, William	WALLS, or WELLS, Nancy	3/19/1819
	Gdn: Benj. CLARK	Warren Cash
PEARMAN, William	TRENT, Sarah	11/26/1834
	F: Benjamin	
PEARPOINT, Jeremiah	GOODIN, Susan	6/25/1844
		Samuel Williams
PECK, Thomas	MCMAHON, Margaret	12/ 4/1820
	F: John MCMAHON	
PEERMAN, Jonas	MAXEY, Mary	9/25/1847
	GDN: Matherly BASIL	C. D. Sheen
PENCE, Jacob W.	HART, Jane	4/ 2/1827
	F: Oliver	

GROOM	BRIDE	DATE
PENCE, Samuel F: Jacob	HART, Balinda F: Oliver	11/ 7/1829
PENDLETON, Thomas G.	BROWN, Mary F: Peter	2/18/1832
PENDLETON, James Henry	TARPLEY, Martha Ann F: William	2/14/1828 William Tarpley
PEOPLES, Bird	BROOKS, Nancy	1/ 5/1818 Hugh Cole
PERCEFULL, Jackson M.	HORNBACK, Susan Robert Martin swore girl 21.	5/ 6/1848 James H. Jenkins
PERCEFULL, John	RUSSELL, Eliza	10/12/1850 James Daugherty
PERCEFULL, William	CHENOWITH, Mariah J. F: James C.	11/27/1828
PERRY, Elisha	PHIPS, Judah cert. girl's father proven by Willis Phips F: John PHIPS	6/26/1822
PERRY, James	ALLEN, Catherine F: Elisha	7/18/1833
PERRY, John	FORD, Sally	3/24/1828 Colmore Lovelace
PERRY, John A.	MORRISON, Matilda F: Henry	12/25/1849
PETERS, Abraham	MILLER, Susan M. Mrs.	5/ 5/1821 James Haycraft
PETERS, James	SHANKS, Ewerine F: Robert	11/ 8/1833 Joseph Armstrong
PETERS, James	MCMAHAN, Jane Thomas Peters says girl is 21.	3/23/1824
PETERS, John M.	PURCELL, Caroline Felix, Lawson swore girl 21.	6/ 3/1848 Ezra Ward
PETERS, William	RICE, Matilda F: Daniel X.	2/19/1849
PETERS, William A.	GOODMAN, Isabella Levi Goodman swore girl 21.	2/ 6/1850 C. Ward
PETRO, Levi	BURKHART, Sally B: Henry Burkhart	2/ 1/1817 Henry Burkart
PEWITT, Joshua	KEEZEE, Jane	6/14/1815 S: Jesse S. Keezee
PEYTON, Samuel F: Charles PEYTON	WICK, Alla cert. Thomas Peyton	12/23/1825
PHELPS, Liberty F: Anthony PHELPS	LONG, Jane F: Andrew LONG	10/13/1821
PHELPS, Robert F: Anthony PHELPS	JENKINS, Elizabeth F: John JENKINS	12/22/1819 David Thurman

GROOM	BRIDE	DATE
PHELPS, Robert	JENKINS, Nancy	7/ 1/1828
	James sw. age	John Hodgen
PHILPS, Josiah	MORRISON, Sally C.	12/26/1831
	F: William	
PHILIPS, Samuel	CAMBRON, Elizabeth	11/14/1829
F: Asa		A. Philips
PHILIPS, William H.	CONN, Nancy	7/14/1823
		Thos. J. Chilton
PHILLIPS, David B.	VERTREES, Elouisa M.	3/23/1847
	Robert H.	
PHILLIPS, David C.	HANDLEY, Mary Ann	8/16/1848
	Hiram Marlin swore	
	girl 21.	
PHILLIPS, John	STADER, Mary Jane	6/ 9/1834
	F: Peter	Colmore Lovelace
PHILLIPS, Isaac C.	FIRKER, Elizabeth	7/14/1823
	F: Ralph FIRKER	
	cert. Ralph Firker	
PICK, Thomas	MAMAHAN, Margaret	12/ 4/1820
PICKERILL, Daniel D.	PETTY, Mildred	11/ 6/1847
	F: John	
PICKERILL, David	MILLEN, Sarah	4/17/1817
F: Samuel		John Baird
PICKRELL, Samuel	MILLEN, Eleanor	4/12/1816
F: Wm.		
PICKRIL, Greenbery	HALL, Sarah	4/30/1822
F: Wm.	cert. proven by	John Baird
	John Hall	
	F: John HALL	
PIERCE, Daniel	GOODMAN, Susan	4/16/1831
	F: Jacob	J. Goodman
PIERCE, William	SKAGGS, Jane	3/ /1825
	M: Hannah SKAGGS	
	consent of girl's mother	
	& boy's father	
PIERMER, Robert	HOBBS, Mary	10/31/1825
	F: Nicholas HOBBS	
PIETY, Austin	MILLER, Polly	3/12/1814
F: Thomas	M: Sarah MILLER S: Robert Miller	
PIETY, James	HERNED, Eleanor	6/29/1818
	F: Enos	
PILE, Francis H.	HARTLY, Elizabeth	12/26/1817
PINDLE, Aaron	BANGAR, Sophia	4/ 1/1819
	consent boy's father Warren Cash	
	age proven 21. by	
	Richard Plyburn	
	S: Jacob Bungar	
PINDLE, Edward	HOWE, Rachel	2/15/1822
	cert. girl's father proven	
	by Bro. Abraham Howe	
	F: John HOWE	

GROOM	BRIDE	DATE
PINDELL, Jacob	NEAFUS, Anna F: John	4/13/1826 con, J. Neafus
PINDLE, James	PENNELL, Nancy F: John	4/17/1828 J. Pennell
PIRTLE, John T.	HENDRICKS, Jane John Rust swore girl 21.	7/12/1847 J. H. Yager
PLYBURN, Francis	BARTLETT, Fanny consent of Thomas MILLER girl's Gdn.	8/ 9/1825 Geo. L. Rogers
POPE, James	WHITE, Elivra M: Catherine	10/27/1834 Alfred Hamilton
POPHAM, Allen	REYNOLDS, Elizabeth F: J. B.	11/18/1850
POPHAM, Job	SETSER, Betsy	1/18/1813 S: John McCollum
POPHAM, John	SETSER, Rebecca	2/ 5/1813 S: John McCollum
PORTER, James	MARSHALL, Jannah Gdn: Wm. MILLER	7/ 5/1830 Isaac Taylor
PORTER, Richard	GILES, Martha G. F: Harvey GILES	10/30/1843
POSTON, Charles D.	HARCRAFT, Margaret J. F: S. HARCRAFT	9/14/1848
POTTER, John W.	ROYALTY, Mary Ann D. Joshua ABNEY and Ann ABNEY M & F: in law consent.	2/ 9/1847 Jacob Rogers
POTTER, Samuel M.	ALLEN, Rebecca SF: John ROGERS	11/ 3/1848 R. L. Thurman
POTTER, William H.	HUMPHREY, Sarah cert. of girl's father, both of age.	3/23/1821
POWER, John	WATTS, Susanah	12/10/1822 Geo. L. Rogers
POWER, Sylvester	JOHNSON, Mary Thos. Johnson swore both of age.	1/29/1847 Robt. A. Abell
PRATES, William	STILWELL, Celia cert. Sally LITTLE, boy's mother proven by V. Hoback who says girl is 21.	10/ 9/1822 John Baird
PRATT, Robert	SCOTT, Nancy Daniel McNeill sw. age.	4/12/1828 Joseph H. Yager
PRESTON, Augustus	COLVIN, Mary Minera F: Luke D.	5/30/1846
PRESTON, James	DRAKE, Nancy F: William	11/10/1845
PRESTON, Micajah	MINTER, Ann F: Mart	3/12/1846

GROOM	BRIDE	DATE
PREWIT, Willis	KEZEE, Tabitha	2/ 4/1819
		Warren Cash
PRICE, Isaac	JACKSON, Eleanor	8/ 1/1814
PRICE, John	GLENN, Rebecca	11/18/1815
PRICE, Thomas	POWELL, Lydia Ann Mrs.	12/31/1834
		James Daugherty
PRICE, Thomas	MCDANIEL, Elizabeth	4/27/1820
	B: Aden Black	
	F: Wm. MCDANIEL	
PRUET, Lamet	SHUMATE, Polly	4/13/1814
	F: Nemrod SHUMATE	
PULLAM, David	NEAFUS, Sally	10/31/1821
		James Cunningham
	S: John Neafus	
PULLAN, Abraham	SUTER, Cynthia	12/23/1818
	cert. Henry Suter	James Cunningham
PULLIAM, Charles	RAGLAND, Lucy	2/22/1817
	S: Gideon	
PURCELL, James	MADCALF, Matilda	10/28/1834
	F: John	
PURCELL, James R.	COFFMAN, Elizabeth	11/11/1844
	F: Henry	
PURCELL, Peter	GOODMAN, Catherine	4/25/1822
	cert. girl's father.	Geo. L. Rogers
	F: Jacob GOODMAN	
PURCELL, Roddy	PURCELL, Drusean	1/22/1818
	F: Wesley PURCELL	
	M: Rebekah PURCELL	
PURCELL, William	VESSELS, Nancy Ann	7/24/1849
	F: Benjamin	
PURCY, Robert C.	HAYWOOD, Rachel	4/ 4/1848
	M: Mary	
PURMER, Robert	HOBBS, Mary	10/31/1825
	F: Nicholas HOBBS	
	cert. girl's father	
PURTLE, Abner	LINDER, Celia	9/18/1824
	F: Nathaniel LINDER	Warren Cash
PYBURN, Francis	CHAPPELL, Polly	4/ 5/1822
	S: Roger Pyburn	
QUICK, Semmon	CARRICO, Teresa A.	3/19/1844
	B.J. Carrico swore	
	girl 21.	
QUIGGINS, John	TULL, Phebe	7/ 3/1827
	Gdn: John QUIGGINS	George L. Rogers
QUINN, Thomas	KENNEDY, Nancy	7/10/1820
	S: Peter Kennedy	Isaac Taylor
RADLEY, Christopher	BOWLIN, Sally	10/ 6/1819
F: Ochabad		Geo. L. Rogers
RADLEY, John	WILLMOUTH, Mary Ann	9/ 8/1828
	Thos. B. Willmouth	James Daugherty
	she was age.	

HARDIN COUNTY, KENTUCKY MARRIAGE RECORDS

GROOM	BRIDE	DATE
RADLEY, Isaac	WELSH, Parmelia Jane M: Deborah LARUE	12/31/1832
RAGLAND, D. Gidson	WELL, Mrs. Ann	5/13/1816
RAGSDALE, Benjamin R.	TAYLOR, Abigail Samuel B. Taylor proved cert.	2/11/1824
RAHM, John	PIKE, Margaret Ann M: Elenor	1/15/1849 C. J. Coomes
RAIN, John A.	BLAND, Mahala F: William	12/15/1834
RAIN, Joseph L.	DILLARD, Mary F: James	1/23/1828 J. Dillard
RAIN, Philip	DILLARD, Sarah F: Isaac	8/14/1826 cert. J. Dillard & James RAIN, Gdn, boy.
RAINE, John A.	PAWLEY, Sarah A. Amasa Pawley proved father's cert.	8/13/1845 G. W. Burris
RAMY, Hercules	MOORE, Mary Elizabeth F: Washington	1/29/1848
RATHBONE, Thos. W.	ENLOW, Mrs. May	3/24/1819 S: Wm. Cesna
RATHBORN, Thomas W.	ENLOW, Abigail	10/6/1819 Geo. L. Rogers
RAWLEY, Wm.	DUNWIDDLE, Elizabeth F. John DUNWIDDLE	7/3/1816
RAWLINGS, Robert	ROBINSON, Elizabeth F: Thomas	9/20/1828 T. Robinson
RAWLINGS, Wilson L.	GILLILAND, Aseneth	3/27/1815 S: Thos. Gilliland
RAY, John	DAZEE, Margaret Gdn: John RAY	2/5/1827
RAYSINGER, Peter or BAYSINGER	RICE, Elizabeth F: Elias	3/14/1832
REACH, Littleberry	BIRKS, Polly J. Hutchinson sw. age.	1/27/1827 Thomas J. Chilton
READ, George A.	MCLURE, Lydia Mrs. widow	9/13/1831 Thurman, David
READ, James Noble F: Archibald	SNELLEN, Christemis M: Ann READ	7/14/1828
READ, John	GRAY, Susannah	7/24/1820 Geo. L. Rogers
READ, Joseph	JACKSON, Susan William sw. age.	9/10/1829 Jacob Enlow
READ, Hensley	HOBACK, Sally	3/6/1816
READ, Hensley, Jr.	HOBACK, Sally F: Michael	3/16/1816
READ, Lewis	BROWN, Aylsey	6/14/1813 S: James Brown

HARDIN COUNTY, KENTUCKY MARRIAGE RECORDS

GROOM	BRIDE	DATE
READ, Thomas	ASH, Mary Ann F: Lawrence	9/26/1831
READ, William W.	HOLBERT, Ann Maria F: John	5/21/1849
READY, Richard	STRADER, Elizabeth	12/ 3/1831 Thomas J. Chilton
REASOR, Anthony	GOATLY?, Susan	3/11/1814 S: John Goatly?
RECSOR, Jacob	MCINTIRE, Elizabeth E.	12/18/1845 Jacob Rogers
REDDING, George M.	MCDOWELL, Ann Eliza F-L: Thos Smith	11/ 7/1833 Colmore Lovelace
REDMAN, George	CARLTON, Eda F: Kimball CARLTON cert. Kimball Carlton proved by H. Carlton	11/21/1821
REDMAN, James	WALTERS, Nancy F: Andrew	4/29/1826 Con, A. Walters
REDMAN, Job D.	MULHALL, Maetha F: Thomas	10/30/1848
REDMAN, Isaac	WALTERS, Mary F: Andrew	7/29/1833
REDMAN, Richard	WALTERS, Susan F: Andrew	5/ 1/1828 A. Walters
REDMAN, William	TRANER, Catherine F: Eleer	11/14/1828 con, Eleer Traner
REDMAN, William	DYE, Rachael F: Job DYE cert. Job Dye	1/26/1824
REED, John	MERRIFIELD, Juliet Robert H. McLure says girl is 21.	5/ 3/1824 Geo. L. Rogers
REED, Peter	GRAY, Nancy F: Jonas GRAY consent of Jonas Gray	12/29/1823
REESOR, Anthony	GOATLY?, Susan	3/11/1814 S: John Ga
REID, Archibald, A.	SNELLING, Anna	4/25/1828 Jacob Enlow
REID, Archibald A.	BAYNE, Margaret F: William	8/25/1830 W. I. Haybe
REID, William P.	HILL, Mary cert. girl's father.	4/ 5/1825 Jacob Enlow
RENO, Charles	LINDER, Letitia consent of boy's father.	11/24/1824
RENO, Christopher	STORK, Elizabeth F: James STORK cert. proven by Wm. Stork	8/22/1825
RENO, William	HAYCRAFT, Martha F: James	2/21/1833

HARDIN COUNTY, KENTUCKY MARRIAGE RECORDS

GROOM	BRIDE	DATE
REYNOLDS, Joseph B.	BURTON, Lydia	4/ 8/1850
	Gdn: Morgan L. LARUE Morgan J. Larue	
REYNOLDS, Philip S.	AUBERRY, Nancy	6/12/1834
	F: John Mrs. Bartlet	
REYNOLDS, William B.	TOWER, Sarah	11/ 5/1819
	F: Mathew TOWER	
RHIN, Anthony	MCMILLEN, Sarah Ann	12/15/1846
	C. J. Coomes	
RHODES, Amos	STICE, Jane	11/20/1835
	David Wright	
RHODES, David	GOODMAN, Rebecca	2/16/1829
	F: Jacob J. Goodman	
RHODES, Jacob	RUE or LARUE, Mrs. Jane	11/12/1823
	John Hodgen	
RHODES, James	PARKER, Eunice	2/10/1821
	cert. Samuel Parker	
	proven by Squire Gilber	
	F: Saml PARKER	
RHODES, Minor	RHODES, Amy	9/12/1825
	M: Dorothy RHODES Stiles Parker	
RICE, Daniel C.	PENNEL, Lucinda	12/31/1825
	F: John PENNEL	
	B: Con. John Pennell	
RICE, Oliver	LARKIN, Mary	9/ 2/1816
	cert. Robert Kirkpatrick	
RICHARDS, Richard	BLAND, Elizabeth	9/15/1824
	cert. James Bland	
RICHARDSON, Amos	JONES, Frances	11/22/1818
RICHARDSON, Bryan	FRANKLIN, Mary	5/16/1850
	Thos. Franklin swore Ezra Ward	
	girl 21.	
RICHARDSON, F. Daniel	SMITH, Nancy	9/15/1824
F: Amos RICHARDSON	cert. boy's father	
RICHARDSON, Daniel L.	DUNCAN, Katherine	8/ 3/1831
	F: Joseph J. Duncan	
RICHARDSON, Daniel S.	FUNK, Lydia Ann	5/ 7/1845
	F: William	
RICHARDSON, Daniel S.	HURD, Mally	4/ 2/1818
	Sam Allen	
	S: Zadoch Hurd	
RICHARDSON, Isaac	GILLELAND, Letitia	10/11/1828
F: Amos	F: James	
RICHARDSON, Jesse	SMITH, Margaret	7/24/1822
F: Amos RICHARDSON	F/M: Christ & Nancy SMITH	
	B-in-law: Nathan Hicks	
RICHARDSON, John	LINDER, Elizabeth	8/23/1815
	F: Daniel, Sr.	
RICHARDSON, John	BOLING, Betsy	1/27/1813
	F: Jonathan S: John Boling	
RICHARDSON, Jonas	SMITH, Margaret	7/24/1822
Amos Richardson cert.	Gdn: Nathaniel HICKS	
of boy's father proved	gave consent	
by James Lawson		

96

GROOM	BRIDE	DATE
RICHARDSON, Jonathan	LAWSON, Lavira F: David	1/13/1832
RICHARDSON, Samuel B.	FUNK, Elizabeth F: William	12/ 1/1845
RICHARDSON, William C.	WALKER, Eliza Ann Geo. H. Hicks	4/25/1850
RICHARDSON, William J.	WILSON, Anna cert. John C. HICKS, girl's Gdn.	11/ 4/1822 Warren Cash
RIDDLE, Benjamin H.	HAYCRAFT, Gilly cert. grandfather Samuel Haycraft	9/15/1819 Geo. L. Rogers
RIDDLE, George	FRANS, Nancy F: John FRANS	9/17/1816
RIDDLE, James	CRUTCHER, Mary Jane Robt. R. Crutcher swore girl 21.	3/ 9/1844 Jacob Rogers
RIDDLE, Simeon B.	PAWLEY, Martha F: James	1/27/1849
RIDDLE, William A.	ADAIR, Mary C. John Morris & Molly Morris cert. proven by D.L. Adair	3/23/1847 H. L. Thurman
RIDEN, Benjamin	BURBA, Sally GDN: John GREEN S: Wm. Burba	12/ 1/1819 Stiles Parker
RIDER, John	MUSLIN, Sally F: John MUSLIN	12/ 1/1819 Stiles Parker
RIDER, Joseph	ROGERS, Pamelia cert. girl's father. S: Elias Rogers	10/ 7/1819 Stiles Parker
RIHN, John	WOODRING, Mahala Ann F: James	12/11/1847
RILEY, John R.	DURBIN, Mary Ann M: Hannah	11/18/1828 H. Durbin
RILEY, Joseph	SMITH, Margaret cert. John Smith	1/18/1822
RILEY, William	BROWN, Elizabeth B.	12/19/1818
RINEY, George A.	GILLINGS, Jane F: James	9/ 4/1828 con, J. Gillings
RINEY, Sylvester	PAWLEY, Elizabeth Stepehn sw. age	5/28/1834 E. A. Clarke
RINGEE, Able F: Cornelius	PEARL, Phebe	9/25/1828
RIVERS, James	BURKHEART, Margaret cert. S.R. Cavan F: Andrew BURKHEART	7/ 8/1817
ROBBS, Gyrus	MARLOW, Jane F: Doug	10/26/1846
ROBERSON, William	GILMOR, Mary F: David GILMORE cert. David Gilmore proven by Sam McCalley	3/19/1824

HARDIN COUNTY, KENTUCKY MARRIAGE RECORDS

GROOM	BRIDE	DATE
ROBERTS, John	ASHCRAFT, Susan	4/21/1831
	F: Jacob	J. Ashcraft
ROBERTS, Joseph	VANMETRE, Elizabeth	5/20/1833
	F: Abisha	
ROBERTS, Thomas	HARRIS, Anna	11/16/1816
		S: John Harris
ROBERTS, Turner	BEWLEY, Phebe	3/15/1830
	F: Kilill	K. Bewler
ROBERTS, William	HOLDREN, Sally	12/ 3/1828
	F: Jacob	H. Holden
ROBERTSON, Andrew	DUCAST, Rebecca	3/10/1829
	Wm. Geeseland sw. age.	James Daugherty
ROBERTSON, George	RADLEY, Sarah	8/29/1819
	cert. from father	Samuel Martin
	F: Icabod	
ROBINSON, Elbert	THOMAS, Dianna	4/25/1835
	M: Sarah BLAND	Thomas J. Chilton
ROBINSON, John	BASHAM, Nancy	11/23/1835
	Gdn: Henry D.	Isaac Hart
ROBINSON, Samuel	MILLER, Polly	2/ 3/1824
	cert. John MILLER Gdn.	Samuel Martin
ROBINSON, Stephen	GRAIN, Mary	8/15/1822
	John Henderson says girl is 21.	
ROBINSON, William	OLIVER, Mary Ann	7/31/1848
F: David	F: Robert J. H.	
ROBINSON, Wm.	EVINS, Nancy	1/ 6/1814
		S: Joseph Howey
ROBINSON, William M.	WHITEHOUSE, Ellena	2/12/1848
	John W. Whitehouse swore girl 21.	Geo. C. Bannon
ROCKWELL, Anthony	BLANSETT, Nancy	6/29/1834
		Isaac Hart
ROGERS, Colmore G.	WOODRING, Margaret	11/ 6/1847
F: Jacob	F: Benjamin	
ROGERS, Elias, Jr.	HOLDEN, Permelia	5/18/1818
ROGERS, Geo. L.	MURRIFIELD, Matilda	11/ 1/1824
	F: Alexander MURRIFIELD cert. girl's father	
ROGERS, Jacob	NALL, Frances Mona	11/20/1849
	Both of age.	Colmore Lovelace
ROGERS, Jenkins	STOCKWELL, Elizabeth	2/23/1820
	cert. by boy's father.	Geo. L. Rogers
ROGERS, John	ALLEN, Lydia	4/ 6/1845
		James Daugherty
ROGERS, John	HOLDEN, Permelia	5/15/1818
ROGERS, John Jr.	STOCKWELL, Lucinda	11/11/1830
F: John Sr.		
ROGERS, Joseph F.	ROGERS, Fatena	1/15/1846
F: Joseph	F: Jacob	

GROOM	BRIDE	DATE
ROGERS, Richard	HANKS, Mary M: Sony HEADRICK SF: Walter HEADRICK	5/24/1813
ROGERS, Shacklet	SOUTH, Elizabeth F: William SOUTH consent Wm. South	9/19/1825
ROGERS, Tadoch F: Jacob	CHENOWITH, Mary F: J.C.	12/15/1833 Colmore Lovelace
ROGERS, Warren J. F: Jacob	COLVIN, Caroline F: William	10/18/1843
ROMANS, Jacob F: Isaac ROMANS	HENSLEY, Sarah F: Saml HENSLEY	3/26/1818
ROOF, Nicholas A.	RHOADS, Rheuby F: Daniel RHOADS	3/ 1/1820
ROSENBOUGH, Jacob	WILLIAMS, Elizabeth Widow of Anthony Young	9/23/1826
ROSS, Simon	BROWN, Susanna F: John W. BROWN S: David Brown M: Sally BROWN	12/ 1/1817
ROSSER, James	CARTER, Nancy M: Casey JOHNSON C. Johnson	8/25/1830
ROUNDTREE, Turner R.	FARGUSON, Polly S: Dudley Roundtree	1/12/1815
ROUSE, William J.	BROWN, Barbara Ann F: Senis	8/ 2/1847
ROUSE, William V.	SULLIVAN, Mary James E. Shelton Isaac Hart swore girl 21.	7/11/1845
ROUT, Richard	JACKSON, Levisa F: Alex JACKSON cert. A. Jackson	10/ 5/1825
ROUTT, John	HOWARD, Sally cert. proven by Thos. J. Chilton Samuel Howard girl's bro. M: Elizabeth HOWARD	4/30/1822
ROYALTY, Isom	STANLEY, Betsey S: Jesse Stanley	12/19/1814
ROYALTY, Thos S.	HUMPHREY, Rachael M. Drusilla R. L. Thurman	12/22/1848
ROYALTY, Thomas S.	BURIS, Delila F: William	12/ 7/1849
ROYALTY, Thos. T.	LARKIN, Ann Mariah F: William	11/25/1844
ROYSE, Ira B.	NOCKES, Nancy D.C. Culley	12/ 3/1850
RUBLE, John B. or R.	GLASSCOCK, Mary cert. proven by Shadrack Brown H. Stovall M: Seney GLASSOCK	5/ 2/1821
RUDE, James	SMITH, Elizabeth cert. John Smith	3/19/1818

GROOM	BRIDE	DATE
RUDE, John S.	STEWART, Amanda M. F: Peter	3/ 8/1847
RUDE, Wm.	KENNEDY, Salley F: Thos. MERRIFIELD	12/29/1819
RUSH, John	BRANDENBURG, Betsy S: Henry Brandenburg	10/ 7/1813
RUSH, Simeon	WHITE, Juliet	10/ 9/1817
RUSSELL, George John Uptgrove sw. age	WELDON, Susan John Baird	10/20/1831
RUSSELL, Joseph	BOLIN, Hannah F: William	3/20/1832
RUSSELL, William	RICHARDSON, Nancy F: Amos	11/18/1831
RUST, Jacob	MCDONALD, Frances	12/21/1813
RUST, John	WALTERS, Gracy S: Coonrod Walters	1/ 2/1815
RYAN, James	BREWER, Mary Jane C. J. Coomes	7/20/1846
RYAN, John	NORRIS, Mary Emily F: William	9/26/1845
RYAN, Joseph	GRAY, Nancy F: John	2/ 3/1847
RYAN, William	NALL, Sarah Ann F: Ignatius	12/23/1845
SALTEMAN, Peter	CONSTANT, Elizabeth	1/ 7/1835
SAMPSON, Benjamin	NEFF, Elizabeth cert, Henry NEFF, Gdn.	4/ 9/1821
SAMUELS, Charles	DORSEY, Polly cert. girl's mother John Stith proven by John Calven M: Nancy P.F. BEAL	10/28/1822
SAMUELS, William T.	MULHOLLAND, Kate F: B. SAMUELS	5/24/1850
SANDERS, Samuel	MORGAN, Ellen Stephen Morgan Wm. M. Howsley swore girl 21.	1/14/1845
SANDERS, Stith	STITH, Betsy cert. girl's father John Stith Jr. F: Richard Sr.	1/16/1819
SCAMABORN, Anthony	KERMICKLE, Elizabeth F: Peter P. Kermickle	10/23/1829
SCANLAND, Benj	WITHENS, Susannah S: Mathew K. Withens	12/20/1813
SCANNABORN, James	WALDREN, Elizabeth Wm. J. Waldren James S. McGill swore girl 21.	6/21/1850
SCHOFFNER, Chad. D.	KELLY, Malvina T. Geo. T. Mahon swore C.D. Shean girl 21.	1/ 4/1849
SCIFERS, Joseph	KOFMAN, Polly F: Abram KOFMAN, cert. by both fathers.	11/22/1820

GROOM	BRIDE	DATE
SCIFREE, David S.	BERRY, Sarah E.	1/16/1849
F: Joseph	F: Levi	
SCIFRES, Mathias	HOWE, Mary	3/15/1822
	F: John HOWE	
	cert. John Howe	
SCIFRES, Simeon	BERRY, Margaret	11/ 3/1845
	F: Morris	
SCINTCLAIR, Geo.	RIEN, Sarah Ann	10/31/1850
	F: William	
SCOTT, Anderson	MAXFIELD, Jane	7/20/1816
SCOTT, Bartley M.	TURNER, Nancy A.	2/25/1850
	William Mattingly	S. Williams
	swore girl 21.	
SCOTT, Bryant Y.	PARKER, Nancy Jane	9/ 3/1846
F: John	F: David	
SCOTT, Elisha P.	HOBACK, Elizabeth	10/ 2/1821
	Hensly Read says	John Baird
	girl is 21.	
	F: Michael HOBACK	
SCOTT, George H.	THURMAN, Sarah	6/ 1/1826
	F: Philip	cert. P. Thurman
SCOTT, Greenberry	WILLIAMS, Ella	12/20/1844
	Gdn: Wm. LASWELL	
SCOTT, Henry W.	PURCELL, Ellen	3/25/1846
	Felix Purcell swore	Abraham Quick
	girl 21.	
SCOTT, James	SMALLWOOD, Polly	10/10/1828
	F: Hezekiah	H. Smallwood
SCOTT, James	SCOTT, Elizabeth	12/28/1829
		Hugh Cole
SCOTT, James	MAXFIELD, Frances	8/23/1820
	cert. girl's mother	Hugh Cole
	M: Margaret MAXFIELD	
SCOTT, Marshall	READ, Nancy	11/17/1819
	cert. gir's father	John Baird
	F: Hansley REED Sr.	
	B: Hansley Reed Jr.	
SCOTT, Peter	RUSSELL, Nancy	12/26/1814
	F: Ezekiel RUSSELL	
SCOTT, Samuel	AMENT, Polly	6/ 1/1818
		James Cunningham
		S: Anthony Ament
SCOTT, Silas	GILMORE, Martha Jane	9/27/1847
		Jacob Rogers
SCOTT, Wm.	AMENT, Catherine	5/21/1814
		S: Henry Ament
SEAMAHORN, Solomon	FORD, Nelly	3/25/1821
	cert, girl's father	
	F: John FORD	
SEDAM, David E.	PERCEFULL, Amanda	4/ 4/1829
	F: James	J. Purcefull

GROOM	BRIDE	DATE
SEELEY, Elisha H.	THOMAS, Lorena	8/19/1819
	F: Samuel THOMAS	
SEGRAND, James H.	HAMMER, Sarah	8/ 9/1833
F: George	F: Henry	
SELBY, Elisha H.	THOMAS, Hurena	8/19/1819
	cert. girl's father	John Stith Jr.
SETZER, Abraham	HOOVER, Rachel	6/31/1826
	Joseph sw. age	James Haycraft
SETZER, Isaac	WILSON, Anne	11/ 5/1827
	F: George	con. Geo. Wilson
SETZER, John	HARRIS, Ruthy	8/18/1818
	proven by Samuel Harris	
SETZER, William H.	HALL, Minerva Jane	12/10/1850
		Jacob Rogers
SETZER, William L.	HOLLOWAY, Elizabeth	11/25/1846
	F: George	
SHACKLEFORD, John	KAZEE, Sally	9/11/1828
	J. Shackleford	Colmore Lovelace
	she was age.	
SHACKLEFORD, John B.	ABELL, Sarah	10/ 8/1835
F: John	F: Samuel	
SHACKLEFORD, John Jr.	WITHERS, Agnes	2/20/1819
		John Stith Jr.
SHACKELFORD, Thos	ENGLISH, Matilda	11/25/1813
F: John Sr.	F: Robert ENGLISH S: John Shackelford	
Witt: Jeremiah Shackleford		
John Shackleford Jr.		
SHACKLEFORD, Thomas	MCNEILL, Eleanor	10/10/1850
	Gdn: John L. HELM	
SHACKLETT, John Sr.	CHALFAN, Susannah	10/ 4/1823
	F: Aaron CHALFAN	
	consent Mr. Chalfan	
SHAW, William	ANDERSON, Sarah	9/10/1845
		James Daugherty
SHAWLER, David	JOHNSON, Nancy	12/28/1832
	F: Hugh	
SHAWLER, Jacob	MONGTOMERY, Julia Ann	9/28/1831
	H. Montgomery sw. age	James Haycraft
SHEBI, John	WALLACE, Elizabeth	10/ 6/1821
		David Thurman
	S: James Wallace	
SHECKLEFORD, Ambrose	DORSEY, Sarah M.	3/ 1/1826
	Chas. S. Dorsey says	Hugh Cole
	girl is 21.	
SHECKLES, Thomas	STOCKWELL, Mrs. Sarah	12/31/1824
SHEETS, Jacob	BALING, Rebecca	6/ 5/1844
	Wesley Baling (bro) swore girl 21.	
SHEHI, John	LARUE, Mary	5/29/1827
		George L. Rogers

GROOM	BRIDE	DATE
SHELTON, Donivan J.	BROWN, Mary Jane	12/15/1845
	Gdn: Isaac HART	Isaac Hart
SHELTON, Andrew M.	SHELTON, Mary Jane	1/27/1845
M: Elizabeth	F: William P.	
SHELTON, Geo. W.	ARMES, Sarah	11/30/1850
	F: Samuel	
SHELTON, Geo. W.	ARMES, Sarah	11/30/1850
	F: Samuel	
SHELTON, Henry	ATCHER, Joanna	9/14/1829
	F: Christopher	C. Atcher
SHELTON, Henry	CAPPS, Rebecca	3/16/1835
	F: Josiah	
SHELTON, Jonathan O.	HARRISON, Catherine	9/18/1850
	F: Henry S.	
SHELTON, William P.	STOVALL, Susan	5/ 3/1824
	cert. both fathers	Colmore Lovelace
SHEPHERD, Samuel	UPTON, Mary	11/21/1831
M: Milly	F: Edward	
SHERLY, Wm.	HOWE, Miliah	8/17/1813
SHERRARD, Warren	GRAY, Mary Ann	6/ 8/1846
	F: Pat. S.	
SHIPLEY, William D.	NEFF, Catherine	3/10/1848
Gdn: A.D. GEOGHEGAN	F: George	
SHOCKLEY, Thos.	DAVID, Elizabeth	8/19/1815
	F: Edw. DAVID	
SHOEMAKER, Jacob	GRAY, Keziah	11/ 9/1828
	Geo. Gray, sw. age.	David Thurman
SHOFNER, Joseph	WILLIAMS, Mary	10/23/1849
SHOWERS, Henry M.	PHILLIPS, Mary E.	7/12/1849
	J.M. Phillips swore	
	girl 21.	
SHOWERS, William	SHACKLEFORD, Mariah	2/18/1850
	Gdn: John ENGLISH	S. Williams
SIGNMASTER, Reubin	GEORGE, Sarah Ann	4/30/1845
	F: John	
SIMMONS, Hiram	CAULKINS, Nancy	8/23/1821
F: Robt. SIMMONS	F: Isaac CAULKINS	
	cert. from father's proven	
	by Enos and Jonathan Simmons	
SIMMONS, James	WHITTINGTON, Anne	10/15/1821
	cert. girl's father.	Alex. McDougal
SIMMONS, Mathew F.	GUM, Mary	4/10/1819
	consent of girl's father.	Geo. L. Rogers
	F: Stephen GUM	
SIMMS, Francis E.	FRENCH, Margaret Mrs.	12/ 1/1845
		C.J. Coomes
SIMON, Joseph	GREENAWALT, Eliza	10/ 1/1827
	M: Eleanor	con. E. Geenawalt
SIMPSON, Francis	MCINTIRE, Mrs. Sarah	1/10/1826
		S. Martin

HARDIN COUNTY, KENTUCKY MARRIAGE RECORDS

GROOM	BRIDE	DATE
SIMPSON, John	BRYAN, Margaret Jane	10/ 4/1845
	James M. Bryan proved, C.J. Coomes	
	father's cert.	
SIMPSON, Robert	FRENCH, Susanna	11/30/1833
	F: Elisha	E.A. Clarke
SIMS, Samuel	BRADLEY, Ellen	10/23/1839
	F: Elijah	E. Bradley
SINGLETON, Allen	ENLOWS, Mary	5/26/1821
		David Thurman
SINGLETON, Allen	WAIDE, Mary	6/22/1824
	cert. Squire LARUE	
	girl's Gdn.	
SINGLETON, John	NEAFUS, Adaline	5/20/1828
F: Benjamin	F: George	
SINGLETON, William Y.	HUNTER, Rachel	10/22/1815
	cert. Benjamin Singleton	
SIPES, Henry	HOWELL, Mary	12/ 2/1826
	F: James	con, J. Howell
SKAGGS, Henry	HOLT, Mary	5/ 2/1831
	F: John	S. Holt
SKEES, Elisha	NOLAN, Olena Ann	7/21/1846
	F: John G.	
SKEES, John	GRIMES, Sally	5/ 3/1828
	James Skees sw. age.	Thomas Ruth
SKEES, Meridel McDeal	CAMLEN, Lucretia	8/ 8/1846
M: Nancy		S. Williams
SKEES, Richard T.	PIERCE, Julia Ann	2/18/1846
	Richard Pierce proved	
	cert. of Wm. Pierce	
SKEETERS, Abraham	GOODEN, Margaret	10/ 7/1822
	cert. girl's father	J. H. Yager
	proven by Christopher BUSH	
	boy's Gdn.	
	F: Isaac GOODIN	
SKEETERS, John	AUBREY, Sally	4/26/1818
	S: Saml Aubrey	James G. Leach
SLACK, Randolph Jr.	COLE, Mary Henrietta	12/29/1849
F: Randolph	M: Mary	
SLACK, Reuben	BUSH, Lettice	7/11/1814
		S: Wm. Bush
SLACK, Richard	WOOLDRIDGE, Sarah	8/ 7/1822
	F: Wm. WOOLDRIDGE	
SLACK, Silas	COLE, Victoria	4/17/1847
	Robert Huff swore	C.J. Coomes
	girl 21.	
SLACK, William	HINTON, Margaret C.	4/ 4/1832
	F: John C.	
SLAUGHTER, John S.	CASH, Mildred	6/10/1831
	F: William	William Cash
SLAUGHTER, Robert C.	CHURCHILL, Lucy C.	10/31/1846
		R.L. Thurman

GROOM	BRIDE	DATE
SLY, Benjamin	GREEN, Tabitha C. Mrs.	11/ 1/1843
		Alex. Guston
SMALLWOOD, Hezekiah	FORD, Lecty	6/ 5/1816
M: Eleanor SMALLWOOD	cert. from father of girl	
	and mother of man.	
	F: Moses FORD	
SMALLWOOD, James S.	IRWIN, S. Rachael	9/30/1844
	Geo. Irwin swore	R. L. Thurman
	girl 21.	
SMALLWOOD, Thomas	SOUTH, Sally	4/29/1822
	cert. girl's father	James Haycraft
	F: Wm. SOUTH	
SMALLWOOD, Thos.	OUSTER, Matilda	1/13/1815
	F: Jacob OUSTER	
SMALLWOOD, Vincent	EDEN, Mary	11/ 4/1822
M: Elender SMALLWOOD	cert. by Elender Smallwood proven	
	by Hezekiah Smallwood, also Gdn.	
	of gir.	
SMALLWOOD, Vincent	MOORE, Mary	12/11/1827
	Gdn: Simeom FORD	Benjamin Keith
SMALLWOOD, Vincent	TULL, Mary	11/ 9/1830
	H. Smallwood sw. age	George L. Rogers
SMITH, Ansel	TUTTLE, Esther	2/17/1821
	cert. by Serajah Stratton	
	Gdn. of girl	Stiles Parker
SMITH, Artemas	GRAYHAM, Delphia	10/20/1829
	SF: Andrew BURKHARD	cert. Turner G.
SMITH, Benjamin	VANMETER, Mary	12/13/1820
	S: Benj. VanMeter	
SMITH, Calvin	NEWTON, Doetha	9/26/1827
	M: Thomas BELKNAP	
SMITH, David	GREY, Mary	11/13/1817
	F & M: Jonas & Hannah GRAY	
SMITH, Edward	OSBURN, Sarah Ann	12/26/1850
	David Osburn swore	Aug. Deganquier
	girl 21.	
SMITH, Frederick	STRICKLER, Grisa Jane	6/ 5/1849
	F: Jacob	
SMITH, Garret	SHANKS, Letitia	12/20/1844
	Wm. E. Shanks swore	Jacob Rogers
	girl 21.	
SMITH, Green	KEELING, Nancy	3/ 6/1826
	F: Wm. FERRIL says	John Baird
	girl is 21.	
SMITH, Hamilton	MCMURTRY, Mrs. Elizabeth	4/16/1833
		Colmore Lovelace
SMITH, Isaac	RUST, Elizabeth	11/18/1844
		Hiram T. Downward
SMITH, James	SMALLWOOD, Elizabeth	5/30/1816
	cert. Elenor Smallwood	

GROOM	BRIDE	DATE
SMITH, James	SWANK, Elizabeth F: Jacob	2/ 6/1832
SMITH, James	HORNBACK, Mary F: Daniel	10/27/1830 D. Hornback
SMITH, James W.	MCGEE, Rachel A.	8/22/1833 Washington Fagg
SMITH, John	DORSEY, Mary C. Amos, sw. age	2/ 8/1833 John Stith Jr.
SMITH, Joseph Jr.	MCCULLUM, Mrs. Sally	1/ 2/1819 Jacob Enlow
SMITH, Lemuel	MERRIFIELD, Cinthia F: Alex	4/12/1819
SMITH, Reuben	PAGET, Lydai	6/18/1834 David Hoskinson
SMITH, Reubin B.	WHITMAN, Sally cert. by John Whitman F: Thomas	8/24/1818
SMITH, Richard	LEE, Phebe cert. Oliver Lee	2/25/1828 Horaxe Brown
SMITH, Robert	SPILLMAN, Nancy	1/19/1825 Mathew Turner
SMITH, Samuel	RUDE, Phebe	3/ 9/1815 S: Wm. Rude
SMITH, Solomon F: William SMITH	STADER, Elizabeth cert. Girl's father proven by Francis Smith F: Francis	1/18/1820
SMITH, Thomas	KNIGHTEN, Sophia SF: Henry GRASS	10/21/1817 Samuel Anderson
SMITH, Thomas	MCDOWELL, Ann J.	7/ 7/1829 William Scott
SMITH, Wm.	GRAY, Jane	11/14/1814
SMOOT, Humphrey	MEEKS, Sarah cert. Henry Butler	8/30/1816
SNEED, James	WRIGHT, Celea M: Tabitha WRIGHT	12/19/1814
SOUTHLARD, Daniel R.	COALE, Anne Maria	5/21/1821 S: Samuel Bleight
SOUTH, Daniel R.	COALE, Anne Maria	5/21/1821 Nathan H. Hall
SOUTH, David	AUBERRY, Margaret F: Lauven	9/30/1834
SOUTH, Henry W.	ROGERS, Nancy F: David	10/ 7/1848
SOUTH, Thornton Y.	KELLY, America A. Wm. M. Burkhead swore girl 21.	11/30/1850 J. F. South
SOUTH, William	SAWYER, Nancy B: Charles Sawyer	9/ 2/1817
SOUTH, William K.	SHIPLEY, Hannah Gdn: Ambrose D. GEOGHEGAN	6/12/1844 W.B. Maxey

GROOM	BRIDE	DATE
SOWELLS, Benjamin	COMFORT, Carmon	5/12/1815
SPENCER, Doctor	MCCULLUM, Elizabeth	10/31/1825
	F: James MCCULLUM	
	consent of girl's father	
SPENCER, Henry	ROGERS, Mrs. Eliza	9/ 3/1831
SPENCER, Isaac	DIVER, Lettice	7/19/1821
	cert. girl's father. Wm. Downs	
		S: Thomas Diver
SPENCER, James	DEAVERS, Sally	6/ 8/1818
		Alex McDougal
		S: Thomas Deavers
SPENCER, Joel	JACKSON, Mary	4/19/1819
	cert. by mother Wm. Downs	
	proven by James Brown	
	M: Sarah JACKSON	
SPENCER, Sharp	JACKSON, Lenice	8/20/1825
	cert. girl's mother	
SPILMAN, James	PAUL, Nancy J.	12/24/1832
	Jno. Carlton, sw. age. H.C. Ulen	
SPINK, Henry	BREWER, Matilda	6/ 7/1823
	cert. of both fathers. Wm. P. O'Brien	
SPINKS, Francis S.	YUTSLER, Phebe	1/ 1/1821
	cert. by Wm. Yeusley	
SPRAULS, Alex	SMITH, Jane	3/ 2/1816
		S: James Smith
SPRIGG, Samuel	LOVELACE, Matilda	4/ 5/1847
	F: Colmore LOVELACE	
SPRIGG, William	CRAWFORD, Sarah	12/22/1849
	F: James	
SPURRIER, Richard	CHECK, Mrs. Susannah	11/25/1822
		Wm. Tarpley
STACK, Richard	WOOLDRIDGE, Sarah	8/ 7/1822
	cert. girl's parents. Jacob Enlow	
	proven by Henry Burcham	
STADER, Jacob	HILL, Nancy	8/ 6/1817
	F: Wm. HILL	
STADER, Henry	BUSH, Elizabeth W.	4/29/1846
F: Peter	F: John	
STADER, John	CROW, Susan	12/11/1832
		Colmore Lovelace
STADER, John Jr.	HILL, Peggy	9/12/1818
		S: Wm. Hill
STADER, Patrick	GUSTON, Rebecca	4/21/1845
	SF: John MILLER Colmore Lovelace	
STADER, William	READ, Mary Ann	6/26/1829
	Joseph Read, sw. age. Colmore Lovelace	
STANDAFORD, Aquilla	HUFFMAN, Catherine	4/15/1829
	F: John J. Huffman	
STANDAFORD, John	WILDER, Julia	12/31/1824
	F: James WILDER	
	consent of girl's father.	

GROOM	BRIDE	DATE
STANDLEY, Jesse	TURNER, Susanna	8/10/1818
	F: Solomon TURNER	
STANDLY, Jesse	AUBREY, Jemina	4/27/1819
	F: Francis AUBREY	Samuel Martin
STANLEY, John	ANDERSON, Ellender	10/28/1828
	F: William	J. Anderson
STANLEY, Pleasant M.	NORTHINGHAM, Margaret	8/ 5/1844
	F: Stephen	
STARK, Daniel	KENNEDY, Abigail	5/ 1/1825
	F: Henry KENNEDY	
	consent of H. Kennedy	
STARK, David	BLAND, Mildred	7/30/1828
F: James	F: Daniel	
STARK, Redham	VANHOCK, Phebe	2/23/1835
		Alfred Hamilton
STATER, Jacob	ROGERS, Rhoady	1/ 6/1829
	F: John	J. Rogers
STEEL, Jakez P.	GARRETT, Betsey R.	10/ 9/1821
	F: Wm. GARRETT	
STEPHENS, Reed	GREENWELL, Anna	7/15/1828
	Stephen G. sw. age.	
STEPEHNSON, Willis	THOMAS, Mary Ann	8/23/1850
M: Margaret	F: Burgess	
STEVENS, Henderson	HAYDEN, Catherine	10/29/1844
F: William	Daniel W. Hayden swore	
	girl 21.	
STEWART, Alexander	MCLURE, Jane	6/ 3/1826
	F: William MCLURE	
STEWART, Charles G.	MCNALLY, Martha J.	5/20/1844
	Gdn: James CORBET	A. C. Dewitt
STEWART, James B.	SMALLWOOD, Sarah	11/22/1827
	F: Hezekiah	cert. M. Smallwood
STEWART, Samuel	BRUNK, Mary	11/25/1820
	Bro. John Brunk	
STEWART. Solomon	SMALLWOOD, Elizabeth	11/22/1827
	F: Hezekiah	cert. H. Smallwood
STEWART, William	WELSH, Nancy	8/19/1820
	F: John WELSH	Wm. Downs
STEWART, William	DANIEL, Fanny	1/ 6/1822
	F: Reuben DANIEL	
	cert. R. Daniel proven by	
	Wm. Withers	
STIBBINS, William	SMITH, Susan	12/ 1/1828
	F: Nash	N. Smith
STILES, Bemas	PURSLEY, Peggy Ann	1/12/1828
	F: Thomas	T. Owsley
STILES, David	GOODMAN, Melcry	1/ 3/1831
	F: Philip	P. Goodman
STILWELL, Joel	PRICE, Mahala	1/14/1830
	M: Martha	M. Price

GROOM	BRIDE	DATE
STITH, Benjamin W.	WOOLFOLK, Polly D.	7/ 5/1823
	James Hardaway proved, John Stith Jr. age of girl	
STITH, Buckner	MOREMAN, Cinderilla	3/ 2/1829
	F: Achilles	
STITH, Felix	PRESTON, Frances Z.	3/16/1850
	Ann Preston cert. proven by Go. Preston	
STITH, Harvey B.	PAWLEY, Elizabeth	12/11/1848
M: Betsy Ann	F: Stephen	
STITH, James	HARRIS, Eliza	10/15/1849
	F: Ben	
STITH, John H.	HARDAWAY, Martha	5/12/1834
	Thomas H. sw. age.	
STITH, Joseph	BOWLING, Amanda	8/10/1845
	Milton Stith proved, A. L. Alderman father's cert.	
STITH, Matthew G.C.	GEOGHEGAN, Comford	2/21/1832
	F: Denton	
STITH, William J.	PHILLIPS, Mary Jane	10/21/1850
	F: Joshiah	
STITH, Richard	MOOREMAN, Elizabeth B.	2/ 2/1833
	F: Achilles	
STITH, Richard	SPRIGG, Sarah	7/10/1819
	cert. girl's father John Stith Jr. F: Leven SPRIGG	
STITH, Richard Jr.	SAUNDERS, Catherine	2/ 7/1817
	F: D. J. SAUNDERS	
STITH, Thomas H.	STITH, Elizabeth	6/14/1819
	cert. by father John Stith Jr.	
STITH, Thomas	MCGUGHIN, Mary	11/18/1823
	F: Samuel MCGUFFIN cert. of S. McCuffin proven by Prior McGuffin	
STOCKWELL, Michael	MARTIN, Drusells	2/23/1820
	cert. boy's mother Geo. L. Rogers	
STONE, John	DAVIS, Alethia	7/ 8/1818
	F: Macklin DAVIS	
STONER, John A.	TABER, Elizabeth	1/ 3/1850
	John W. Pearman John Rodes swore girl 21.	
STORMS, James A.B.	HORN, Mersilla	10/18/1847
	F: David WISE J.C. Denton	
STOUR, Waters J.	PURDY, Sarah Forcas	4/16/1834
	F: Edmund Benjamin Keith	
STOUT, Jonathan	WEST, Mrs. Patsey	10/ 3/1817
	Martin Utterback	
STOVALL, Hezekiah L.	GLASSCOE, Serry	5/21/1821
	M: Sency GLASSCOE cert. S. Glasscoe proven by J. R. Rubles	

GROOM	BRIDE	DATE
STOVALL, Hezekiah A.	MCCULLUM, Masa	7/24/1826
	F: James	con. J. McCullum
STOVALL, Hezekiah	BRASHEAR, Mrs. Sarah Elenor	1/20/1835
		Colmore Lovelace
STOVALL, James	RUST, Sarah	10/11/1831
	Matthew R. sw. age	George L. Rogers
STOVALL, James	STANDIFORD, Nancy	3/27/1820
	by father's consent.	Warren Cash
STOVALL, John	ATCHER, Susan	3/14/1834
F: Hezekiah	Cornelius A. sw. age.	
STOVALL, John O.	NEWMAN, Rachel	7/ 3/1845
	Hardin Newman swore	Jacob Rogers
	girl 21.	
STOVALL, Luther	SELBY, Mary Jane	9/29/1846
	F: William	
STOVALL, Thomas	HIBBS, Christina	10/31/1820
F: Hezikah STOVALL	cert. boy's father	
STOVALL, William	SHELTON, Elizabeth	1/11/1818
	F: Henry SHELTON	
STRADER, Jesse	HENDRIX, Ruanna	10/21/1815
STRADER, Larkin	MATHERLY, Lucy	10/31/1825
F: Francis STRADER	F: Samuel MATERLY	
	cert. of parents	
STRADER, Wm.	HILL, Elizabeth	8/ 9/1815
	F: John HILL S: Wm. Hill	
STRANCY, Lee	BROWN, Margaret	10/23/1849
	F: Lewis	
STRANGE, Joseph	SCOTT, Mary	2/12/1831
		George L. Rogers
STRANGHAM, Bennet	COOMBS, Urith	4/ 7/1823
	cert. SF. of girl	Thos. J. Chilton
STRICKLER, Geo. W.F.	ARTHUR, Frances Emily	8/26/1847
	F: Meredith	
STRINGLER, Jacob	NICHOLS, Edney	3/27/1817
STRINGER, Wesley A.	ROBINSON, Rhode	12/ 2/1843
	F: William	
STUART, Alex	MCLURE, Jane	6/3 /1816
	F: Wm. MCLURE S: Robert McLure	
STUMP, Geo. W.	MILLER, July Ann	12/25/1845
F: George	F: John	
STURGEON, Alfred	DORSEY, Katherine S.	5/22/1846
		John C.C. Thompson
STURGEON, James	PAGET, Betsey	11/12/1814
		S: Reuben Paget
STURGEON, John	BERRY, Elizabeth	7/11/1815
SULLIVAN, Daniel	ROGERS, Elizabeth	2/12/1821
	cert. girl's father.	Stiles Parker
	S: Elias Rogers	
SULLIVAN, Samuel	UPTON, Sarah C.	8/ 1/1850
	Isham C. Upton	Silas Lee
	swore girl 21.	

GROOM	BRIDE	DATE
SUMMERS, Thos	NORRIS, Susanna	2/20/1819
SUMMERS, John	ROBINSON, Jane	10/19/1816
SUMMERS, Thomas	NORRIS, Susanna	2/19/1819
	cert. Elisha French Anthony Garnish	
SUMMERS, Thomas E.	HAMILTON, Susan E.	6/10/1850
		P. B. Samuels
SUMMERS, Valentine M.	MCLURE, Rachel Elizabeth	4/ 2/1850
	F: Enoch	
SUTTON, Campbell	CALDWELL, Mrs. Elizabeth	10/15/1832
		Wm. Bolding
SWAN, Alexander	BUCKLES, Phebe	10/ 9/1827
		Hugh Cole
SWAN, John	KENNEDY, Sarah	12/17/1827
		George L. Rogers
SWAN, Julius	HAYDEN, Sophia	6/10/1829
	F: Daniel D. Hayden	
SWEET, Benjamin F.	ROBINSON, Jane	9/20/1830
	F: Thomas T. Robinson	
SWEETS, Allen B.	ROBINSON, Mary	1/27/1830
	F: Thomas T. Robinson	
SYMPSON, James	BOMAR, Jane	1/ /1831
		R. Bomar
SYMPSON, Thomas	PHELPS, Lavina	12/10/1827
	F: Anthony cert. A. Phelps	
TABB, Edmund C.	UPTON, Elizabeth	11/10/1817
F: Robt. TABB		S: Jacob Van Metre
TABB, John	MILLER, Sarah C.	12/19/1849
F: N.C.	M: Malinda	
TABER, Hiram H.	BOWLEY, Polly	3/21/1829
F: Jutus	F: Christopher	
TABER, Jesse R.	COLEMAN, Caroline M.	4/16/1847
	Elizabeth Coleman cert.	
	proved by Wilson Coleman	
TABER, John	HOSKINS, Elenor	12/10/1827
F: Justus		con. J. Taber &
		Jno. Mabus, g.s.f.
TABER, William H.	PEARMAN, Elizabeth	3/19/1845
		T.B. Williams
TALBOT, Thomas	HOBACK, Margaret	3/30/1827
	F: Isaac I. Hoback	
TATE, Jesse M.	MCMILLEN, Lucinda	8/11/1846
	Geo. H. & Rachen Colmore Lovelace	
	McMillen proved father's cert.	
TARRANT, Henry	DODGE, Deadmia	2/27/1822
	M: Sophia DODGE	
	John Mills says mother	
	states girl is age 21.	
TAYLOR, George	KENNEDY, Nancy W.	4/23/1832
	F: John	
TAYLOR, James	SMITH, Elizabeth	1/23/1818
TAYLOR, John	KESSINGER, Nancy	4/25/1818
	F: Solomon KESSINGER	

GROOM	BRIDE	DATE
TAYLOR, Ninicen	LUCAS? Achey	3/ 7/1814
TAYLOR, Richard A.	MCGEE, Sally	7/ 2/1818
	Gdn: Thos MCGEE	
TAYLOR, Samuel	ASHBAUGH, Mary	9/13/1831
	Jonathan Brady sw. age.Colmore Lovelace	
TAYLOR, Zachariah	WILLIAMS, Frances S.	9/ 5/1850
	F: Daniel	
TERRY, Absolem	RICHARDSON, Catherine	11/30/1819
	cert. boy's father Hugh Cole	
TERRY, Andrew B.	WAGGONER, Margaret	2/11/1823
	cert. Jasper Terry & Wm.	
	WAGGONER girl's Gdn.	
TERRY, David	LAWSON, Amelia D.	10/18/1845
	Isaac Hart	
TERRY, Isaac	PENSE, Betsey	1/17/1824
	F: Jacob PENSE	
	cert. Jacob Pense proven	
	by John Hein	
TERRY, James F.	GILLELAND, Phillena	1/ 7/1828
	F: James J. Gilleland	
TERRY, Josiah	AKERS, Barbara	8/29/1833
	F: Josiah	
TETRICK, George W.	AUBRY, Mariah	3/23/1825
	F: Crow	
THARP, Green B.	GADDIE, Hannah	11/17/1818
	cert. Jesse Gaddie	
THERGEAN, Albert	SLAUGHTER, Mary L.	10/18/1828
	F: Robert E. Slaughter	
THOMAS, Benjamin	STONE, Hepsabeth	12/20/1823
	F: John STONE	
	cert.-John Stone	
	proven by Liston T. Bell	
THOMAS, Eleazar	HAMMOND, Polly	12/ 4/1813
	S: Joseph Hammond	
THOMAS, Enoch	BROWN, Margaret	2/ 5/1831
	F: jonathan C. J. Brown	
THOMAS, Hardin	LARUE, Sarah	5/29/1821
	F: Jacob LARUE	
	cert. Jacob Larue proven	
	by I. Larue	
THOMAS, Henry	THOMAS, Sarah	5/24/1816
THOMAS, Henry C.	THOMAS, Mary	9/19/1846
	F: Joseph S.	
THOMAS, Hezekiah	THOMAS, Lucretia	3/ 6/1826
	cert. Nancy Walker John Hodgen	
	proven by Jacob Larue	
THOMAS, Hosea	BEALES, Elizabeth	7/26/1817
	F: Butts BEALES	
THOMAS, Isaac	HAMMOND, Rhoda	11/12/1816
THOMAS, Isaac	ATT, E. Mary	2/ 9/1849
	Nicholas Hoff swore girl 21.	

GROOM	BRIDE	DATE
THOMAS, Jack	DURBIN, Rebecca	1/28/1820
SF: Elias DRURY	cert. boy's father Robert Abell	
	Bro. Christ V. Durbin	
THOMAS, James Richard	PENDLETON, Eliza Ann	10/ 5/1850
	F: Thos. C.	
THOMAS, Joseph	PRICE, Charlotte	8/ 2/1813
THOMAS, Joseph	PAULEY, Ann	9/13/1820
	cert. girl's father. Geo. L. Rogers	
	F: John PAULEY Sr.	
THOMAS, Joseph	DAVENPORT, Mrs. Nancy	12/ 5/1823
	Wm. P. Tarpley	
THOMAS, Joseph B.	ROOF, Alice	1/25/1845
	Joseph R. Dillingham Alexander Guston	
	swore girl 21.	
THOMAS, John	BROWN, Mary J.	10/10/1849
	Gdn: Charles CECIL Aug. Deganquier	
THOMAS, John	MORELAND, Rachael	2/ 1/1834
	J.C.M. sw. age. Colmore Lovelace	
THOMAS, John	JONES, Margaret	7/1 /1845
	Jones, Rust proved C.J. Coomes	
	parents, cert.	
THOMAS, John C.	SMITH, Mary M. J.	1/22/1849
	F: John J.	
THOMAS, Melzar	MILLER, Eleanor	5/ 7/1825
	F: Samuel SMALLWOOD, Gdn	
	James Haycraft	
THOMAS, Miles	MILLER, Sally	1/ 3/1827
	F: C. G. Miller, con.	
THOMAS, Miles, N.	PARKER, Elizabeth Mrs.	10/21/1844
	A.L. Alderson	
THOMAS, Moses	BEALES, Elizabeth	7/26/1817
	John Stith, Jr.	
THOMAS, Moses	RUST, Gracey	7/ 1/1834
THOMAS, Robert H.	MILLER, Lettice	10/ 2/1817
	Samuel Anderson	
THOMAS, Richard	SKEES, Nancy	5/17/1849
	Richard T. Skees Aug. Deganquier	
	swore girl 21.	
THOMAS, Samuel	BRANDENBURGH, Hester	2/23/1818
THOMAS, Samuel	YOUNG, Loryanda M.	9/18/1833
	F: James	
THOMAS, Silas	HAGAN, Elizabeth	9/27/1843
F: John	Gdn: Sylvester RINEY	
THOMAS, Thomas	JONES, Cassendra	8/16/1849
	F: Zachariah	
THOMAS, Twyman	READ, Belinda	3/24/1834
	F: Simis John Barard	
THOMAS, William	ARRANDER, Cyrena	7/28/1833
F: Alexander	F: Mathew	
THOMAS, William H.	MILLER, Catherine	8/3/1835
	Issac sw. age. Colmore Lovelace	

GROOM	BRIDE	DATE
THOMAS, William M.	LUCAS, Lucinda	7/20/1849
		Alexander Guston
THOMAS, Zepherriah	APRAGENE, Emily	9/11/1835
		Brown, Wm. H.
THOMPSON, Ambrose	QUINN, Celia Mrs.	11/27/1847
		C. J. Coomes
RHOMPSON, Charles	BURRIS, Mary	10/28/1848
M: Delia ALLEN	F: Will	
THOMPSON, Clem A.	LAUNDERS, Mary	8/11/1828
	SF: John GUSTER	Wagginer, H. G.
THOMPSON, Greenberry	SCOTT, Martha Ann	8/30/1849
	F: James D.	
THOMPSON, Harrison	MILBURN, Levilla H.	6/ 9/1847
	F: Edwan	
THOMPSON, Isaac	LASWELL,(Thompson),Elizabeth	8/20/1814
THOMPSON, James	DULEY,? Dolly	11/11/1815
		S: James Duley
THOMPSON, James	BURRIS, Delila	12/ 7/1822
	cert. girl's grand-	Jacob Enlow
	father Ben Lapwell, Sr.	
	F: Charles BURRIS	
THOMPSON, James	MOORE, Sarah	1/ 2/1845
F: Lewis	F: Alexander	
THOMPSON, John	ROLL, Mary	7/24/1820
	F: John ROLL	Geo. L. Rogers
THOMPSON, Lewis	FRYREAR, Sebra	4/29/1822
	F: Jeremiah FRIREAR	
	cert. girl's father.	
THOMPSON, Silas J.	BALLINGER, Louisa	5/24/1850
	Gdn: Wm. CROWN	Colmore Lovelace
THOMPSON, Washington	THOMPSON, Judah Ann	3/ 5/1845
M: Delilah	F: Lewis	
THOMPSON, William	MILBURN, Mary Ann	8/ 2/1847
	F: Euan	
THORNBERRY, Benjamin	ALVEY, Magdelen	12/13/1833
	F: James	Ed. A. Clarke
THORNBERRY, John	HAGEN, Nancy	5/19/1831
	Wm. Cole, sw. age.	Charles J. Cecil
THORP, Silas	LONG, Molly	12/ 3/1828
	Tobas sw. age.	
THORP, William	SMALLWOOD, Mariah	12/25/1827
	F: Hezekiah	
THURMAN, Richard	DAVIS, Jiney	12/26/1831
	Tandy J. sw. age.	David Thurman
TOBIN, Benjamin	SLEWELLYN, Celia	12/10/1829
		Colmore Lovelace
TOBIN, Benjamin	HAYNES, Martha A.	1/14/1834
		Thomas J. Chilton
TOBIN, Thomas	HAYDEN, Maria C.	2/ 5/1833
	John S. sw. age.	Colmore Lovelace

GROOM	BRIDE	DATE
TOMKINSON, Septemus	SMITH, Lucy	8/18/1830
	S: Noah	W. Smith
TONEY, Jesse	SHAW, Mrs. Polly	10/ 6/1829
		Cole, Hugh
TORRANCE, William	HUBBARD, Matilda J.	12/31/1847
	F: T. J.	
TOWER, Cotton	EDSON, Hannah	12/ 3/1816
F: Mathew TOWER	M: Sarah EDSON	
Nathan Tucker Sr.		
TRANDER, William Jr.	MCDOWELL, Nancy	4/10/1827
	F: John	
TRENT, Benjamin	JOHNSON, Malinda	9/ 7/1848
	F: William	
TRENT, Pleasant	PEARMAN, Mary	2/23/1834
	M: Nancy	Jacob Rogers
TRIGGER, Solomon	WISEHART, Sarah	2/ 5/1817
		S: John Wisehart
TRIPLETT, Annanias J.	PRESTON, Elonisa	9/12/1835
F: Frederick		
TRIPLETT, Bailis	JENKINS, Polly	11/ 4/1820
		S: B-in-L: Rich. Walker
TRIPLETT, Franklin	DOWDALL, Elizabeth C.	3/16/1833
	F: William	
TRIPLETT, Grenville H.	EMERY, Mary	3/ 8/1845
	F: Isaac	
TRIPLETT, James	ENGLISH, Elizabeth	3/ 7/1850
	Elisha Pearman	Geo. H. Hicks
	swore girl 21.	
TRIPLETT, Lewis	MORN, Barbara	3/10/1817
		Wm. G. Hays
TRIPLETT, Sanford L.	COFFMAN, Matilda	9/14/1822
	cert. girl's father.	Daniel Walker
		S: Abraham Coffman
TRIPLETT, Wm.	KENNEDY, Elizabeth	2/25/1823
TRIPLETT, Frederick F:	F: Henry KENNEDY	
TRUMAN, William M.	CASH, S. Emily	12/25/1843
	Warren T. Cash Jr.	
	swore girl 21.	
TRUMBO, Samuel Moore	LARUE, Mary	11/28/1829
	Gdn: John MORRIS	James Daugherty
TUCKER, Nathan	HART, Elizabeth	3/28/1821
	cert. Samuel Price	Geo. L. Rogers
	with whom Miss. Hart lived.	
TUCKER, Nathan	FRAKES, Hannah	9/14/1822
TUCKER, Nathan Sr.	TREDWELL, Mrs. Mary	8/17/1820
		Geo. L. Rogers
TUCKER, Thomas	CECIL, Mary	12/ 1/1847
		Geo. H. Hicks
TUCKER, Thomas C.	CARTWRIGHT, Elizabeth	3/ 3/1826
	F: Richard	R. Cartwright

GROOM	BRIDE	DATE
TUCKER, William M: Mary TUCKER & SF: Nathan TUCKER	TWEDEL, Mary	9/26/1825
TULL, Nicholas	DUNN, Mary Ellen Thos. C. Tucker swore girl 21.	3/29/1848
TULL, Nicholas	MCNEILL,_____ F: Daniel D. McNeill	8/17/1830
TUNNELL, David	MCLURE, Elizabeth Geo. L. Rogers	5/26/1829
TUNSDALE, Richard B.	HOLM, Anne Maria cert. of girl's mother proven by Peter A. Holm	6/11/1823
TURLEY, Sampson	STOVALL, Sarah F: Ralph STOVALL cert. Ralph Stovall	3/11/1822
TURNER, Alfred	WRIGHT, Mary F: David	6/ 5/1833
TURNER, Daniel M: Cassandra	CARVER, Milly M: Pleasant	5/ 4/1826
TURNER, John	DAVIS, Sally F: Theodosia DAVIS Bedan Davis says girl is 21.	7/17/1822
TURNER, Joshua	LIPSEY, Rebecca S: Gdn: Wm. THOMAS	1/10/1818
TWEEDELL, Benjamin	PEARPOINT, Sarah F: Jeremiah J. Pearpoint	4/ 5/1826
TWEEDELL, Nathan	BROWN, Sarah F: Frederick F. Brown	8/19/1830
TWEEDELL, Joseph	BANT, Nancy G: Benj. TWEEDELL Geo. L. Rogers	10/11/1830
TWEEDELL, Joseph	COY, Phebe F: Daniel	10/19/1835
TWEDELL, Micajah	PEARPOINT, Jane F: Jeremiah	5/ 4/1833
TWEDELL, James	WEST, Elizabeth M: Catherine	9/ 6/1832
TWYMAN, Paschel	WILSON, Mariah B. F: William E.	5/ 5/1846
TYRES, Saterwhite	STANDAFORD, Belinda F: Israel STANDAFORD cert. girl's father.	1/19/1826
UPTON, Daniel	BURKS, Saley	3/15/1819
UPTON, Edw. Jr. F: Edward UPTON Sr.	MURLIN, Anna F: John MURLIN	3/20/1820
UPTON, Geo. W.	FLANDERS, Elizabeth Silas Lee	7/14/1845
UPTON, John	SPURNIER, Rachael S: Joseph Spurnier	4/27/1821

GROOM	BRIDE	DATE
UPTON, Joseph T.	BRASHEAR, Eveline F: Andrew	3/24/1849
UPTON, Samuel S.	BRASHEAR, Sarah A. Andrew Brashear swore, Silas Lee girl 21.	2/27/1849
UPTON, Thomas	RIDER, Mahetable Wm. Sullivan swore, Silas Lee girl 21.	11/14/1845
UPTON, William	VERTREES, Amelia Herbert Wagginer	11/15/1830
UTTERBACK, Benj.	UPTON, Sarah	6/27/1815
UTTERBACK, Elijah M.	BRACKETT, Rebecca F: John	10/24/1849
UTTERBACK, Thos. D.	BRACKETT, Emily A. Jane Ben C. Brackett Silas Lee swore girl 21.	11/25/1844
UTTERBACK, Upton F: Ben	BRACKETT, Barbara F: John	3/25/1844
VANDERGRIFT, Samuel	HUGHES, Poley S: Samuel Vandergrift	6/25/1813
VAN MATRE, Abraham	DORSEY, Salley F: Beal DORSEY	5/18/1814
VANMETRE, Abraham	MORRISON, Mary F: Isaac	2/22/1847
VANMETER, Ben Jr.	SMITH, Keziah Jonathan sw. age. J. H. Nager	1/20/1830
VANMATRE, Daniel S.	ABELL, Elizabeth consent of girl's father.	10/ 3/1825
VANMATRE, Edward Jr. F: Jacob VANMATRE	BAIRD, Mary S: Jacob Baird says girl is 21.	2/ 7/1821
VANMETRE, Henry R.	FARLINE, Hope V. Robert R. Crutcher John Stith Jr. says girl is 21.	9/ 1/1823
VAN METER, Hubbard	BUSH, Sarah F: Wm. BUSH consent Wm. Bush	2/14/1826
VANMETER, Isaac	CARSON, Jane James Haycraft	4/ 4/1825
VANMETRE, John	VANMETRE, Hannah H. F: Wash.	11/ 3/1846
VAN MATRE, John	WATSON, Rachel S: Robert Watson	2/12/1813
VAN METRE, Jonathan	TABB, Marry proven by Abraham VanMetre	8/23/1817
VANMETRE, Joseph W.	LAWSON, Caroline J.W. Cralle proved Creed Meador father's cert.	7/14/1845
VANMATRE, Miles C.	MCANTIRE, Jane S. Thos. sw. age. David Thurman	8/ 4/1830
VANMETRE, Moses H.	RICHARDSON, Amanda E. F: Daniel S.	9/13/1850

GROOM	BRIDE	DATE
VANMETRE, Nathaniel	DORSEY, Carrena	1/ 5/1838
	Gdn: A. VANMETER	Colmore Lovelace
VANMETRE, Vincent	MORRISON, Susan	10/ 5/1845
	F: Joel A.	
VANMATRE, William	GOODIN, Elizabeth	3/24/1826
	Christopher Bush	Geo. L. Rogers
	says she was age.	
VANMETRE, William	CREAGER, Margaret	2/ 8/1847
	F: Christy	
VANMETRE, William	BLAND, Ann B.	5/12/1847
	F: John H.	
VANSMATRO, Jacob	BUSH, Susan	6/18/1821
Jacob Vansmatro on	S: Wm. Bush	
on otter creek		
VAUGHN, George	CONNER, Eliza	8/ 6/1832
	John Davis sw. age.	
VAN WINKLE, James	DEAVERS, Elizabeth	6/28/1813
		S: Thomas Deavers
VEACH, Elliott L.	MASON, Sophia	12/20/1830
	James sw. age.	Thomas J. Chilton
VEACH, Isaac	SPRIGGS, Mary	4/17/1823
	cert. girl's father, S. Buchanan	
	proven by Abraham Lewis.	
VEACH, James	HART, Susan	9/25/1845
	F: Isaac	
VEIRS, John	MCWILLIAMS, Sally	3/25/1818
		Jacob Enlow
		S: James McWilliams
VEIRS, John H. D.	MASON, Sophia	2/10/1830
	James sw. age.	Thomas J. Chilton
VEIRS, John H. D.	CARROLL, Martha Jane	2/10/1830
	M: Jane	J. Carroll
VENDERR, Robert	MONIN, Lavina	6/16/1827
or VERDER		
VERDER, Robert	MONIN, Lavina	6/16/1827
or VENDERR		
VERNON, Alfred B.	SWAN, Ruth	11/14/1845
		John C.C. Thompson
VERNON, Thomas	SWANK, Ellender	8/28/1828
	F: Jacob Sr.	J. Swank Sr.
VERTREES, Amos	MAXFIELD, Grozzle	3/21/1812
		S: Acve? Williams
VERTREES, Charles	VERNON, Milley	4/19/1816
	F: Author VERNON	
VERTRUS, James A.	BRADLEY, Ellen	11/10/1849
	F: Samuel	
VERTREES, John	GEOGHIGAN, Margaret	10/29/1823
	F: Denton GEOGHIGAN	
	cert. D. Geoghigan proven	
	by W. Geoghigan	
VERTREES, Thomas W.	JIPER, Lyida Elizabeth	4/17/1849
	F: Henry	

GROOM	BRIDE	DATE
VERTREES, Thomas	TYRES, Polly	2/ 2/1818
		S: Thomas Tyrees
VERTREES, William	HAYDEN, Rachel	3/ 3/1834
	F: Daniel	Colmore Lovelace
VESSELS, Alexander	VESSELS, Luvina Jane	4/ 2/1850
	Wm. Mattingly swore	Thomas Fife
	girl 21.	
VESSELS, Charles	BROWN, Matilda Ann	5/ 3/1849
	F: William	
VESSELS, George	MILLS, Susanna	11/23/1835
	M: Elledner VESSELS	
VESSELS, Martin	PETERS, Lucy	1/ 3/1834
	F: Thomas	
VICTOR, John	MCLURE, Martha	7/28/1828
		George L. Rogers
VIERS, Benjamin	EMERY, Melinda	8/30/1834
	F: Isaac	Colmore Lovelace
VIERS, Elisha	STEVALL, Mary	7/16/1827
	F: Heze	H. Stovall
VIERS, William	DONDALL, Sarah	7/21/1834
		cert. H. Dendall
VINCENT, Obidiah	SCOTT, Elizabeth	7/ 2/1827
	Gdn: James	George L. Rogers
VITTITOE, William	VOWLES, Eliza	2/ 3/1836
	Thos. Johnson sw. age.	
VITTITOE, James	LAFALLET, Ann	1/ 2/1827
	F: Isaac	con. J. Lafollet
VITTITOE, William	FIELD, Mrs. Ann	10/18/1844
		Jacob Rogers
WADLEY, Adam	WALLS, Polly	3/ 9/1833
	William Edlin sw. age.	G. C. Ulen
WADDLE, David	BUTLER, Sarah	6/14/1813
		S: Wm. Clements
		S: Able Butler
WADLEY, Jordan	CASTLEMAN, Nancy	11/15/1828
	F: James	con. J. Castleman
WAGGONER, Adam	TERRY, Polly	12/20/1820
	cert. girl's father.	James Haycraft
	F: Jasper TERRY	
WAGGONER, Herbert	BEST, Elenor	7/25/1827
		Warren Cash
WAGGONER, James M.	SHEPHERD, Gelly	10/27/1830
	M: Amelia	
WAGGONER, William	GOFORTH, Sarah	2/10/1823
	Jasper Terry swore girl 21.	
WAIDE, John	CASTLEMAN, Maria	6/ 8/1818
	S: Benj. Castleman	Alex. McDougal
WAID, Solomon	REED, Polly	3/26/1817
		Jacob Enlow
WALDEN, Isaac	DRURY, Sarah	9/ 7/1825
	F: Timothy F. DRURY	Warren Cash

GROOM	BRIDE	DATE
WALKER, Daniel	WALSH, Malinda F: Stirdy JONES	12/23/1815
WALKER, Edward	OWENS, Sally M: Elizabeth OWENS cert. E. Owens proven by Samuel Owens	2/16/1821
WALKER, Feliz	WATTS, Rachel M: Prudence	8/ 5/1826
WALKER, James W.	WHITE, Mary Ann F: Edward	9/22/1849
WALKER, John	DYE, Amelia S: John Dye	5/13/1813
WALKER, William	TRIPLET, Salina cert. Lewis Triplet	10/31/1818
WALL, William	JACKSON, Sally F: Alex	1/ 4/1833
WALLACE, James	MCCLURE, Nancy girl's age proven Elijah Summers by John Ashcraft	5/ 6/1822
WALLS, Thomas	MILLER, Mary Miles Thomas sw. age. Colmore Lovelace	8/24/1830
WALTERS, Amos	MARSHALL, Rebecca con. John MARSHALL, Geo. L. Rogers Gdn. girl	12/31/1825
WALTERS, Jacob W.	FUNK, Lydia F: Alex	1/ 6/1846
WALTERS, James	WILSON, Mary M: Rose Ann R. A. Wilson	9/22/1830
WALTERS, Jediah	MIDDLETON, Sarah cert. by Andrew Walters F: Hendley MIDDLETON	10/ 6/1818
WALTERS, John	FRIEND, Catherine F: Charles	12/ 7/1830
WALTERS, Mary Gdn: Amos WALTERS	WALTERS, Barney David Thurman	6/20/1831
WALTERS, William	BAYNE, Nancy F: Thomas BAYNE Sr. Wm. Downs	7/24/1820
WALTERS, William	REDMAN, Catherine F: Richard	5/ 3/1830
WALTERS, Quillan	BAYNES, Elizabeth F: Thomas BAYNE cert. T. Bayne Sr. says Thomas Bayne Jr.	9/29/1821
WARFIELD, Caleb	BARNETT, Mrs. Leah John Bards	6/11/1828
WARNER, Ephriam	CANN, Mary Michael sw. age. Batchly S. Wood	10/27/1832
WARD, Jenkins	HURT, Louisiana Jas. Daugherty	7/ 2/1850
WARD, Solomon	READ, Polly M: Ann READ	3/26/1817

120

```
GROOM                          BRIDE                          DATE
WARD, William                  PATTERSON, Mary Ellen          3/ 8/1847
                               Christian Patterson cert.
                               proved by Jacob Ward

WASHER, Jacob                  BRUCE, Polly                   8/10/1818
WASHINGTON, Thomas             MCINTIRE, Mary                 1/ 3/1834
                                             James Noll
WASHBURN, William              SHARPENSTENN, Mrs. Hanah       5/16/1827
                                             George L. Rogers
WATHEN, Charles                PURCY, Elizabeth               3/25/1844
                                             Aug. Deganquier
WATHEN, Gabriel                NITTE, Sony                    5/19/1814
                               NETTE? Sary
WATHEN, George W.              LARUE, Martha                  9/26/1844
                                             S.S. Deering
WATHEN, Thomas I.              SLAUGHTER, Sarah C.            1/16/1823
                               F: Reuben C. SLAUGHTER
                               cert. R. Slaughter
WATHEN, William A.             BLAND, Susan A.                7/11/1831
                               M: Sesan          S. Bland
WATKINS, James J.              RIDER, Mariah                  4/16/1850
                               F: Joseph M.
WATKINS, Samuel                BRASHEAR, Rachel               2/15/1833
                               F: Edwin
WATKINS, Torrance              STACKETT, Elenor               7/19/1821
                                             Geo. L. Rogers
WATSON, Isaac                  LONG, Frances                  4/20/1835
                               Daniel sw. age.
WATSON, James                  SETZER, Celia                  1/ 5/1830
                               William sw. age.   Hugh Cole
WATSON, John                   VAN METRE, Lettice             3/ 2/1814
F: James WATSON                F: Jacob VAN METRE S: John Van Metre
WATT, James M.                                                3/29/1847
F: George                                    Jacob Waylor
WATTS, George                  MCMAHON, Mary                  2/ 1/1825
                               F: John MCMAHON
                               cert. J. McMahon
WATTS, John B.                 MCMAHON, Rebecca               4/ 8/1815
                               F: John MCMAHON
WATTS, John Sr.                ENLOW?, Mary                   4/24/1825
                               John Harrison says  Wm. Gurrn
                               girl is 21.
WAYLER, Jacob                  RAHM, Margaret                 2/15/1845
                               F: John
WEEKLY, John                   DENBO, Mrs. Polly              5/20/1818
WELCH, James                   VANMATRE, Sarah                5/20/1818
                                             S: Benj. VanMatre
WELCH, John                    SIMMONS, Mrs. Elizabeth       12/29/1821
                                             S: Enos Simmons
WELLER, Samuel                 LARUE, Phebe                   8/10/1824
                               F: Wm. LARUE
                               consent Wm. Larue
```

HARDIN COUNTY, KENTUCKY MARRIAGE RECORDS

GROOM	BRIDE	DATE
WELLS, Lewis	SCOTT, Peggy	10/21/1822
	M: Mary SCOTT	
WELLS, Thomas	CASWELL, Elizabeth	7/ 2/1817
G: Lewis WELLS	F: John CASWELL	
WELLS, William	KESSINGER, Polly	3/10/1817
	B: Lewis Wells	
	F: Joseph KESSINGER	
WEST, James	WATKINS, Sarah	7/14/1817
	F: Samuel WATKINS	
WEST, John	MCLEAN, Mrs. Nancy	10/14/1815
WEST, Silvester	REDMAN, Rebecca	3/17/1829
	George sw. age.	Thomas J. Chilton
WEST, Thomas	SELF, Eleanor	10/16/1822
	proven by Baird People	
WEST, Wm.	JONES, Orphy	7/ 1/1815
	Gdn: Jasper TERRY S: John Hart	
	Witnesses:	
	Aaron Terry	
	John Hart	
WHALING, John	FIELD, Nancy	6/ 6/1833
	Reuben R. Jones	John Rush
	sw. age.	
WHEATLEY, John Sylvester	JOHNSON, Eliza	9/30/1829
	F: John	J. Johnson
WHEATLEY, Richard	GRAY, Elizabeth	7/28/1849
	James Carlisle swore,	L.L. Hodgen
	girl 21.	
WHITE, Bassel	DRURY, Polly	4/13/1822
	cert. father proven	John Stith Jr.
	by Christopher Durben	
	F: Elias DRURY	
WHITE, William	LEWIS, Catherine	12/14/1822
	F: Alijah LEWIS Sr.	
	cert. A.K. Lewis	
	proven by A. Lewis Jr.	
WHITEHEAD, George	MCDOUGAL, Dorcas	9/26/1825
WHITEHEAD, John	DEWITT, Delila	2/ 2/1819
		S: Isaac Dewitt
WHITESTONE, John	WHETSTONE, Elizabeth	8/18/1822
	cert. girl's father	John Hodgen
	proven by John Collins	
	F: Peter WHITESTONE	
WHITMAN, Christopher	LUCAS, Patsey	10/16/1815
		S: Cornelius Lucas
WHITMAN, John	CASH, Martha	10/ 6/1818
		S: Abraham Cash
WHITMAN, Richard	LUCAS, Tabitha	10/26/1819
		S: Cornelius Lucas
WILDER, James	BROWN, Nancy	5/13/1823
	cert. Dixon Brown	

HARDIN COUNTY, KENTUCKY MARRIAGE RECORDS

GROOM	BRIDE	DATE
WILKERSON, Michael	MONTGOMERY, Mrs. Salley	10/18/1815
	S: Isaac Kessinger	
WILKERSON, Robert	LOGADON, Mary	4/ 2/1818
	F: Thomas LOGADON	
WILKES, John W.	LOGADON, Rebecca	8/12/1816
	B: Humphrey Smoot	
	F: Wm. LOGADON	
WILKES, Samuel	GEORGE, Margaret R.	7/23/1831
	F: William	William George
WILKINS, Henry	STRADER, Polly	8/22/1825
	F: Francis STRADER	
WILKINS, James	WALKER, Fanny	10/ 4/1819
	F: Richard	John Baird
WILLHEIM, Alexander	HARRIS, Eleander	2/19/1823
	M: Nancy HARRIS	
WILLHEIM, Martin	BRADLEY, Rachel	9/21/1816
	S: Wm. Bradley	
WILHELM, Charles	BLANCET, Arreny	6/ 1/1847
	cert. by A. Rockwell	Jas. W. Pence
WILHITE, Presley	HAMILTON, Malinda	10/ 3/1834
	F: Hance	
WILLET, Maxfield	HARRISON, Elizabeth	7/21/1823
	cert. girl's father	Stiles Parker
	proven by John M. Riddle	
	F: Cuthbert HARRISON	
WILLETT, James	HARRINGTON, Elizabeth	9/14/1832
	F: David	
WILLIAMS, Acne?	MAXFIELD, Hester	4/ 1/1814
WILLIAMS, Charles	MCCULLUM, Jane	10/ 1/1814
	S: James McCullum	
WILLIAMS, Constant	SCOTT, Mrs. Elizabeth	2/24/1827
	George L. Rogers	
WILLIAMS, Daniel	VERNON, Sarah	9/ 1/1813
WILLIAMS, Elisha	MCCULLUM, Sally	2/13/1827
	James sw. age.	Colmore Lovelace
WILLIAMS, Felix	SHECKLES, Ageline	9/18/1832
	F: Thomas	
WILLIAMS, Green B.	CLINGINSMITH, Margaret	4/29/1828
	F: George	
WILLIAMS, Humphrey	KELLY, Mary	1/19/1847
	M: Margaret	
WILLIAMS, Jacob	HARTLEY, Amy	6/ 4/1825
	consent of John Hartley	
WILLIAMS, Jacob L.	PAUL, Susan	6/25/1844
	Geo. H. Hicks	
WILLIAM, Jacob T.	GLAZEBROOKS, Abigail	3/15/1850
	G. I. Clandell	
WILLIAMS, James	MCWILLIAMS, Ann	9/28/1825
	F: James MCWILLIAMS	
	consent of father.	
WILLIAMS, James	FAIRLEIGH, Lettice	5/11/1830
	Colmore Lovelace	

HARDIN COUNTY, KENTUCKY MARRIAGE RECORDS

GROOM	BRIDE	DATE
WILLIAMS, James Gdn: Henry B. PECK	THOMPSON, Lucinda M: Delila	8/19/1850
WILLIAMS, John	CLEVELAND, Hannah cert. of Isaiah Jackson girl's SF.	10/26/1819 Jacob Enlow
WILLIAMS, John	COOMBS, Tacy Mrs. S: Henry Williams	9/28/1820 Thos. J. Chilton
WILLIAMS, John	CHILTON, Lee F: Thomas J. CHILTON cert. T. Gilten proven by Burr W. Owsley	10/21/1822
WILLIAMS, John	EMERY, Martha G: John MCWILLIAMS	2/10/1830 George L. Rogers
WILLIAMS, John	PECK, Elizabeth F: John W.	7/26/1834 Colmore Lovelace
WILLIAMS, John	FRYREAR, Amanda Mrs.	1/19/1835 William Tarpley
WILLIAMS, John	MORRISON, Lucinda F: Henry	8/10/1845
WILLIAMS, John F.	VERNON, Mary F: Anthony VERNON	2/11/1822
WILLIAMS, John F.	FRYREAR, Somirel F: Francis Sr.	4/ 3/1848
WILLIAMS, John C.	CASEMAN, Elizabeth J.F. sw. age.	4/ 7/1831 Thomas J. Chilton
WILLIAMS, Joseph	WRIGHT, Elizabeth Joseph sw. age.	2/12/1827 Thomas J. Chilton
WILLIAMS, Joseph	PETERSON, Martha	5/10/1845 Alexander Guston
WILLIAMS, Joseph	JEFFRIES, Mary F: James	5/ 2/1849
WILLIAMS, Owen	LARKIN, Catherine Geo. K. Larkin swore girl 21.	1/18/1847
WILLIAMS, Thomas	HAYCRAFT, Peggy	11/18/1817 Warren Cash S: Saml Haycraft Jr.
WILLIAMS, Thomas	ARNOLD, Polly	1/ 6/1817 S: John Arnold
WILLIAMS, Wm.	JOSEPH, Nancy	12/16/1815 S: Thos. Lincoln
WILLIAMS, William	JOHNSON, Seelia F: John	7/19/1833
WILLIAMS, Vinson D.	GILMORE, Mary F: Smith	5/15/1848
WILLIAMS, Zachariah	SCOTT, Catherine Samuel Williams prved cert.	1/17/1848 S.L. Hodgen
WILLIAMSON, Robert	WALKER, Sylvania cert. girl's mother Nancy WALKER prvn. by Wm. Martin	9/10/1822 John Hodgen

GROOM	BRIDE	DATE
WILLIAMSON, William	BIGGER, Elizabeth Alex Fulks says girl is 21.	5/30/1822 Geo. L. Rogers
WILLIS, John	MORMON?, Nancy F: Jesse MORMON? B: Joel A. Mormon?	11/ 5/1821
WILLIS, John	HARRISON, Nancy F: Jesse HARRISON cert. J. Harrison proven by Joel A. Morrison	11/ 5/1821
WILLIS, Isaiah F: John	SKEETERS, Elenor F: John	1/27/1845
WILLSON, Jonathan	CASH, Mary	11/25/1822 S: Claborn Cash
WILLSON, Silas	MOOR, Susan W. Moore say she is 21.	6/11/1823 John Stith Jr.
WILLYARD, Elijah	MORRISON, Margaret F: Isaac	10/18/1834 James Haycraft
WILLYARD, George	HAYCRAFT, Polly cert. John Daugherty SF: Gamiel WILLYARD proved cert.	12/ 3/1824 James Haycraft
WILLYARD, Henry	CASH, Eliza F: Clabourn	10/18/1832
WILLYARD, John	ADAMS, Amanda F: William	10/ 3/1845
WILLYARD, Samuel	CASH, Susan F: Clabourn	1/10/1827
WILSON, Christy	KIRKPATRICK, Mary Ann Robt. Martin sw. age.	3/27/1832 H. C. Ulen
WILSON, George	SHEPHERD, Mary M: Amelia	6/ 1/1833
WILSON, James	JONES, Elizabeth	8/18/1816
WILSON, James	WALTERS, Hanna	5/ 3/1817 S: Jacob Booker
WILSON, James	WATTLES, Elizabeth John Booker, made oath that parent were willing	10/ 5/1818
WILSON, James	SHAVER, Barbary M: Nancy SHAVER	10/ 5/1818
WILSON, James	JOHNSON, Rosey	4/ 9/1825 Samuel Martin
WILSON, Jeremiah	TURNER, Emily M: Jane	11/ 7/1832
WILSON, John	WATTLES, Mrs. Hannah	5/ 3/1817
WILSON, John	JONES, Mrs. Elizabeth	9/18/1816 S: Benj. Pulliam
WILSON, Jonathan	CASH, Mary F: Clabourn CASH cert. C. Cash proven by Golden Hicks	3/25/1822

GROOM	BRIDE	DATE
WILSON, Joseph A.	LAWSON, Mary Ann	9/22/1845
		Geo. H. Hicks
WILSON, Joseph G.	GOODMAN, Susan T.	5/11/1850
	Gdn: James GOODMAN	Colmore Lovelace
WILSON, William A.	WRIGHT, Elizabeth	11/18/1833
	George sw. age.	James Daugherty
WILSON, Samuel	COFFMAN, Parmelia	5/11/1847
	F: Hermon	
WIMP, Daniel	WELCH, Rachel	9/16/1815
	SF: & M: Wm. &	S: John Wimp, Jr.
	Susanna WILLET	
WINCHESTER, John	MILLER, Margaret	10/10/1814
		S: John Miller
WINCHESTER, Jordan	THOMAS, Elizabeth	4/ 4/1825
F: Richard WINCHESTER	F: Isaac THOMAS	
WINDERS, Earhart	MCDONALD, Malvina	4/22/1829
	F: James	J. McDonald
WINDER, James G.	HARRIS, Ruth	11/22/1817
	F: John HARRIS	
WINDER, William	OVERALL, Elizabeth	12/30/1825
	M: E. OVERALL	
WINTERSMITH, Horace G.V.	BLAND, Elmira	11/26/1850
	F: Henry	
WINTERSMITH, Horatie G.	WINTERSMITH, Margaret	10/13/1835
	G: Charles G.	James Nall
WISE, David E.	HORN, Mrs. Ellen	11/28/1835
		Aug. Deganquier
WISE, David E.	HAYDEN, Elizabeth	3/ 4/1848
	Wm. Hayden cert. proven	
	by Ben G. Hayden	
WISE, Elisha	FRENCH, Lucinda	12/28/1828
	F: Elisha	E. French
WISE, Thos. H.	DORSEY, Nancy	6/12/1817
	M: Sarah, 23 yrs old	
WISEHEART, John	MILLER, Eliza	6/10/1813
		S: James Van Winkle
WISEHEART, John H.	HARNED, Susan	3/ 4/1831
	William sw. age.	Benjamin Keith
WISEMAN, Philip C.	COLE, Mary Ellen	12/27/1847
	Henry F. Cole proved	
	father's cert.	
WITHERS, Albert G.	GRIGSBY, Mary N.	6/ 9/1847
	John A. Grigsby	Colmore Lovelace
	swore girl 21.	
WITHERS, Alphonso B.	HOTON, Providence Jane	2/15/1850
	married before	Colmore Lovelace
WITHERS, Isaac C.	FIELD, Artridge	3/22/1847
	F: Ezekiel	
WITHERS, James A.	GRIGSBY, Elivra H.	8/ 9/1847
	John A. Grigsby	Colmore Lovelace
	swore girl 21.	

HARDIN COUNTY, KENTUCKY MARRIAGE RECORDS

GROOM	BRIDE	DATE
WITHERS, Lewis	BOON, Eliza F: Enoch BOONE	7/14/1820 Shadrack Brown
WITHERS, Loanna M.	ROGERS, Fetna M: Frances	3/10/1847
WITHERS, William Jr.	LUSK, Alzina	1/12/1819 Shadrack Brown S: Wm. Ditto
WOODFOLK, Fleming	MOREMAN, Judith cert. girl's father. F: Jesse MOREMAN	10/29/1819 John Stith Jr.
WOODFORD, Howard	DESHA, Jane M: Milly	3/ 7/1831 M. Desha
WOOD, Hawkins,	JOHNSON, Mrs. Jane	5/29/1826 Robert Byrn
WOOD, John	HANKS, Mary F: Wm. HANKS	12/18/1815
WOOD, Jonathan	LYON, Martha M: Rebecca	2/26/1831 R. Lyon
WOOD, Jonathan	KENDALL, Frances	5/27/1844 S.S. Deering
WOOD, Norman G.	LYONS, Elizabeth C. M: Rebecca	1/ 8/1833
WOOD, Parley	SUDDES, Susan Plimeas Gilbert says girl is 21.	12/31/1822
WOOD, Solomon S.	BURBA, Sovina F: William	2/16/1845
WOOD, Thomas W.	SMITH, Celista T. F: Rufus	10/ 7/1848
WOOD, William D.S.T.	STURGEON, Sarah S. F: Alfred	7/23/1850
WOODS, Joseph	THOMAS, Elizabeth M: Ann THOMAS	6/25/1818 John Stith Jr.
WOODRING, Allen	BROWN, Lydia Ann David E. Wise swore girl 21.	2/12/1845 Geo. H. Hicks
WOODRING, Charles	HARTLEY, Matilda G: Benj. WOODRING	2/14/1834 Colmore Lovelace
WOODRING, James	THOMAS, Sarah	2/13/1828
WOOLDRIDGE, John A.	SKEES, Malvina John A. Skees swore girl 21.	4/ 3/1849 Aug. Deganquier
WOOLDRIDGE, John D.	ALLSTON, Mahala F: Jeremiah	10/12/1847
WOODRING, Joseph	THOMAS, Malvina F: John	1/ 3/1846
WOODRING, Samuel	SHACKLEFORD, Jane G: Hiram B. ENGLISH	8/26/1835 Colmore Lovelace
WOOLDRIDGE, Thomas	OVERTON, Mahala Louisa W.H. Hays swore both of age.	2/15/1847 Jacob Rogers

127

HARDIN COUNTY, KENTUCKY MARRIAGE RECORDS

GROOM	BRIDE	DATE
WOODRIS, William	HOBACK, Elenor F: Isaac HOBACK	10/ 4/1825
WOODRUFF, John	VANDERGRIFT, Elizabeth Both of age.	1/23/1850 C. Ward.
WOODWARD, Finis M.	YAGER, Sarah E. Lhdia cert. proven by Benj. Yager	5/19/1844
WOODWARD, John Q.	YAGER, Mary D. M: Lydia	1/28/1847
WOOLF, Peter	MCCULLUM, Nancy Mrs. S: James McCullum	1/27/1819 Jacob Enlow
WOOLF, Henry	MCMULLUM, Keziah F: James	2/13/1827 Colmore Lovelace
WOOLDRIDGE, Jesse	HAYES, Susan M: Mary	8/13/1827 cert. M. Hayes
WOOLFOLK, Jos.	VANMETRE, Susanna S: John VanMetre	1/12/1818 John Stith Jr.
WOOLFOLK, Joseph	THRELKIELD, Elizabeth Mrs.	12/30/1818 John Stith Jr.
WOOLDRIDGE, Joseph	TRENT, Catherine F: Benjamin	2/23/1830 B. Trent
WOOLDRIDGE, Lot F: William	COUCHOUSE, Mary Ann F: John	12/13/1831
WOODRING, J. Benjamin	DAUGHERTY, Polly cert. by brother S: John Daugherty	9/2/ 1819
WORLAND, William R.	MARRIOTT, Isabella Ephriam sw. age.	11/12/1835 Joseph Rogers
WORLEY, John	BIGLER, Julian R. F: John BIGLER	1/26/1818 Warren Cash
WORTHAM, Charles H. F: Samuel	COOK, Margaret F: James	7/20/1835
WORTNEY, Ephriam G.	JENKINS, Jane F: Allison JENKINS	11/ 9/1817
WRIGHT, Carter	FINLEY, Indiana cert. John Wright F: Isreal FINLEY	1/ 8/1819
WRIGHT, Eliazar G.	BARBER, Alta M: Margaret	3/ 6/1827
WRIGHT, George	STEPHENS, Betsy Ann F: Thomas	10/21/1826 con. T. Stephens
WRIGHT, Geo. Edwin	KENNELY, Marygaret Jane	4/18/1850 James H. Jenkins
WRIGHT, James	DAUGHERTY, Nancy Lorenzo D. Wright swore girl 21.	12/10/1846 Alexander Guston
WRIGHT, Jonathan	LEE, Eliza F: John LEE & Sally LEE cert. John Lee proven by Alven Newton	1/27/1819

GROOM	BRIDE	DATE
WRIGHT, Laban	COLLINS, Mary Ann	9/ 8/1846
	Gdn: Philip B. HOWARD Jas. Daugherty	
WRIGHT, Lovira J.	SMOOT, Minerva Jane	5/ 8/1846
	F: Eligale	
WRIGHT, Martin G.	CECIL, Elizabeth	6/22/1844
	M: Susan	
WRIGHT, Oaty	WRIGHT, Perlina	8/ 1/1831
F: David	F: Martin	
WRIGHT, Stephen D.	HARREL, Sarah Ann	12/20/1847
	Wm. W. Bland	Alexander Guston
	swore girl 21.	
WRIGHT, William	GOODIN, Rebecca	12/18/1835
	F: James	
WRIGHT, William	DAUGHERTY, Jane	12/27/1830
	M: Nancy	cert. James Daugherty
YATES, Elias	COFFMAN, Margaret Ann	10/14/1840
	Gdn: Wm. HOLLAND	
YATES, Elias	DRAKE, Mary	12/20/1844
		Jacob Rogers
YATES, Francis G.	WOOD, Susannah	1/29/1813
	F: Isaac WOOD	
YATES, Greenberry	WRIGHT, Clarenda	3/30/1846
	F: Martin C.	
YATES, Ignatius Peter	DRURY, Rebecca Ann	10/ 6/1846
	John R. Drury swore	C.D. Shean
	girl 21.	
YATES, John B.	SCIFERS, Margaret	10/29/1849
	married before	
YAGER, John W.	DORSEY, Lydia	5/22/1821
	F: Richard DORSEY	
YATES, Jonathan	RICHARDSON, Amanda	6/12/1845
		Geo. H. Hicks
YAGER, Stephen	THOMAS, Kitty	7/14/1818
F: Cornelius YAGER	cert. Robert Michell Sr.	
M: Elizabeth YAGER		
YATES, Thomas E.	BOWLES, Frances	10/ 7/1848
	Thos. Armsbay	Geo. H. Hicks
	swore girl 21.	
YEAMAN, William P.	SHACKLEFORD, Eliza	12/10/1850
F: Stephen M.	John English	
YEAKEY, Henry	ISLER, Caroline M. Mrs.	8/31/1824
		Geo. L. Rogers
YORK, Job	HOWELL, Sarah	3/23/1822
	cert. girl's father	John Baird
	and boy age proven by	
	Thomas York	
	F: John HOWELL	
YORK, John	LARKIN, Mrs. Elizabeth	8/20/1821
YORK, Zadoc	DEWIT, Mehuria	7/14/1823
	cert. of parent proven	Geo. L. Rogers
	by Seth Duncan	

GROOM	BRIDE	DATE
YOUNG, Jacob	HICKS, Savena or Serena	10/ 5/1849
	Wilson Hicks swore	Jacob Rogers
	sw. 21.	
YOUNG, John	PATTERSON, Lydia	1/12/1849
		Jacob Rogers
YOUNG, James	HATFIELD, Phebe	3/18/1848
	John Young swore	Ezra Ward
	both 21.	
YOUNG, James	WARD, Misilva	10/16/1830
	F: John	J. Ward
YOUNG, John	SAWYER, Tilly?	3/ 7/1822
Susannah Young	F: Charles SAWYER, Jr.	
YOUNG, Thomas	BOLING, Eliza	10/19/1843
	Wesley Boling swore	
	girl 21.	
YOUNG, William	COX, Sally	10/23/1819
	cert. by father John FOX	
YOUNG, William	DAUGHERTY, Mrs. Nancy	3/19/1832
		William Cash
YOWELL, William	MILBURN, Elizabeth Ann	10/29/1834
	M: Nancy	James Haycraft
YULZTER, Jacob	COUTS, Mrs. Sarah	10/ 2/1819
		S: Samuel Haycraft Jr.

A
ABELL, Elizabeth, 117.
ABELL, Lucy, 50.
ABELL, Rebecca, 36.
ABELL, Sarah, 102.
ABELL, William 72.
ADAIR, Mary C., 97.
ADAMS, Amanda, 125.
AKERS, Barbara, 112.
AKERS, Sarah, 7.
ALEXANDER, Lydia, 12.
ALLEN, Catherine, 90.
ALLEN, Delila, 4.
ALLEN, Elizabeth, 65.
ALLEN, Ellis, 65.
ALLEN, Lydia, 98.
ALLEN, Martha, 67.
ALLEN, Martha A., 38.
ALLEN, Mary, 20.
ALLEN, Patsey, 81;88.
ALLEN, Rebecca, 92.
ALLEN, Sally Ann, 2.
ALLEN, Sarah, 55.
ALLEN, Susan, 53;58.
ALLSTIEN, Polly, 40.
ALLSTON, Lucinda, 9.
ALLSTON, Mahala, 127.
ALLY, Nancy, 4.
ALVEY, Elizabeth, 51.
ALVEY, Magdelen, 114.
ALVEY, Nancy, 54.
AMENT, Abigail, 71.
AMENT, Cahanice, 30.
AMENT, Catherine, 101.
AMENT, Elizabeth, 1.
AMENT, Mary Ann, 75.
AMENT, Polly, 101.
ANBERRY, Eliza, 18.
ANDERSON, Betsey, 5.
ANDERSON, Eliza, 18;24.
ANDERSON, Ellender, 108.
ANDERSON, Jane, 38.
ANDERSON, Nancy, 3.
ANDERSON, Sarah, 102.
ANGEL, Elizabeth, 53.
ANTEMCA?, Dawson, 81.
APRAGENE, Emily, 114.
ARMER, Ann Jane, 53.
ARMES, Sarah, 103.

ARMOUR, Nancy, 15.
ARNOLD, Elizabeth, 11.
ARNOLD, Julian, 33.
ARNOLD, Katherine, 48.
ARNOLD, Lydia, 31.
ARNOLD, Mary Ann, 39.
ARNOLD, Mary E., 84.
ARNOLD, Nancy, 36.
ARNOLD, Polly, 124.
ARRANDER, Cyrena, 113.
ARTHUR, Ann H., 64.
ARTHUR, Frances Emily 110.
ARVIN, Elizabeth Jane, 5.
ASH, Hellon, 36.
ASH, Maria, 45.
ASH, Mary Ann, 95.
ASH, Nancy, 12.
ASHBAUGH, Mary, 112.
ASHBAUGH, Sophia, 86.
ASHBOUGH, Sally, 17.
ASHBOUGH, Sophia, 78.
ASHBROUGH, Martha, 56.
ASHBY, Rachel, 52.
ASHCRAFT, Julian, 51.
ASHCRAFT, Margaret, 51.
ASHCRAFT, Susan, 98.
ASHLEY, Polly, 44.
ATCHER, Joanna, 103.
ATCHER, Susan, 110.
ATHERTON, Elizabeth, 29.
ATHERTON, Letticia, 25.
ATHERTON, Lucinda, 6.
ATHERTON, Lydia, 84.
ATHERTON, Margaret, 37.
ATHERTON, Nancy, 43.
ATT, E. Mary, 112.
ATTERBURY, Levisa ?, 5.
ATWELL, Jane, 46.
AUBERRY, Jane, 87.
AUBERRY, Margaret, 106.
AUBERRY, Nancy, 96.
AUBREY, Jemina, 108.
AUBREY, Sally, 104.
AUBREY, Sally R., 31.

AUBRY, Ellender, 89.
AUBRY, Mariah, 112.
AUBRY, Nancy, 40.
AUCHER, Margaret, 35.
B
BACON, Elizabeth N., 30.
BACON, Rebecca, 52.
BAIRD, Mary, 13;117.
BAIRD, Sarah, 78.
BALDWIN, Susanna A., 29.
BALING, Rebecca, 102.
BALL, Betsy, 73.
BALLINGER, Elizabeth, 26.
BALLINGER, Louisa, 114.
BALLOW, Christena, 41.
BANGAR, Sophia, 91.
BANT, Nancy, 116.
BARBER, Alta, 128.
BARKER, Martha, 64.
BARLOW, Frances, 13.
BARNES, Nancy Ann, 51.
BARNETT, Leah (Mrs.) 120.
BARRON, Elizabeth, 46.
BARTLETT, Fanny, 92.
BASHAM, Nancy, 98.
BASKET, Susan, 42.
BAYNE, Elizabeth, 48.
BAYNE, Margaret, 95.
BAYNE, Nancy, 120.
BAYNES, Elizabeth, 120.
BAYNES, Sarah, 66.
BEAGLER, Polly, 55.
BEALES, Elizabeth, 112;113.
BEALL, Christena, 45.
BEARD, Eliz A., 68.
BEARD, Sarah, 31.
BEARD, Willimina, 7.
BEAVERS, Elizabeth, 44.
BEAVERS, Nancy, 81.
BEELER, Margaret, 46.
BEIGLER, Agatha, 79.

BEIGLER, Elizabeth, 29.
BEIGLER, Lucretia, 33.
BENNET, Judah, 9.
BENNETT, Mavinda, 10.
BENNETT, Nancy G., 30.
BERRY, Elizabeth, 82.
BERRY, Elizabeth, 110.
BERRY, Margaret, 101.
BERRY, Martha, 4.
BERRY, Nancy S., 69.
BERRY, Sarah E., 101.
BERRYMAN, Louise, 35.
BEST, Elenor, 119.
BEST, Elizabeth, 88.
BEWLEY, Esther, 22.
BEWLEY, Phebe, 98.
BIDDLETCOME, Laura, 89.
BIGGER, Elizabeth, 125.
BIGGER, Mary, 41.
BIGLER, Julian R., 128.
BIRD, Sally, 26.
BIRKS, Polly, 94.
BISSER, Polly, 46.
BLACKFORD, Jane, 64.
BLANCET, Arreny, 123.
BLAND, Ann B, 118.
BLAND, Anna Eliza, 40.
BLAND, Augustian, 9.
BLAND, Elizabeth, 96.
BLAND, Elmira, 126.
BLAND, Jane 36.
BLAND, Katherine, 79.
BLAND, Mahala, 94.
BLAND, Mary A., 35.
BLAND, Mildred, 108.
BLAND, Nancy, 70.
BLAND, Sarah, 6.
BLAND, Susan A., 121.
BLANSETT, Nancy, 98.
BLEDSOE, Sally, 64.
BLEVINS, Lydia, 84.
BLISSIT, Nancy, 76.
BLUE, Nancy, 20.
BOAG, Aseneth, 54.
BOAG, Rebecca, 15.
BOARMAN, Susan Eliza-

beth, 14.
BOARMAN, Susannah, 15.
BOGUE ?, Deborah, 15.
BOLD, Tresy, 11.
BOLDING, Elizabeth, 60.
BOLIN, Hannah, 100.
BOLIN, Jane, 43.
BOLIN, Mariah, 86.
BOLIN, Mary, 57.
BOLING, Betsy, 96.
BOLING, Eliza, 130.
BOMAR, Jane, 111.
BOMAR, Katherine, 12.
BOMAR, Polly, 14.
BOMAR, Sally, 66.
BOOKER, Margaret E., 34.
BOON, Eliza, 127.
BOON, Mildred, 62.
BOON, Nancy, 7.
BOONE, Amanda, 84.
BOWLES, Frances, 129.
BOWLEY, Polly, 111.
BOWLIN, Sally, 93.
BOWLING, Amanda, 109.
BOWLING, Rebecca, 23.
BOYD, Matilda, 10.
BRACHERR, Elizabeth, 3.
BRACKETT, Barbara, 117.
BRACKET, Emily A. Jane, 117.
BRACKETT, Rebecca, 117.
BRACKETT, Sarah E., 19.
BRADLEY, Ellen, 104; 118.
BRADLEY, Mary, 45.
BRADLEY, Rachel, 123.
BRADLEY, Susan, 80.
BRADLY, Rebecca, 85.
BRANDENBURG, Betsy, 100.
BRANDENBURG, Nancy, 7.
BRANDENBURG, Hester, 113.
BRASHEAR, Amanda, 11.
BRASHEAR, Eveline, 117.
BRASHEAR, Margaret, 88.

BRASHEAR, Mary, 71.
BRASHEAR, Milly, 71.
BRASHEAR, Rachel, 121.
BRASHEAR, Sarah A., 117.
BRASHEAR, Sarah Elenor, 110.
BRAW or BROWN, Rachael, 56.
BRESHEAR, Elizabeth A., 26.
BREWER, Catherine A., 56.
BREWER, Elizabeth, 1.
BREWER, Mary Jane, 100.
BREWER, Matilda, 46; 107.
BRIAN, Mary, 5.
BRISCOE, Mary Jane, 75.
BRISCOE, Sally, 35.
BROOKS, Jane, 30.
BROOKS, Margaret, 46.
BROOKS, Nancy, 90.
BROWN, Aylsey, 94.
BROWN, Barbara Ann, 99.
BROWN, Elizabeth, 31; 80;86.
BROWN, Elizabeth B., 97.
BROWN, Elizabeth C., 53.
BROWN, Ellen, 56.
BROWN, Elsey W., 88.
BROWN, Frances B., 54.
BROWN, Ignatia, 13.
BROWN, Lydia Ann, 127.
BROWN, Margaret, 33; 110;112.
BROWN, Mary, 4;90.
BROWN, Mary J., 113.
BROWN, Mary Jane, 103.
BROWN, Mary T.S., 20.
BROWN, Matilda A., 73.
BROWN, Matilda Ann, 119.
BROWN, Nancy, 58;61; 122.
BROWN, Omimdia, 6.
BROWN, Patsey, 63.
BROWN, Polly, 55.
BROWN, Rachel, 40.

BROWN, Rebecca, 59.
BROWN, Sally, 9;39;56;
80.
BROWN, Sarah, 116.
BROWN, Sarah A., 20.
BROWN, Sarah H., 66.
BROWN, Susan, 6.
BROWN, Susanna, 99.
BROWNFIELD, Nancy, 51.
BRUCE, Polly, 121.
BRUMFIELD, Elizabeth,
84.
BRUMFIELD, Joanna, 88.
BRUMFIELD, Lucretia,
3.
BRUNK, Mary, 108.
BRYAN, Ann, 74.
BRYAN, Ellenor, 74.
BRYAN, Margaret Jane,
104.
BRYAN, Mary, 39.
BRYANT, Elizabeth, 86.
BRYANT, Joysey, 28.
BRYON, Mary Ellen, 22.
BUCKHEART, Polly, 32.
BUCKLES, Elizabeth,
23;63.
BUCKLES, Nancy, 64.
BUCKLES, Phebe, 111.
BUCKLES, S. Emily, 61.
BUCKNER, Elizabeth,
46.
BUCKNER, Lauretta, 27.
BUCKNER, Louisana, 84.
BUMMEL, Mary, 15.
BUNGAR, Susannah, 58.
BUNGER, Elizabeth, 70;
77.
BUNGER, Mary, 79.
BUNGER, Nancy, 9.
BUNNEL, Sarah, 57.
BUNNELL, Martha, 22.
BUNTON, Elizabeth, 13.
BURBA, Azuba, 15.
BURBA, Harriet, 60.
BURBA, Sally, 97.
BURBA, Sovina, 127.
BURCH, Dorcas, 8.
BURCHAM, Rebecca, 3.
BURCHAN, Sarah, 24.
BURIS, Delila, 99.
BURK, Elizabeth, 27.
BURKAHRT ?, Cath., 25.

BURKART, Polly, 14.
BURKHART, Pheby, 70.
BURKHART, Sally, 90.
BURKHEAD, Eleanor, 22.
BURKHEART, Margaret,
97.
BURKS, Mary Elizabeth,
58.
BURKS, Saley, 116.
BURNET, Susanna, 24.
BURRIS, Delila, 114.
BURRIS, Elizabeth Jane,
20.
BURRIS, Mary, 114.
BURTON, Lydia, 96.
BUSAN, Katherine, 7.
BUSH, Elizabeth, 34.
BUSH, Elizabeth W.,
107.
BUSH, Juliet Ann, 12.
BUSH, Katherine E.,
88.
BUSH, Lettice, 104.
BUSH, Lydia, 39.
BUSH, Sarah, 117.
BUSH, Sarah R., 59.
BUSH, Susan, 118.
BUSON, Mary, 73.
BUTLER, Sarah, 119.
BUZAN ?, Phebe, 64.
C
CALDWELL, Elizabeth,
111.
CALDWELL, Enode, 40.
CALVERT, Conny, 83.
CALVIN, Elizabeth, 76.
CALVIN, Sarah, 51.
CALVIN, Susan E., 67.
CALVIND, Milly, 60.
CAMAHORN ?, SEAMAHORN,
Margaret, 16.
CAMBRON, Elizabeth, 91.
CAMLEN, Lucretia, 104.
CANDA, Irena, 31.
CANN, Mary, 82;120.
CANNAWAY, Martha, 53.
CAPPS, Rebecca, 103.
CARBY, Mary Margaret,
17.
CARDIN, Caroline H.,
88.
CARDIN, Elizabeth, 15.
CARLEY, Margaret, 7.
CARLISLE, Penelope, 4.

CARLTON, Eda, 95.
CARLTON, Elizabeth,
54.
CARMAN, Anne, 33.
CARMAN, Elizabeth,
82.
CARR, Elizabeth, 80.
CARR, Sarah, 35.
CARRICA, Sarah, 74.
CARRICO, Nancy, 4.
CARRICO, Susan, 85.
CARRICO, Teresa A.,
93.
CARRICO, Theresa, 17.
CARRICOL, Barbara,
74.
CARROLL, Martha Jane,
118.
CARSON, Jane, 117.
CARSON, Polley, 49.
CARTER, Anna, 12;64.
CARTER, Elizabeth A.,
5.
CARTER, Nancy, 71;99.
CARTWRIGHT, Elizabeth,
115.
CARTWRIGHT, Mary, 28.
CARVER, Milly, 116.
CASAWAY, Sarah, 12.
CASEMAN, Elizabeth,
124.
CASH, Angeline, 18.
CASH, Eliza, 125.
CASH, Elizabeth, 63.
CASH, Lucretia W.,
72.
CASH, Martha, 122.
CASH, Mary, 125.
CASH, Mildred, 104.
CASH, S. Emily, 115.
CASH, Susan, 125.
CASH, Susan M, 76.
CASTEEL, Elizabeth,
47.
CASTEEL, Leticia, 40.
CASTLEMAN, Evaline,
75.
CASTLEMAN, Grace Ann,
72.
CASTLEMAN, Margaret,
7.
CASTLEMAN, Maria, 67;
119.

DOUGHERTY, Hannah, 13.
DOUGHERTY, Matilda, 61.
DOUGHERTY, Nancy, 50.
DOUGHERTY, Susan, 23.
DOWDALL, Elizabeth C., 115.
DOWDALL, Rebecca B., 78.
DOWNS, Frances, 58.
DOWNS, Malinda, 7.
DRAKE, Elizabeth, 37.
DRAKE, Kitty, 61.
DRAKE, Mary, 129.
DRAKE, Mary Jane, 44.
DRAKE, Nancy, 92.
DRAKE, Permelia, 76.
DRAKE, Sally, 2.
DRANE, Mary, 75.
DRURY, Catherine, 44.
DRURY, Eley, 17.
DRURY, Polly, 122.
DRURY, Rebecca Ann, 129.
DRURY, Sarah, 119.
DUCAST, Rebecca, 98.
DUFFEY, Ruth Ann, 66.
DUFNER, Ann, 39.
DUFNER, Mary, 22.
DUGAN, Elizabeth, 57.
DULEY ?, Dolly, 114.
DULEY, Sarah, 18.
DUMWIDDIE, Elizabeth, 89.
DUNCA, Klen, 71.
DUNCAN, Agnes F., 7.
DUNCAN, Agnes R., 57.
DUNCAN, Amanda, 59.
DUNCAN, Cynthia, 32.
DUNCAN, Katherine, 96.
DUNCAN, Martha, 17.
DUNCAN, Rosannah, 41.
DUNDIFF, Sarah Ann, 44.
DUNN, Elizabeth, 34.
DUNN, Lydia, 6.
DUNN, Mary Ellen, 116.
DUNN, Nancy, 7;57.
DUNN, Phebe, 6.
DUNN, Rosanna, 32.
DUNWIDDLE, Elizabeth, 94.
DURBIN, Emily, 32.

DURBIN, Hannah, 51;70.
DURBIN, Mary, 33.
DURBIN, Mary Ann, 97.
DURBIN, Rebecca, 113.
DURBIN, Secilly, 61.
DURKIN, Margaret, 70.
DURKIN, Ruth, 62.
DUVAL, Lydia, 18.
DUVALL, Ann, 10.
DUVALL, Kitty, 18.
DUVALL, Nancy, 66.
DUVALL, Sarah, 82.
DYE, Amelia, 120.
DYE, Rachael, 95.
E
EDEN, Anny, 59.
EDEN, Jane, 5.
EDLEN, Polly, 43.
EDLEN, Sally, 68.
EDLIN, Carziah, 36.
EDLIN, Elizabeth, 5;15.
EDLIN, Ellen, 14.
EDLIN, Jane, 6.
EDLIN, Margaret, 74.
EDLIN, Mary, 84.
EDLIN, Rose Ann, 1.
EDLIN, Sarah, 44;79.
EDLIN, Susan, 43.
EDSON, Hannah, 115.
EDWARD, Elizabeth, 81.
ELIOT, Ruth E., 85.
Ellenor CISSELL, 15.
ELLIT, Mariah, 57.
ELLIT, Mary, 78.
ELMORE, Nancy, 40.
EMANNE, Charlotte, 86.
EMERY, Martha, 124.
EMERY, Mary, 115.
EMERY, Melinda, 119.
EMHLEY, Ruthey, 2.
EMRY, Mary, 6.
ENGLISH, Adah Ann, 9.
ENGLISH, Adaline, 9.
ENGLISH, Elizabeth, 48;115.
ENGLISH, Lydia L, 46.
ENGLISH, Mahala, 56.
ENGLISH, Malvina, 60.
ENGLISH, Mariah, 9.
ENGLISH, Matilda, 102.

ENGLISH, Susan, 31.
ENLOUIS, Louisa Ann, 13.
ENLOW, Abigail, 94.
ENLOW, Amy S., 59.
ENLOW alias BERRY, Malinda, 36.
ENLOW, Betsy, 18.
ENLOW, Genota, 1.
ENLOW, Lydia, 83.
ENLOW, Malvina, 82.
ENLOW ?, Mary, 121.
ENLOW, May, 94.
ENLOW, Polly, 30.
ENLOW alias BERRY, Sally, 69.
ENLOWS, Elizabeth, 36.
ENLOWS, Mary, 104.
ENLOWS, Sally, 11.
ERRELS, Jane, 45.
EVANS, Labina Patterson, 5.
EVENS, Eliza, 23.
EVINS, Nancy, 98.
F
FAIRLEIGH, Elizabeth, 88.
FAIRLEIGH, Lettice, 123.
FARLEIGH, Mary, 64.
FAIRLEIGH, Mary L., 1.
FARGUSON, Polly, 99.
FARLINE, Hope V., 117.
FARMER, Elizabeth, 48;60.
FARMER, Nancy, 82.
FEDGETT, Elizabeth M., 40.
FELTCHER, Ann Eliza, 85.
FERGUSON, Sally, 76.
FERLEY, Elizabeth, 19.
FERREE, Matilda, 31.
FIELD, Ann, 119.
FIELD, Artridge, 126.
FIELD, Maria, 82.
FIELD, Mary Ann, 50.
FIELD, Nancy, 122.
FINLEY, Indiana, 128.
FIRKER, Elizabeth, 91.

GOODMAN, Rebecca, 96.
GOODMAN. Susan, 91.
GOODMAN, Susan T.,
126.
GOODMAN, Vian, 23.
GOODMEN, Rebecca, 5.
GOODWIN, Polly, 16.
GORE, Matilda, 49.
GRABLE, Sarah, 25.
GRACEY, Hetty Ann,
85.
GRADY, Polly, 13.
GRAHAM, Susan, 15.
GRAIN, Mary, 98.
GRAVEN, Anna, 2.
GRAY, Elizabeth, 79;
122.
GRAY, Hannah, 72.
GRAY, Jane. 33;106.
GRAY, Mary Ann, 103.
GRAY, Nancy, 95;100.
GRAY, Polly, 50;53.
GRAY, Sarah, 71.
GRAY, Susannah, 94.
GRAYHAM, Delphia, 105.
GRAYHAM, Mary Ann, 36.
GRAYHAM, Susan, 9.
GREEN, Minerva, 38.
GREEN, Peggy, 59;85.
GREEN, Perthena, 60.
GREEN, Tabitha C., 105.
GREEN, Trecy, 69.
GREENAULT, Lewisa, 55.
GREENAULT, Mary, 28.
GREENAULT, Mary Ann,
14.
GREENAWALT, Catherine,
42.
GREENAWALT, Eliza, 103.
GREENAWALT, Levina, 61.
GREENAWALT, Rachel, 60.
GREENSULT, Katherine,
39.
GREENWALT, Polly, 55.
GREENWALT, Rebecca,
8;79.
GREENWELL, Anna, 108.
GREENWELL, Mary Amelia,
26.
GREENWOOD, Ann, 42.
GREENWOOD, Polly, 43.
GREGORY, Sarah Ann,
28.

GREY, Mary, 105.
GRIGSBY, Elivra H.,
126.
GRIGSBY, Mary N.,
126.
GRIGSBY, Sally, 78.
GRIMES, Sally, 104.
GRISTY, Elizabeth,
10.
GUM, Mary, 103.
GUM, Sally, 65.
GUNDIFF, Permelia, 86.
GUSLER, Elizabeth, 55.
GUSTON, Rebecca, 107.
H
HABAXK, Nancy, 76.
HACKLEY, Frances Maria,
23.
HAGAN, Bahenny, 89.
HAGAN, Elizabeth, 11;
113.
HAGAN, Henlen W., 77.
HAGAN, Julia Ann, 8.
HAGAN, Mary Elizabeth,
70.
HAGAN, Susan, 47.
HAGAR, Monica, 47.
HAGAEN, Nancy, 114.
HALDRON, Mary Jane,
8.
HALL, Martha, 2.
HALL, Minerva Jane,
102.
HALL, Sarah, 91.
HAMILTON, Malinda,
123.
HAMILTON, Susan E.,
111.
HAMMER, Sarah, 102.
HAMMOND, Polly, 112.
HAMMOND, Rhoda, 112.
HANAN, Mary, 13.
HANDLEY, Celia Ann,
9.
HANDLEY, Laura Ann,
9.
HANDLEY, Mary Ann,
91.
HANKINS, Nancy, 66.
HANKS, Mary, 99;127.
HANNA, Elizabeth, 69.
HANNA, Louisa Ann, 3.
HARCRAFT, Margaret J., 103.

92.
HARD, Susan, 28.
HARDAWAY, Martha, 109.
HARDIN, Ann, 57.
HARDIN, Betsy, 49.
HARDIN, Mary, 22.
HANKINS, Mary Jane,
29.
HARDIN, Patsey, 86.
HARDING, Alice V.,
9.
HARDING, Sarah, 36.
HARE, Mary, 20.
HARGAN, Prudence, 50.
HARGAN, Sarah Ann,
75.
HARGIN, Mary or Polly,
52.
HARLAN, Elizabeth, 2.
HARLAND, Elizabeth, 67.
HARLE, Sarah Ann, 70.
HARLEY, Lucy, 55.
HARNED, Amy, 68.
HARNED, Elizabeth, 8.
HARNED, Nancy, 56.
HARNED, Patsy, 24.
HARNED, Sally, 28;31.
HARNED, Susan, 126.
HARREL, Sarah Ann, 129.
HARRIET, Elizabeth,
70.
HARRINGTON, Elizabeth,
123.
HARRINGTON, Samira,
30.
HARRIS, Anna, 98.
HARRIS, Catherine, 12.
HARRIS, Eleander, 123.
HARRIS, Eliza, 109.
HARRIS, Elizabeth, 82.
HARRIS, Hannah, 18.
HARRIS, Lidia, 42.
HARRIS, Martha, 12.
HARRIS, Mary, 51.
HARRIS, Nancy, 2;8;70.
HARRIS, Rachael, 43.
HARRIS, Ruth, 126.
HARRIS, Ruthy, 102.
HARRIS, Sally, 85.
HARRIS, Sarah, 28.
HARRIS, Susannah, 88.
HARRISON, Catherine,

HARRISON, Elizabeth, 87;123.
HARRISON, Isabel, 69.
HARRISON, Nancy, 125.
HART, Amelia, 49.
HART, Balinda, 90.
HART, Belinda, 14.
HART, Charity, 45.
HART, Elizabeth, 44; 115.
HART, Jane, 89.
HART, Milly, 14.
HART, Nancy, 20.
HART, Olive, 59.
HART, Polly, 38.
HART, Susan, 118.
HARTLEY, Amy, 123.
HARTLEY, Elizabeth, 68.
HARTLEY, Matilda, 127.
HARTLEY, Rachael, 17.
HARTLEY, Susan, 53.
HARTLY, Elizabeth, 91.
HARVEY, Sarah, 30.
HASKETT, Frances, 9.
HASKETT, Kitty, 42.
HATFIELD, Labitha, 45.
HATFIELD, Martha, 78.
HATFIELD, Mary, 11.
HATFIELD, Phebe, 130.
HAWKINS, Nancy, 36;87.
HAWKINS, Ruth F., 1.
HAYCRAFT, Gilly, 97.
HAYCRAFT, Hiram, 88.
HAYCRAFT, Lettice, 28.
HAYCRAFT, Martha, 95.
HAYCRAFT, Palmira, 43.
HAYCRAFT, Peggy, 124.
HAYCRAFT, Polly, 125.
HAYDEN, Catherine, 108.
HAYDEN, Elizabeth, 126.
HAYDEN, Maria C., 114.
HAYDEN, Mary, 31.
HAYDEN, Rachel, 119.
HAYDEN, Rosa Ann, 4.
HAYDEN, Sophia, 111.
HAYES, Susan, 128.
HAYNES, Martha A., 114.
HAYS, America, 10.

HAYS, Mary, 15.
HAYS, Mary F., 85.
HAYWOOD, Cynitha, 29.
HAYWOOD, Rachel, 93.
HAYWOOD, Sally, 41.
HAYWOOD, Susan, 27.
HELM, Elizabeth C., 67.
HELM, Emily E., 11.
HELM, Louisa, 76.
HELM, Luiretia, 41.
HELM, Margaret, 44.
HELM, Mary Jane, 66.
HENCK, Phebe, 64.
HENDERSON, Alley, 76.
HENDERSON, Ally, 80.
HENDERSON, Margaret, 41.
HENDERSON, Margaret A., 4.
HENDERSON, Phebe, 19.
HENDERSON, Prudence, 1.
HENDLEY, Sally, 9.
HENDRICKS, Drewsilla, 30.
HENDRICKS, Jane, 92.
HENDRICKS, Mitilda, 64.
HENDRIX, Ruanna, 110.
HENRY, Martha Jane, 72.
HENSLEY, Sarah, 99.
HENTON, Hetty, 66;69.
HERNED, Eleanor, 91.
HIBBS, Belinda, 52.
HIBBS, Christina, 110.
HIBBS, Mary Ann, 65.
HIBBS, Nancy, 52.
HIBBS, Sally, 52.
HICKMAN, Elizabeth, 31.
HICKMAN, Polly, 24.
HICKS, Elizabeth, 69; 78.
HICKS, Mary Ann, 40.
HICKS, Nancy, 21.
HICKS, Savena or Serena, 130.
HILL, Elizabeth, 110.
HILL, Martha, 86.
HILL, Mahatable, 42.
HILL, Mary, 95.
HILL, Nancy, 107.
HILL, Peggy, 107.
HILL, Sally, 58.
HILTON, Angeline, 31.

HILTON, Ellen Ann, 17; 27.
HILTON, Frances, 61.
HINCH, Eveline, 75.
HINCH, Phoebe, 63.
HINTON, Margaret C., 104.
HINTON, Nancy, 33.
HIRCH HINCH, Eveline, 75.
HISHFIELD, Polly, 55.
HITTSON, Alice, 7.
HOBACK, Elenor, 128.
HOBACK, Elizabeth, 101.
HOBACK, Margaret, 111.
HOBACK, Mariah, 70.
HOBACK, Sally, 94.
HOBBS, Elizabeth, 49.
HOBBS, Mary, 66;91;93.
HOBBS, Nancy, 22.
HODGES, Ann Elizabeth, 88.
HOLBERT, Ann Maria, 95.
HOLDEN, Permelia, 98.
HOLDREN, Harmony, 3.
HOLDREN, Sally, 98.
HOLLAND, Agens, 58.
HOLLOWAY, Elizabeth, 63;102.
HOLM, Anne Maria, 116.
HOLSTON, Sally, 25.
HOLT, Mary, 104.
HOMES, Elizabeth, 63.
HOOKER, Ihrena, 28.
HOOVER, Elizabeth, 31.
HOOVER, Margaret, 48.
HOOVER, Rachel, 102.
HOOVERM, Katherine, 45.
HORN, Ellen, 126.
HORN, Mary, 66.
HORN, Mersilla, 109.
HORNBACH, Marian, 40.
HORNBACK, Amy, 76.
HORNBACK, Kitty, 55.
HORNBACK, Margaret, 40.
HORNBACK, Mary, 106.
HORNBACK, Phebe, 14.
HORNBACK, Susan, 90.
HOSKINS, Elenor, 111.
HOSKINS, Rachael, 63.

McCLURE, Nancy, 120.
McCLURE, Sarah, 70.
McCULLUM, Elizabeth, 45;107.
McCULLUM, Jane, 123.
McCULLUM, Mary, 70.
McCULLUM, Masa, 110.
McCULLUM, Nancy, 128.
McCULLUM, Polly, 86.
McCULLUM, Sally, 52; 106;123.
McDANIEL, Elizabeth, 93.
McDANIEL, Mary, 56.
McDANIEL, Nancy, 16.
McDONALD, Frances, 100.
McDONALD, Malvina, 126.
McDONALD, Mary, 67; 87.
McDOUGAL, Dorcas, 122.
McDOUGALL, Elizabeth, 75.
McDOWELL, Ann Eliza, 95.
McDOWELL, Ann J., 106.
McDOWELL, Kitty, 26.
McDOWELL, Margaret, 26.
McDOWELL, Mary, 10.
McDOWELL, Mary S., 26.
McDOWELL, Nancy, 29; 115.
McDOWELL, Suan, 34.
McELROY, Easter, 20.
McELROY, Mary, 33.
McELROY, Susan, 87.
McENTIRE, Eliza, 35.
McGALLION, Martha Ann, 7.
McGEE, Eliza J., 19.
McGEE, Rachel A, 106.
McGEE, Sally, 112.
McGEEHEE, Louisa, 27.
McGRAN, Mary, 29.
McGREW, Hannah E., 72.
McGUFFIN, Aley, 48.
McGUGHIN, Mary, 109.
McINTIRE, Elizabeth E., 95.
McINTIRE, Mary, 121.

McINTIRE, Nancy M., 73.
McINTIRE, Sarah, 103.
McINTIRE, Sarah C., 87.
McINTIRE, Sarah E., 28.
McLEAN, Mary, 42.
McLEAN, Nancy, 122.
McLURE, Ann M., 36.
McLURE, Cloa, 64.
McLURE, Elizabeth, 116.
McLURE, Jane, 108; 110.
McLURE, Lydia, 94.
McLURE, Mariah, 30.
McLURE, Martha, 119.
McLURE, Rachel Elizabeth, 111.
McMAHAN, Jane, 90.
McMAHAN, Susan, 35.
McMAHON, Margaret, 89.
McMAHON, Mary, 121.
McMAHON, Purmelia, 23.
McMAHON, Rachel, 48.
McMAHON, Rebecca, 121.
McMAHON, Rosannah, 72.
McMAHON, Savina, 72.
McMILLEN, Eliza Ann, 36.
McMILLEN, Letitia, 1.
McMILLEN, Lucinda, 111.
McMILLEN, Rebecca, 67.
McMILLEN, Sarah Ann, 96.
McMULLUM, Keziah, 128.
McMURTRY, Elizabeth, 50;105.
McNALLY, Martha J., 108.
McNEALL, Lelvina, 78.
McNEILL, 116.
McNEILL, Eleanor, 102.
McVAY, Rachael, 75.
McVEY, Betsey, 85.
McVEY, Cynthia Ann, 8.
McVEY, Mary, 75.
McVEY, Nancy, 78.
McWILLIAMS, Ann, 123.
McWILLIAMS, Martha, 83.

McWILLIAMS, Mary Jane, 67.
McWILLIAMS, Sally, 118.
MEDHAM, Abilgail, 25.
MEEK, Elizabeth, 16.
MEEK, Levicy, 7.
MEEKS, Rebecca, 45.
MEEKS, Sarah, 106.
MELTON, Lucy, 25.
MELTON, Lydia, 2.
MELTON, Sary, 69.
MERIDETH, Elizabeth, 86.
MERRIFIELD, Adaline, 78.
MERRIFIELD, Cinthia, 106.
MERRIFIELD, Jemima, 56.
MERRIFIELD, Juliet, 95.
METCALF, Elizabeth, 34.
MIDDLETON, Jane, 62.
MIDDLETON, Sarah, 120.
MIKLES, Silvey, 75.
MILBOURN, Rachel, 38.
MILBURN, Elizabeth Ann, 130.
MILBURN, Levilla H., 114.
MILBURN, Mary Ann, 45; 114.
MILES, Ruth, 37.
MILLE, Laney also Sena, 3.
MILLEN, Eleanor, 91.
MILLEN, Sarah, 91.
MILLENDER, Martha, 11.
MILLER, Barbary, 4.
MILLER, Catherine, 63; 113.
MILLER, Eleanor, 113.
MILLER, Elender, 22.
MILLER, Eliza, 126.
MILLER, Elizabeth, 35; 38;78.
MILLER, Gilly G., 8.
MILLER, Jane, 73.
MILLER, July Ann, 110.
MILLER, Lettice, 113.
MILLER, Lucetia Ann, 58.
MILLER, Lucetta, 3.

INDEX

INDEX

ROBERTSON, Mary, 23.
ROBERTSON, Sarah, 25;
71.
ROBINSON, Angeline S.,
27.
ROBINSON, Cofrona, 68.
ROBINSON, Cynthia, 79.
ROBINSON, Elizabeth,
94.
ROBINSON, Jane, 111.
ROBINSON, Katherine,
48.
ROBINSON, Mary, 29;
111.
ROBINSON, Rhode, 110.
ROBINSON, Sarah, 9;12.
ROBISON, Martha, 34.
ROBY, Marian, 83.
ROGERS, Anna, 58.
ROGERS, Cynthia, 5.
ROGERS, Eliza, 107.
ROGERS, Elizabeth, 110.
ROGERS, Fatena, 98.
ROGERS, Fetna, 127.
ROGERS, Frances C., 23.
ROGERS, Mary, 83.
ROGERS, Nancy, 106.
ROGERS, Pamelia, 97.
ROGERS, Rachel, 72.
ROGERS, Rebecca, 49.
ROGERS, Rhoady, 108.
ROLL, Lena, 57.
ROLL, Mary, 114.
ROOF, Alice, 113.
ROOF, Nancy, 45.
ROOF, Rebecca, 10;76.
ROOT, Cynthia, 58.
ROSE, Sarah, 45.
ROSEBERRY, Frances,
30.
ROSS, Frankey, 35.
ROSSON, Martha Ann,
43.
ROUNDTREE, Betsy, 37.
ROUSE, Martha M., 42.
ROUT, Prudence, 3.
ROW, Elizabeth, 70.
ROYALTY, Amanda, 58.
ROYALTY, Elizabeth,
63.
ROYALTY, Mary Ann D.,
92.
RUDE, Phebe, 106.

RUDE, Susannah, 39.
RUE or LaRue, Jane,
96.
RULER, Mary Ann, 41.
RUNNELLS, Polly, 69.
RUNNER, Frances, 45.
RUSH, Elizabeth, 82.
RUSSELL, Eliza, 90.
RUSSELL, Nancy, 101.
RUST, Elizabeth, 105.
RUST, Gracey, 113.
RUST, Margaret, 48.
RUST, Mary, 28.
RUST, Matilda, 71.
RUST, Sarah, 110.
RUTHERFORD, Malinda,
68.
RUTHERFORD, Mary, 68.
RYAN, Martha, 39.
S
SAMUELS, Mary, 3;76.
SAND, Catherine, 6.
SANDER, Sally, 59.
SANDERS, Ann, 1.
SANDERS, Nancy, 46;
79.
SAUNDERS, Catherine,
109.
SAWYER, Nancy, 106.
SCAMABORN, Keziah,
55.
SCHULTZ, Darah W.,
41.
SCIFERS, Margaret,
129.
SCIFES, Endamile, 59.
SCIFRES, Martha Ann,
8.
SCIFRES, Mary Malvina,
74.
SCOTT, Catherine, 124.
SCOTT, Elizabeth, 101;
119;123.
SCOTT, Louisa, 18.
SCOTT, Mahalia, 16.
SCOTT, Martha Ann,
114.
SCOTT, Mary, 39;110.
SCOTT, Nancy, 92.
SCOTT, Peggy, 122.
SCOTT, Sally, 45.
SCOTT, Virginia, 60.
SEDLEY, Mary Jane, 36.

SEIFRES, Barbara, 50.
SEIFRES, Lucinda, 89.
SELBY, Mary Jane, 110.
SELF, Eleanor, 122.
SELF, Lydia, 11.
SELSON, Rachel, 58.
SETSER, Betsy, 92.
SETSER, Rebecca, 92.
SETZER, Celia, 121.
SETZER, Louisa, 53.
SHACKLEFORD, Eliza,
129.
SHACKLEFORD, Elizabeth,
78.
SHACKLEFORD, Jane, 127.
SHACKLEFORD, Mariah,
87;103.
SHACKLEFORD, Sarah,
32.
SHACKLETT, Barbara,
31.
SHAKLET, Sally, 89.
SHALTON, Sally, 88.
SHANKLIM, Jaines, 5.
SHANKS, Ewerine, 90.
SHANKS, Letitia, 105.
SHANKS, Mary, 84.
SHANKS, Susannah, 71.
SHARPENSTEEN, Mary Ann,
58.
SHARPENSTENN, Hanah,
121.
SHAVER, Barbary, 125.
SHAVER, Polly, 61.
SHAW, Polly, 115.
SHAWLER, Elizabeth,
33.
SHAZE, Catherine, 40.
SHEARUM, Mary, 54.
SHECKLES, Ageline,
123.
SHECKLES, Hester, 67.
SHEETS, Elizabeth, 20.
SHEETS, Mary, 18.
SHEETS, Providence Jane,
56.
SHEETS, Rebecca, 56.
SHEETS, Sarah, 70.
SHEHI, Eliza, 81.
SHEILD, Eliza, 71.
SHELTON, Ann, 26.
SHELTON, Elizabeth,110.
SHELTON, Mary Jane, 103.

147

SHELTON, Susanna, 50.
SHEPHERD, Gelly, 119.
SHEPHERD, Mary, 125.
SHERRARD, Ann, 87.
SHIECKLES, Fanny, 83.
SHIPLEY, Hannah, 106.
SHOEMAKER, Nancy, 54.
SHREWSBURG, Ann A.,
42.
SHREWSBURRY, Mary D.,
10.
SHUMATE, Polly, 93.
SIMMONS, Elizabeth,
121.
SIMON, Ann, 70.
SIMS, Elizabeth, 18.
SINGLETON, Mahala,
52.
SINGLETON, Polly, 50.
SITTH, Katharine, 62.
SITTLE, Debby, 21.
SKAGGS, Jane, 91.
SKEENS, Lacinda, 63.
SKEES, Malvina, 127.
SKEES, Nancy, 113.
SKEETERS, Elenor, 125.
SLACK, Catherine, 22.
SLACK, E. Letitia, 22.
SLACK, Eliza Jane, 49.
SLACK, Penelope, 17;
39.
SLACK, Polly, 55.
SLACK, Susan, 39.
SLAUGHTER, Abegail,
75.
SLAUGHTER, Elizabeth,
20.
SLAUGHTER, Mary L.,
112.
SLAUGHTER, Sarah C.,
121.
SLEWELLYN, Celia, 114.
SLY, Live Anne, 23.
SMALLWOOD, Eleanor,
105.
SMALLWOOD, Elender,
105.
SMALLWOOD, Elizabeth,
82;105;108.
SMALLWOOD, Harrietta,
60.
SMALLWOOD, Lidia, 29.

SMALLWOOD, Mariah,
114.
SMALLWOOD, Polly,
101.
SMALLWOOD, Sarah, 108.
SMITH, Amanda, 7.
SMITH, America, 56.
SMITH, Anna, 45.
SMITH, Betsy, 15.
SMITH, Catherine, 80.
SMITH, Celista T.,
127.
SMITH, Elizabeth, 57;
73;76;99;111.
SMITH, Ellen, 72.
SMITH, Frances, 5;47.
SMITH, Jane, 107.
SMITH, Katherine, 19.
SMITH, Keziah, 117.
SMITH, Letticia, 19.
SMITH, Lucretia, 59.
SMITH, Lucy, 115.
SMITH, Margaret, 96;
97.
SMITH, Martha, 77.
SMITH, Martha Ann,
28.
SMITH, Mary,19;20;72;
89.
SMITH, Mary M. J., 113.
SMITH, Mathilda, 2.
SMITH, Matilda, 2.
SMITH, Nancy, 89;96.
SMITH, Rachel R., 68.
SMITH, Rebecca, 80.
SMITH, Sarah, 44.
SMITH, Susan, 2;108.
SMITH, Susan Jane, 8.
SMITH, Susan S., 51.
SMITHER, Catherine,
3.
SMITHER, Susan, 84.
SMITHERS, Elizabeth,
50.
SMOOT, Emily, 8.
SMOOT, Minerva Jane,
129.
SNELLEN, Christemis,
94.
SNELLING, Anna, 95.
SNELLING, Hannah, 5.
SNELLING, Nancy, 16.

SOIFREE, Margaret, 56.
SOIFREE, Sarah Ann,
12.
SOUTH, Elizabeth, 99.
SOUTH, Hannah, 25.
SOUTH, Rebecca, 74.
SOUTH, Sally, 105.
SPALDING, Mary Jane,
86.
SPARKS, Polly, 85.
SPAULDINGS, Nancy, 44.
SPENCER, Eunice, 67.
SPENCER, Margaret, 70.
SPENCER, Martha, 24.
SPILLMAN, Nancy, 106.
SPINK, Eliza Jane, 89.
SPRIGG, Sarah, 109.
SPRIGGS, Mary, 118.
SPURNIER, Rachael, 116.
SPURRIER, Corilla, 16.
SPURRIER, Eliza, 9.
STACKETT, Elenor,
121.
STADER, Anna, 28.
STADER, Betsy, 28.
STADER, Catherine A.,
16.
STADER, Elizabeth,
106.
STADER, Hannah, 30.
STADER, Margaret, 59.
STADER, Mary Jane, 91.
STAIGHTER, Amanda, 11.
STANDAFORD, Belinda,
116.
STANDAFORD, Cinderella,
71.
STANDAFORD, Hannah,
40.
STANDIFORD, Mary, 39.
STANDIFORD, Nancy, 49;
110.
STANDLY, Emily Jane,
86.
STANLEY, Betsey, 99.
STARK, Margaret M.,
26.
STATER, Lydia Ann,
77.
STATER, Sally, 4.
STEPHENS, America,
50.

27.
WINTERSMITH, Mary S., 26.
WINTERSMITH, Sarah E., 35.
WISE, Elizabeth, 39.
WISE, Julia Ann, 17.
WISE, Matilda, 11.
WISE, Rozella, 17.
WISE, Sarah M., 54.
WISEHART, Lettice, 29.
WISEHART, Sarah, 115.
WISEMAN, Nancy, 51.
WISEMAN, Rosella, 47.
WITHENS, Susannah, 100.
WITHERS, Agnes, 102.
WITHERS, Ann Eliza, 81.
WITHERS, Margaret, 30.
WITHERS, Martha F., 9.
WITHERS, Marty, 37.
WITHERS, Mary, 80.
WITHERS, Narcissa E., 30.
WITHERS, Polly, 77.
WOLF, Polly, 38.
WOOD, Matilda, 57.
WOOD, Rebecca, 57.
WOOD, Susannah, 129.
WOOD, Trifman, 37.
WOOD, Unis, 48.
WOODRING, Lucinda, 47; 79.
WOODRING, Mahala Ann, 97.
WOODRING, Margaret, 98.
WOODRING, Nancy, 53.
WOODRING, Susan Catherine, 22.
WOOLEY, Lydia, 55.
WOOLDRIDGE, Harriet C., 12.
WOOLDRIDGE, Mary, 13.
WOOLDRIDGE, Sarah, 104;107.
WOOLF, Ester, 35.
WOOLFOLK, Elizabeth B., 38.
WOOLFOLK, Polly D., 109.
WOOLFOLK, Susan, 26.

WRIGHT, Celea, 106.
WRIGHT, Clarenda, 129.
WRIGHT, Elizabeth, 124; 126.
WRIGHT, Laury, 12.
WRIGHT, Martha, 13.
WRIGHT, Mary, 116.
WRIGHT, Nancy, 23.
WRIGHT, Perlina, 129.
WYLEY, Sarah, 16.
WYMP, Mary 31.
Y
YAGER, Elizabeth F., 35.
YAGER, Leatitia S.H., 6.
YAGER, Lydia, 89.
YAGER, Mary D., 128.
YAGER, Sarah E., 128.
YAGES, Martha, 71.
YATES, Ann, 72.
YATES, Jane, 72.
YEATES, Patience, 65.
YATES, Rhoda, 16.
YEAGER, Sarah Jane, 70.
YOUNG, Eliza P., 47.
YOUNG, Elizabeth Ann, 47.
YOUNG, Ellen V., 30.
YOUNG, Lavina, 1.
YOUNG, Loryanda M., 113.
YOUNG, Maria L., 41.
YOUNG, Mary, 46.
YOUNG, Nancy, 42;47.
YOUNG, Polly, 75.
YOUNG, Rebecca, 7.
YOUNG, Ruth, 12.
YOUNG, Sarah Elenor, 10.
YOUNG, Susan, 64.
YOUNG, Susannah, 130.
YUTSLER, Phebe, 107.

Misfiled
CISSELL, Ellenor, 15.
GRAY, Keziah, 103.
HURD, Mally, 96.
KELLY, Tempy, 42.
SMOOT, Suckey, 13.

Heritage Books by Frances T. Ingmire:

Arkansas Confederate Veterans and Widows Pension Applications

Citizens of Missouri Territory: 1787-1810, Grants in Present Day Missouri, Arkansas and Oklahoma, Vol. 1

Citizens of Missouri Territory: 1810-1812, Grants in Present Day Missouri, Arkansas and Oklahoma, Vol. 2

Citizens of Missouri Territory to-1835, Grants in Present Day Missouri, Arkansas and Oklahoma, Vol. 3

Hamilton County, Indiana Marriage Records Book A, 1833–1843

Hardin County, Kentucky Marriage Records, 1813–1850

Hardin County, Kentucky Will Book B, 1810–1816

Hardin County, Kentucky Will Book C, 1816–1821

North Carolina Marriage Bonds and Certificates Series: Craven County, North Carolina, Marriage Records, 1780–1867

North Carolina Marriage Bonds and Certificates Series: Cumberland County, North Carolina, Marriage Records, 1803–1878

North Carolina Marriage Bonds and Certificates Series: Guilford County, North Carolina, Marriage Records, 1771–1868

North Carolina Marriage Bonds and Certificates Series: Lincoln County, North Carolina, Marriage Records, 1783–1866

North Carolina Marriage Bonds and Certificates Series: Orange County, North Carolina, Marriage Records, 1782–1868

North Carolina Marriage Bonds and Certificates Series: Randolph County, North Carolina, Marriage Records, 1785–1868

North Carolina Marriage Bonds and Certificates Series: Rowan County, North Carolina, Marriage Records, 1754–1866

North Carolina Marriage Bonds and Certificates Series: Stokes County, North Carolina, Marriage Records, 1783–1868

North Carolina Marriage Bonds and Certificates Series: Surry County, North Carolina, Marriage Records, 1783–1868

North Carolina Marriage Bonds and Certificates Series: Wake County, North Carolina, Marriage Records, 1781–1867

North Carolina Marriage Bonds and Certificates Series: Wilkes County, North Carolina, Marriage Records, 1779–1868

Texas Ranger Service Records, 1838–1846

Texas Ranger Service Records, 1847–1900, Volume 1: A-C

Texas Ranger Service Records, 1847–1900, Volume 2: D-G

Texas Ranger Service Records, 1847–1900, Volume 3: H-K

Texas Ranger Service Records, 1847–1900, Volume 4: L-N

Texas Ranger Service Records, 1847–1900, Volume 5: O-S

Texas Ranger Service Records, 1847–1900, Volume 6: T-Z

www.ingramcontent.com/pod-product-compliance
Lightning Source LLC
Chambersburg PA
CBHW080333270326
41927CB00014B/3204